GLOBAL GOVERNANCE UNDER FIRE

PRINCETON STUDIES IN INTERNATIONAL HISTORY AND POLITICS

Tanisha M. Fazal, G. John Ikenberry,
William C. Wohlforth, and Keren Yarhi-Milo, Series Editors

Global Governance Under Fire

HOW INTERNATIONAL ORGANIZATIONS RESIST THE POPULIST WAVE

ALLISON CARNEGIE AND
RICHARD CLARK

PRINCETON UNIVERSITY PRESS
PRINCETON & OXFORD

Published by Princeton University Press
41 William Street, Princeton, New Jersey 08540
99 Banbury Road, Oxford OX2 6JX

press.princeton.edu

GPSR Authorized Representative: Easy Access System Europe – Mustamäe tee 50, 10621 Tallinn, Estonia, gpsr.requests@easproject.com

All Rights Reserved

ISBN 9780691276205
ISBN (pbk.) 9780691276212
ISBN (e-book) 9780691276229

Library of Congress Control Number: 2025944041

British Library Cataloging-in-Publication Data is available

Editorial: David McBride and Alena Chekanov
Production Editorial: Natalie Baan
Cover Design: Karl Spurzem
Production: Lauren Reese
Publicity: William Pagdatoon
Copyeditor: Eric Newman

This book has been composed in Arno

10 9 8 7 6 5 4 3 2 1

CONTENTS

ILLUSTRATIONS

Figures

Tables

ACKNOWLEDGMENTS

WE WERE fortunate to engage with a tremendous and diverse group of scholars who read portions of the book, offering suggestions and helpful conversations. We especially thank Sabrina Arias, Jennie Barker, Ryan Brutger, Don Casler, Sarah Daly, Lindsay Dolan, Jeff Frieden, Page Fortna, Nikhar Gaikwad, Stephan Haggard, Ayse Kaya, Christian Kreuder-Sonnen, Anna Meyerrose, Vicky Murillo, Jack Snyder, Calvin Thrall, Keren Yarhi-Milo, and Noah Zucker. Participants at the IPES conference, GRIPE workshop, and talks at Columbia University, New York University, Princeton University, Rice University, the University of California Berkeley, the University of California San Diego, the University of Mannheim, and Vanderbilt University also provided useful comments. We also thank the editorial team at Princeton University Press and the anonymous reviewers whose comments greatly improved this book.

We acknowledge the *Journal of Politics* and *World Politics* for allowing us to include portions of articles that we previously published in their journals and especially thank the reviewers and editors who suggested improvements throughout the publication process. We are also extremely grateful to our co-authors on those papers, Austin Carson, Ayse Kaya, and Noah Zucker, as well as our co-authors on related works-in-progress, Lisa Fan and Seowoo Chung, for their significant contributions and support of this project. We received excellent research assistance from Elden Griggs and Melinda Zhang.

As we developed the manuscript, we spoke to policymakers and practitioners who shared their knowledge, experiences, and insights. Though we do not list them by name to protect their anonymity, we are incredibly grateful for their willingness to engage with the work.

Last, we thank our families and friends for their support—without them, none of this would be possible.

GLOBAL GOVERNANCE UNDER FIRE

1

Introduction

THE ORGANS of global governance, painstakingly constructed through decades of diplomatic negotiation and multilateral agreements, face unprecedented threats. Chief among them is the rise and spread of anti-globalization sentiment. An array of challenges has fueled opposition to global governance: rising economic inequality, mass migration, a global pandemic, the existential threat of climate change, technological disruptions, and the shifting international balance of power. People around the world feel forgotten, resentful, and disenchanted by the traditional political order—especially in working-class areas of many developed, deindustrializing, and decarbonizing democracies.

Those discontented with the globalized world increasingly coalesce around populist political ideologies. Charismatic populist leaders amplify these sentiments, promising a return to a bygone era. They lambaste the corrupt elite, blaming incumbent politicians and international actors alike for runaway globalization. These leaders argue that their countries should break loose from the shackles of economic interconnectedness and multilateralism that have sapped state sovereignty and diluted democracy. Across continents, populists advancing such messages have gathered political strength with fiery rhetoric that taps into longstanding fears and promises swift solutions to difficult problems.

As such leaders rise to power, their policies and ideas increasingly threaten established global networks and governing bodies. Populists preach nationalism, isolationism, and protectionism to their domestic audiences. In their quest to champion the people, they seek to diminish the international organizations (IOs) and treaties that states have gradually forged since the conclusion of World War II. Strikingly, many of the architects of the liberal international order have become its staunchest critics under populist regimes.

Global Governance Under Fire cuts to the heart of this storm, exploring the effects of populists' attacks on the foundations of the international order. The book confronts several pressing questions: Can international cooperation survive despite the rise and persistence of populism? If so, what form will it take, and what are the implications for the quality of global governance?

This book spotlights international organizations' attempts to fight back against detractors. We show that IOs are not helpless but rather have several powerful tools at their disposal that can allow them to persevere and even thrive. Yet their methods can also have unintended consequences, at times eroding their legitimacy and fueling additional populist resistance. We provide recommendations for policymakers and practitioners seeking to make their institutions more "populist-proof" while avoiding these negative side effects.

1.1. Populism and Global Governance

Scholars and policymakers often react to the spread of populism with pessimism regarding the future of global governance. They express concern that as populism surges around the globe, globalization will stagnate or reverse, and the international organizations that support it will incur significant damage. This is because, as we describe subsequently, populists are highly pro–state sovereignty and anti-elite. Because international organizations are staffed by elites and place constraints on their members, populists typically oppose them.

For example, Goldstein and Gulotty (2021, 553) observe, "Today, American commitment to the [trade] regime may be at a watershed moment, facing both anti–trade treaty populism at home and skepticism from its founders abroad." Others suggest that the World Trade Organization (WTO)—the largest and most important multilateral trade body—has incurred fatal damage: "The WTO was a lovely promise of a more rational, predictable, and fairer global economic order. Its death should be mourned."[1]

Indeed, populists frequently criticize the international elites that dominate bodies like the WTO, refusing to cooperate with such institutions and prioritizing their own countries' needs (Copelovitch and Pevehouse 2019). They express concern about relative rather than absolute gains, wishing to increase their share of the pie rather than to expand the size of the pie as a whole; such a preference undercuts international collaboration (Mearsheimer

---

1. *CFR*, 2018, https://www.cfr.org/blog/trump-china-and-steel-tariffs-day-wto-died.

2001). Campaign statements, including "America First";[2] "We are for local, against global";[3] and "Brazil Above Everything,"[4] make clear that populists decry international cooperative efforts and prefer to turn inward.

Populists portray the global elite as corrupt and out-of-touch and IOs as infringing on their national sovereignty. For example, US president Donald Trump, in his first term, asserted that one of his political opponents was "the candidate of . . . globalists . . . ripping off the United States with bad trade deals and open borders."[5] Similarly, former British prime minister Boris Johnson felt "very, very frustrated by people being told what to do by nanny in Brussels" and wanted to "take back control . . . of our money, our borders, and our laws" from the EU.[6]

Given populists' repeated calls to tear down the global architecture, it is no wonder that the rise of populism has spread fears of international calamity among nonpopulists. At stake are no less than the unprecedented levels of peace and global economic prosperity that have been driven, in part, by globalization and international cooperation (Russett and Oneal 2001; Gartzke 2007; Ikenberry 2011a). Critics worry that if populists upend the trade regime, for example, the global policies and processes that practitioners have refined over decades to guide global commerce will fall apart, with enormous economic and political consequences. If populists undercut global development institutions or organizations tasked with maintaining peace between rivals, they could thrust many individuals into poverty, forced migration, or conflict. Should populists block cooperation on environmental degradation and climate change, the planet may become engulfed in irreversible heat and biological devastation (Barnett and Adger 2007; Colgan, Green, and Hale 2021).

Yet others argue that populists offer a necessary corrective for an international order that has expanded too fast and intruded too far into issues that should be under countries' purviews (Rodrik 2017). Critics point to IOs' sprawling bureaucracies and large budgets and argue that their waste and inefficiency must be tamed. They charge that IOs have become too powerful and

---

2. Donald Trump, 2016 campaign slogan.

3. Marine Le Pen, 2022 campaign speech.

4. Jair Bolsonaro, 2022 campaign speech.

5. Marc Levy, "Oz's Ties to Turkey Attacked in Pennsylvania's Senate Race." AP. May 6, 2022.

6. Jennifer Rankin and Jim Waterson, "How Boris Johnson's Brussels-Bashing Stories Shaped British Politics." *The Guardian.* July 14, 2019.

have evolved far past their original mandates. Populism may bring such important issues back into the public sphere for discussion (Mudde and Rovira Kaltwasser 2017). Still others, however, argue that even if populists make valid points, the solution is not to undermine or destroy existing systems of global governance but to reform them.

These issues are regularly debated, as populist parties are popular in virtually every region of the world. Figure 1.1 displays all countries with populist executives in 1990 compared with 2018; the number of populist heads of state increased from 5 to 22. More recent examples abound as well, including the 2022 election of far-right populist Giorgia Meloni as prime minister of Italy, the 2023 election of populist anarcho-capitalist Javier Milei as president of Argentina, and the 2024 reelection of Donald Trump as US president.

As a result of populism's popularity and anti-IO orientation, many have concluded that the international order is under severe duress (Copelovitch and Pevehouse 2019; Voeten 2020; Borzel and Zürn 2021). While some bemoan IOs' perceived downfall and others cheer it on, the idea that global governance faces critical challenges is generally accepted. Yet despite its importance, we know little about the nature of the populist threat to international cooperation, and how global governance is changing as a result. In this project, we take up these essential topics. In short, we conclude that the notion that populism is decimating the liberal international order is misguided; instead, we ask *how* populism is changing the global order.

To do so, we recognize that IOs have agency, and we investigate the specific strategies they adopt in response to populist attacks. We then explore how these defensive measures are altering global governance. While we discuss and briefly test how populists undermine IOs, the book focuses primarily on how IOs shift their policies as a result. Our theory is generalizable, though our empirics center primarily, but not exclusively, on international financial institutions. This concentration enables us to compare findings across empirical analyses and to speak to the large literature analyzing the effects of IOs in this realm (Stone 2011; Schneider and Tobin 2016; Lipscy 2017; Pratt 2021).

This book addresses several important scholarly debates, including how IOs can or cannot foster cooperation, the effects of the populist resurgence on such cooperation, and the degree to which states and institutions of global governance possess power in the international system. Further, our study carries lessons for practitioners who seek to strengthen multilateral cooperation in the face of widespread resistance.

(a) 1990

(b) 2018

FIGURE 1.1. The rise of populism. These maps show countries with populist leaders in 1990 and 2018, highlighting populism's spread. Data comes from Funke, Schularick, and Trebesch (2023).

Our primary contention is that IOs are strategic actors that can—and do—combat attacks by hostile actors, allowing them to remain much more resilient than they are often given credit for. We thus push against the considerable scholarship on global governance that overlooks IO agency, which argues that IOs "do not take on a life of their own, and thus . . . are simply tools of the great powers" (Mearsheimer 2019). Others argue that IOs possess authority only within narrow bounds, restricted by the limited degree to which member states delegate responsibilities to them (Keohane 1984; Pollack 1997; Abbott and Snidal 1998). Even when IOs' agency is acknowledged, scholars have difficulty applying these insights to derive specific, testable predictions about IO behavior.

In contrast, we show that IOs leverage and innovate tools to push back against detractors. We adapt insights from organizational sociology and the study of bureaucracies to the international context to identify the tools in IOs' foreign policy toolkits. Unlike countries' coercive strategies, IOs' instruments can target two levels of actors: member states and their domestic publics. Our theory highlights four main methods that IOs use to defend themselves, which span both of these levels: sidelining or appeasing unfriendly leaders and sidelining or appeasing their constituents. IOs sideline populist leaders by relying on them less heavily for things they need, like funding and information. Or, IOs marginalize or obscure activities from populists' constituents so that populists can avoid domestic penalties associated with cooperation. IOs also appease populists by providing them with greater benefits and reduced costs or mollify constituents by appealing directly to them.

This framework enables us to analyze how IOs evolve systematically and to generate testable predictions. In the empirical chapters, we leverage new data to rigorously evaluate each of these mechanisms, providing evidence to support our theoretical claim that IOs can maintain resilience in the face of external threats. Our findings demonstrate that populist challenges compel IOs to confront status quo biases and adopt meaningful reforms.

However, while populist hostility drives IOs to defend themselves in order to remain viable, these methods have unintended consequences. While some tactics can make IOs more responsive to the public and efficacious, others can have pernicious effects. For instance, IOs' forays into secrecy and bribery can make them less legitimate, less transparent, and overextended, thereby threatening the normative pillars of global governance. Indeed, in their struggle to combat populism, IOs may inadvertently sow the seeds of further populist backlash, undermining the very legitimacy they seek to protect. Throughout this book, we discuss how IOs can avoid such negative outcomes, remaining vibrant despite ongoing populist resistance.

1.2.   Why Populism?

Scholars and policymakers frequently bemoan the many barriers confronting international institutions (Gray 2018; von Borzyskowski and Vabulas 2019b; Lake, Martin, and Risse 2021; Dellmuth and Tallberg 2023) and the liberal international order more broadly (Borzel and Zürn 2021; Farrell and Newman 2021; Weiss and Wallace 2021). Indeed, a plethora of hostile actors actively work against international cooperation. A variety of factors cause negative perceptions of IOs, including perverse economic experiences (Kiratli 2021), elite cues (Dellmuth and Tallberg 2023), limited knowledge (Rho and Tomz 2017; Dolan and Milner 2023), political ideology (Brutger and Clark 2022; von Borzyskowski and Vabulas 2024a), core values (Brutger 2021), and low levels of empathy (Casler and Groves 2023). Many states, such as those in the former Soviet bloc, Latin America, and others, have long questioned certain IOs' legitimacy and abilities to represent ordinary people. But while many detractors oppose specific facets of IOs (e.g., procedures, authority, or performance), most do not oppose international cooperation altogether. Those that do typically are not large enough in number or power to fundamentally threaten IOs. Populism, however, offers a popular and widespread ideology to explain why IOs should not constrain states, and thus represents a potent challenge (Voeten 2021).

Because many political ideologies and core values are compatible with populism, its appeal crosses party and ideological lines, boosting its popularity. Populism's congruence with other beliefs helps populists attract support at the ballot box relative to other skeptics of international cooperation. Thus, while our theory applies to many of globalization's detractors, we focus on populists as a particularly salient and prevalent set of actors who consistently oppose global governance (Ikenberry 2018; Voeten 2020; Broz, Frieden, and Weymouth 2021).

While populists differ on many dimensions, they share two defining characteristics: 1) a belief that a country's "true people" are locked into conflict with outsiders and elites, and 2) opposition to constraints on the will of the true people.[7] The meaning of "the true people" can vary based on context, but it generally refers to a perceived authentic, idealized majority that populist leaders claim to represent while excluding those who are seen as outsiders or part of the establishment. These true people are portrayed as good and hardworking, in contrast to corrupt elites. Populists claim they will provide power to these people at the expense of elites.[8]

Populists accuse IOs of standing in the way of this goal because IOs typically comprise elites and constrain national sovereignty. IOs are staffed by unelected, highly educated, lifelong bureaucrats who epitomize the global elites whom populists disparage. Such bureaucrats are rewarded for acquiring elite skills and experience—often receiving their education from top Western universities (Weaver 2008; Chwieroth 2015) and working for other elite organizations, whether public or private (Novosad and Werker 2019; Adler-Nissen 2021). These workers possess specialized knowledge and technical expertise in areas such as economics, law, diplomacy, and development. While they need this training to perform their jobs, it also can make them seem out-of-touch with common people who tend to value lived experience over "book smarts." IO staff also hail from a diverse mix of foreign countries and thus do not represent the "true people" that populists privilege, that is, the native, working-class members of their country (Mudde and Rovira Kaltwasser 2017; Copelovitch and Pevehouse 2019; Carnegie, Clark, and Zucker 2024).

This perception is reinforced by IOs' complex decision-making processes that involve negotiations among member states or appointed representatives (cf. Putnam 1988), and that appear far removed from the general public. IOs have their own rules and norms, with a focus on technical knowledge that seems far removed from people's everyday experiences. The involvement of diplomats, bureaucrats, and other high-ranking officials, who interact with multinational corporations, governments, and influential state actors, contributes to these perceptions of privileged and exclusive groups making decisions that affect—but are not shaped by—ordinary people.

---

7. Our definition draws on recent pieces on populism and its microfoundations—see Muller (2016); Mudde and Rovira Kaltwasser (2017); Mudde and Rovira Kaltwasser (2018); Copelovitch and Pevehouse (2019); Broz, Frieden, and Weymouth (2021); Funke, Schularick, and Trebesch (2023).

8. The framing of the "true people" often has a racial or ethnic element, especially for right-wing populists—see Copelovitch and Pevehouse (2019).

In addition to appearing as elite organizations, IOs threaten populists' prioritization of state sovereignty because they explicitly seek to constrain and alter state behavior (Keohane 1984; Copelovitch and Pevehouse 2019). IOs establish norms, standards, and rules for their members that encompass a wide range of issues, including human rights, trade, environmental protection, and security. IOs often enforce these regulations through monitoring, reporting, and applying international pressure.[9] They gather data, conduct investigations, and publish reports highlighting violations or areas of concern. Many have formal dispute-resolution mechanisms to adjudicate potential violations of their rules. IOs also offer economic incentives to influence state behavior, such as financial assistance, trade benefits, or market access.

These activities help IOs encourage states to adhere to their agreements and facilitate cooperation, yet they also drive populist anger because they constrain states' behavior. Populists often feel that the areas IOs govern should fall within states' purviews. They see these institutions as lacking compatibility with domestic priorities (Snyder 2019). As IOs' remits have grown, populists have pushed back on what they see as IO overreach.

Unlike resistance from other types of leaders, populists' resistance is often credible because populist leaders and their constituents ideologically oppose international cooperation. Moreover, populism is so widespread that IOs cannot afford to ignore it. If populists' grievances are not addressed, populists can credibly threaten to undermine or even exit IOs. Because their constituents are also skeptical of ceding sovereignty to international bureaucrats, they do not penalize leaders who disengage from these bodies and may even reward them.

However, populist leaders vary in the strength of their anti-IO beliefs. We conceptualize populists as falling on a continuum between those who genuinely take anti-elite, pro-sovereignty stances, and those who merely perform populism. In the latter category, leaders adopt populist positions including opposition to IOs solely to appeal to domestic audiences. These politicians often use populism as a part of their political strategy to win and retain office, but their anti-IO positions are insincere (e.g., when politicians scapegoat the International Monetary Fund for needed economic reforms, see Vreeland 1999; Handlin, Kaya, and Günaydin 2023). For them, the main cost of publicly embracing IOs is backlash from supporters who oppose IOs and observe

---

9. For example, through naming and shaming; see Hafner-Burton 2008; Tingley and Tomz 2022; Casler, Clark, and Zucker 2024.

inconsistency between populists' stated anti-elitism and their cooperation with international bodies (cf. Fearon 1994; Brutger and Kertzer 2018). Bashing IOs is then a way to bolster populists' anti-elite and anti-globalist bona fides. Genuine populists, in contrast, are often political outsiders who sincerely distrust the global elite and thus have both ideological and domestic political incentives to oppose IOs.

In reality, most populists fall somewhere in the middle of this spectrum, incurring domestic and ideological costs from engaging with IOs to varying degrees. While the sincerity of their beliefs is unobservable, the point is that populists across this spectrum take anti-IO stances and actively undermine these bodies. Of course, certain types of IOs may activate populists' concerns more than others; we discuss the organizations to which our theory best applies later in this chapter.

1.3.   Populist Tactics to Oppose IOs

Populists' opposition to IOs manifests in a variety of ways. Because the main contribution of this book is to uncover how IOs respond to populist attacks, we must first understand the nature of these attacks. We therefore discuss how populists oppose IOs briefly here, providing further explanation in chapter 2 and empirical testing of these tactics in chapter 3. We also touch on several key examples to fix ideas in this chapter, which we flesh out in the case studies found in chapter 8.

The populist backlash against IOs ranges from subtle resistance to dramatic actions. Some populists seek to reshape IOs from within, while others endeavor to dismantle them from the outside. Unfortunately for IOs, populists often implement a multitude of these strategies simultaneously. Moreover, different leaders adopt diverse approaches, subjecting IOs to a barrage of such measures.

The specific strategies chosen by a given populist are contingent on the populist's objectives and constraints. For example, state power is one important factor that shapes the form of populist resistance. Powerful states have many levers they can pull to weaken IOs, such as cutting off funds or reducing their participation in the organizations. Weaker states, meanwhile, typically affect IOs to a lesser extent. That said, small countries that oppose IOs can band together to damage organizations (Helfer 2004; Pratt 2021); for example, several smaller states joined forces to counter the International Criminal

Court (ICC), as we show in chapter 8. Defections by small states can also trigger chain reactions, and small states may possess outsize power given institutional rules such as unanimous decision making and leadership rotation (Arias, Clark, and Kaya 2024). Indeed, Hungary often blocks the EU's actions because of requirements of unanimity, and temporary members of the UN Security Council wield significant influence. As such, both the number of populist member states resisting an IO and the collective power possessed by such states can determine the potential harm inflicted on an organization. We discuss these considerations further in chapters 2 and 3.

1.3.1. Insights from Organizational Sociology

In exploring how populist actors resist international organizations (IOs), we draw on insights from organizational sociology, which examines how hostile participants disrupt the institutions they inhabit. These disruptions often occur through withholding critical resources and fostering toxic environments, behaviors labeled as "organizational deviance" or "workplace aggression" (Likert 1967; Pfeffer and Salancik 1978). However, when applied to IOs, this framework becomes more complex, as both domestic and international dynamics come into play. This section outlines general tactics hostile actors use to harm organizations, adapting these insights to the unique context of IOs. While not exhaustive, it highlights key strategies populists use to destabilize these bodies.

It is worth noting that many of these tactics are not exclusive to populists; nonpopulist actors also employ them when they wish to weaken IOs. However, populists' resistance is often more systematic and has stronger ideological underpinnings. Their persistent willingness to challenge IOs stems from the lower political and ideological costs they face when disengaging from or undermining these bodies.

A primary way hostile actors disrupt IOs is by withholding resources, a tactic organizational sociology identifies as critical to undermining an institution's vitality. One such resource is effort—the basic engagement required for an organization to function. Hostile actors may intentionally underperform, withhold expertise, or refuse to contribute to collective goals (Robinson and Bennett 1995; Lawrence and Robinson 2007). These behaviors not only stymie productivity but also tarnish the organization's reputation and effectiveness (Fombrun and Shanley 1990; Ambrose, Seabright, and Schminke 2002).

Effort withdrawal often manifests as noncompliance, wherein actors challenge institutional authority, disregard its rules, or actively obstruct organizational processes (O'Leary 2010). This type of resistance disrupts IOs' ability to coordinate and execute initiatives, leaving them vulnerable to both internal dysfunction and external criticism. Indeed, compliance, performance, and reputation are often tightly interconnected (Heinzel and Liese 2021).

Another critical resource in this context is information and communication, which hostile actors can exploit to create confusion and mistrust. Tactics such as spreading misinformation, circulating rumors, and selectively disclosing information undermine trust within the organization (Kramer 1999; Bordia et al. 2006). These actions fuel toxic communication patterns, ranging from passive-aggressive behavior to outright personal attacks, which foster a contentious and conflict-ridden environment (Tucker 1993; Giacalone and Greenberg 1997; Neuman and Baron 2005). As a result, interpersonal relationships suffer, organizational cohesion erodes, and collaboration is stifled (Pearson, Andersson, and Wegner 2001).

Beyond withholding resources, hostile actors amplify their impact by fostering negative environments within IOs. One effective strategy to this end is the formation of dissident coalitions, where actors ally with other dissatisfied members to mobilize opposition and promote subversive agendas (Brown 2003; Mechanic 1962). These alliances can challenge established power structures, erode leaders' authority, and disrupt organizational hierarchies, all while advancing alternative agendas (Clemens and Cook 1999; Ezzamel, Willmott, and Worthington 2001; Fleming and Spicer 2007).

Hostile coalitions often exploit organizational vulnerabilities to great effect. They may engage in bureaucratic obstruction, procedural manipulation, or strategic nonparticipation to block decision making and sabotage initiatives they oppose (Ackroyd and Thompson 2003). By exploiting such institutional loopholes, they create inefficiencies and undermine the organization's credibility and operational capacity.

1.3.2. *Populists as Organizational Disruptors*

Populist actors apply these tactics with a distinct intensity. Their ideological commitment to resisting globalism and their ability to rally domestic support against IOs can embolden them to take extreme measures. Unlike other actors, populists often perceive fewer costs associated with disengagement or noncompliance, enabling them to pursue disruption unfettered.

One of the most visible ways populists challenge IOs is by withholding effort. They may disengage entirely—skipping meetings, refusing to comply with IO rules, or even exiting altogether. For example, Britain's decision to leave the EU, spurred by a populist-led referendum, highlights how domestic constituents can drive disengagement. Similarly, Hungary and Poland have actively blocked the EU's plans under populist leaders (Kelemen 2017), while India under Modi has stalled WTO negotiations on key trade reforms.[10] These actions sap IOs of critical resources and momentum, creating significant roadblocks to progress.

Populists also undermine IOs by creating competing institutions that draw away funding, influence, and participation. These rival organizations dilute the power of established IOs and complicate global governance (Alter and Meunier 2009; Clark 2022). For instance, some populist-led states have opted to support new forums that reflect their narrower national interests, leaving existing IOs to navigate diminished relevance.[11]

Populists frequently disregard IO rules, regulations, and policies, fostering a culture of noncompliance. Such behavior can trigger a domino effect as other states become reluctant to comply, fearing they will be the sole adherents (see Barrett 2003). Under Donald Trump's leadership, for example, the United States flouted WTO rules, which had ripple effects across the global trade regime (Carnegie and Carson 2019). Additionally, populists often exploit IOs' decision-making rules, blocking initiatives or staffing appointments that are unaligned with their interests. They may also replace expert bureaucrats with loyalists, muting the professionalism and expertise needed for IOs to function effectively (Eichengreen 2018; Sasso and Morelli 2021; Bellodi, Morelli, and Vannoni 2024).

International organizations thrive on active member participation. Without state representatives engaging in discussions, contributing expertise, and formulating policy, IOs risk becoming "zombies"—entities that exist in name but lack meaningful influence (Gray 2018). Populists exacerbate this risk by withholding not just effort but also funding. Most IOs rely on member-state contributions, whether providing loans, deploying peacekeepers, or adjudicating disputes. The Trump administration's decision to withdraw US funding

10. Tom Miles, "Nine reasons why India's WTO veto shocked the world." Reuters, August 1, 2014.

11. See, e.g., India's co-sponsorship of the New Development Bank. On competitive IO creation, see Urpelainen and Van de Graaf (2015); Pratt (2021).

from the WHO during the COVID-19 pandemic is a stark example of how financial withdrawal can cripple IO activities. Jair Bolsonaro of Brazil similarly cut funds to an array of IOs promoting environmental cooperation during his tenure as president, including the Amazon Cooperation Treaty Organization.

Another critical resource that populists manipulate is information. IOs depend on accurate data from member states to implement policies and ensure compliance. By withholding or distorting this information, populists hinder IOs' ability to function effectively. For example, populists like Donald Trump and Viktor Orbán have weakened scientific bureaucracies by replacing experts with loyalists, thereby obstructing data collection and undermining the flow of information to IOs (Carnegie, Clark, and Zucker 2024).

This tactic isn't limited to withholding information; populists actively weaponize communication to sow distrust in IOs. Anti-globalist rhetoric, fiery speeches, and campaigns blaming IOs for domestic problems erode public confidence in these institutions (Dellmuth and Tallberg 2023; Handlin, Kaya, and Günaydin 2023). By vilifying IOs as symbols of elitism and external meddling, populists cultivate domestic backlash and raise the political costs of cooperation with these organizations.

Importantly, populists do not always disengage completely from IOs. Sometimes they stay within such institutions but seek to repurpose them to advance domestic agendas. By reshaping an organization's mandate or exploiting procedural loopholes, populists redirect IO efforts to align with their priorities, weakening the institution's broader mission (Gray 2018; Spandler and Söderbaum 2023). Orbán has sought to do so with various EU immigration initiatives, for instance.

These tactics can sow toxic environments within IOs, fostering inefficiency, division, and the erosion of legitimacy. Whether through disengagement, noncompliance, or deliberate manipulation, populists hollow out institutions, reducing their capacity to serve as effective global governance actors. However, as the following section explores, IOs are not passive in this battle; they actively develop strategies to push back against populist resistance.

1.4.   IOs as Strategic Agents

The central focus of our theory and empirical analysis is to uncover how IOs respond to populist attacks. While much is known about the array of tactics countries use to defend themselves against external threats, far less attention has been paid to the defensive toolkits possessed by IOs. What tools do these institutions wield in their efforts to counter hostility and maintain cooperation among their members? We argue that IOs' strategies diverge in important ways from those employed by states within institutions, reflecting their unique nature and constraints.

Countries enjoy a vast array of foreign policy instruments to project power and achieve their objectives. From manipulating trade policies and foreign aid to providing military protection or imposing sanctions, states can leverage both rewards and threats to influence allies and adversaries alike. Great powers often use aid or investments as carrots to secure policy alignment (e.g., aid-for-votes exchanges in the UN General Assembly; Dreher, Sturm, and Vreeland 2015), while simultaneously wielding sticks with which to punish states that stray from their agendas (e.g., through sanctions or tariffs). These tools allow states to assert dominance, build coalitions, and deter opposition.

Like states, IOs deploy a variety of tools to foster cooperation, neutralize opposition, and retain member participation. However, IOs' strategies and capabilities differ markedly from those of states. Unlike nations, IOs cannot mobilize armies or enforce their mandates through territorial control. They operate within narrower issue areas, their funding depends on member contributions, and their authority often lacks enforceability. Threats to IO budgets—such as the Trump administration's efforts to defund key institutions—underscore their vulnerability to external pressures. Indeed, by virtue of their accountability to member-state principals, IOs seemingly possess limited room in which to maneuver.

Yet IOs are not passive bystanders. Far from being mechanical responders, they possess significant agency and deploy it strategically. Scholars have examined many of the individual tactics IOs use to incentivize cooperation, such as adjusting voting rules, modifying conditionalities, or engaging in diplomatic persuasion (Copelovitch 2010; Stone 2011; Carnegie and Clark 2023). However, there is a surprising lack of research on how these tools are combined into cohesive strategies to counter threats, punish hostile members, and nurture long-term cooperation.

IOs face structural and operational constraints that limit their ability to coerce or compel. As supranational entities, they are coalitions of diverse member states, each with their own policy priorities and domestic pressures. Decision making within IOs often requires internal bargaining, making enforcement inconsistent and subject to compromise. Moreover, IOs typically lack direct control over populations or traditional governance organs, further distinguishing their tools from those of states.

However, one overlooked dimension of IOs' power is their relationship with domestic publics. While IOs often operate out of the public eye, their legitimacy hinges on perceptions of their responsiveness and value among ordinary citizens (Dellmuth 2018; Dellmuth and Tallberg 2023). Critiques of a "democratic deficit" argue that IOs are detached from the will of the people (Dahl 1999), but we build on existing work on IO legitimacy and instead contend that these institutions actively seek public buy-in, just as populist leaders often mobilize public opposition to IOs. Such institutions do so because they recognize that cultivating public support can indirectly influence state leaders, incentivizing greater engagement with global governance.

In sum, the prevailing narrative in much of the existing literature assumes that IOs are passive actors, mechanically reacting to state actions and operating within limited bounds. We challenge this assumption. IOs wield extensive agency and strategically deploy their resources to build positive relationships with member states, partner organizations, and even domestic publics. While their tools differ from those of states, IOs employ them with a similar goal: to maintain cooperation and fulfill their mandates despite opposition.

Understanding IOs as proactive, resourceful players in the international system re-frames common perspectives on global governance. Far from being mere instruments of state power, these institutions actively shape the dynamics of interstate cooperation, demonstrating resilience and adaptability in the face of populist challenges.

1.4.1. *Key Players in the Fight for IOs*

This book grapples with urgent questions: What tools do international organizations have at their disposal with which to assert authority, attract support, and rein in opposition from populist member states? How do their actions shape the broader landscape of global governance? To address these questions, we delve into the inner workings of IOs, exploring the motivations and actions of the key players within them. Four main groups shape IO behavior: IO staff and management, nonpopulist member states, populist actors, and domestic publics.

Indeed, IOs are not just collections of member states but dynamic entities driven by mission-focused bureaucrats and leaders who are deeply committed to their survival and the preservation of the international order. This conceptualization draws on political sociology, which highlights how IO staff are socialized into their organization's unique culture and practices, transforming them into stewards of the IO's mission rather than mere representatives of their home countries (Chwieroth 2015; Honig 2018). Career concerns loom large—when populist states retreat or disengage, IOs often face resource constraints that lead to program cuts, staff layoffs, and, in extreme cases, organizational collapse (von Borzyskowski and Vabulas 2024b). Populist obstruction also undermines field operations, as staff rely on state cooperation to achieve performance targets. For instance, World Bank staff are evaluated using quantitative benchmarks, which can become unattainable when member states refuse to share critical data or hinder program implementation.

But beyond career pressures, IO bureaucrats and leaders are ideologically driven. Many staff join IOs out of a genuine commitment to international cooperation and causes, often sacrificing higher-paying private sector opportunities (Honig 2018). Once inside, they are steeped in the organization's norms and practices, developing a deep loyalty to its mission (Weaver 2008; Clark and Dolan 2021). IO leaders, meanwhile, often pursue agendas shaped by their ideological beliefs (Copelovitch and Rickard 2021). These personal and professional motivations make IO personnel determined to resist populist efforts to undermine their institutions.

For nonpopulist member states—and especially for powerful state backers of global governance—IOs are critical tools for advancing their interests. These states often use IOs to promote economic and political liberalization in target countries, attaching policy conditions to aid or loans and socializing governments into adopting liberal norms (Li, Sy, and McMurray 2015; Kentikelenis, Stubbs, and King 2016). Such states benefit from the stability and predictability of the existing international order and have a clear incentive to maintain IOs as vehicles for their influence (Johnston 2008; Ikenberry 2011a). The United States and many Western European states, who were the primary architects of the liberal order, have historically benefited from international cooperation in these ways. Such states may thus view populist attacks on IOs as direct threats to their strategic interests. These attacks disrupt the mechanisms through which nonpopulist states exercise soft power, or influence others without resorting to coercion. This jeopardizes the benefits such states derive from the current global system.

Populists' attempts to dismantle IOs are not idle provocations; they are credible threats rooted in their pro-sovereignty, anti-elite ideology. Populist leaders are often rewarded domestically for resisting what they frame as overreaching or illegitimate IOs, making their opposition both ideologically consistent and politically advantageous. Such domestic pushback against IOs can harm their legitimacy and limit their ability to achieve their missions, especially during periods of crisis or upheaval when IOs become particularly salient in the public's minds (e.g., the WHO during the COVID-19 pandemic). Together, states and individuals that lead IOs have strong incentives to resist populist attacks, using the available tools and strategies to protect their organizations, maintain their missions, and uphold the international order.

1.5.   IOs' Defensive Playbook

Given their agency and incentives, IOs are far from passive entities in the face of populist attacks. On the contrary, they possess a diverse set of tools with which to preserve their roles and influence on the global stage. While these strategies can be used against various types of opposition, this book focuses on how IOs employ them in concert to combat the unique, large-scale threat of populism. Unlike external challenges, which may call for different approaches, populism presents an internal, ideologically driven disruption that strikes at the very heart of IOs' missions.

Drawing from organizational sociology and international relations, we examine the defensive playbook of IOs, reimagining the classic tools of "carrots" (incentives) and "sticks" (punishments) for IOs. In organizational sociology, carrots and sticks are essential mechanisms for managing conflict and fostering compliance. Within IOs, these mechanisms can be tailored to meet the challenges posed by populist leaders and their constituents. Punishments are designed to sideline detractors and bring them back into compliance, while incentives aim to integrate hostile actors into the organization's norms and culture. Importantly, IOs wield these tools strategically across two key targets: populist leaders and the domestic populations that empower them. By using these strategies, IOs can neutralize opposition, foster cooperation, and adapt to evolving political landscapes.

We conceptualize IOs' defensive tactics within a framework of four strategies: sidelining or appeasing populist leaders, and sidelining or appeasing their constituents (see table 1.1). These approaches are often employed simultaneously, comprising a multifaceted response to populist challenges.

When IOs sideline populist leaders, they minimize reliance on such leaders' cooperation and proceed with reduced participation. This strategy often

TABLE 1.1. IOs' defensive toolkit

	Sideline	Appease
Populists	Reduce reliance on populists; improve capacity; cooperate with other IOs, states, NGOs	Make policy concessions; reform to benefit populists (e.g., increase vote share)
Constituents	Engage populists covertly; empower nonpopulist actors	Cue the public; employ populist language

involves sanctions, suspensions, or other penalties to punish noncompliance and deter similar behavior from others. IOs can also strengthen their independence by developing in-house expertise or focusing on areas where they are less reliant on populist states. Further, by building self-sufficiency or fostering partnerships with nonpopulist states, NGOs, or other IOs, they mitigate the impact of populist disengagement. For example, after the first Trump administration withheld energy-related data from the World Bank, the organization turned to Arab multilateral development banks for information, bypassing the United States entirely—an example we return to in chapter 4.

Appeasing populist leaders involves concessions to these leaders, such as offering favorable terms, material benefits, or reforms that address their grievances. For instance, international financial institutions like the World Bank and the IMF have historically provided lenient conditions to secure populist cooperation, as we show in chapter 5. Similarly, the WTO proposed reforms to its voting and procedural structures in response to the Trump administration's criticisms. These measures aim to mollify populist leaders and prevent further disruptions to IO operations.

IOs can also sideline populists' constituents. Populist leaders often face domestic backlash for engaging with IOs, as cooperation can appear inconsistent with their anti-globalist rhetoric. IOs exploit this vulnerability by engaging populists covertly or empowering domestic actors who oppose local populist policies. For example, leaders like Silvio Berlusconi and Hugo Chávez continued to collaborate with the IMF in private while publicly denouncing it. Alternatively, IOs can strengthen domestic counterweights to populist agendas by supporting nonpopulist groups within a country. By fostering alliances with civil society organizations or subnational governments, IOs can create alternative pathways for engagement and diminish populist influence.

Finally, IOs can appease populists' constituents. To reduce populists' ability to leverage anti-IO rhetoric, organizations can work to win over domestic populations. This involves public outreach, emphasizing the tangible benefits that IOs provide, such as foreign aid, infrastructure projects, or economic support. Branding aid projects with IO logos, as seen with many UN initiatives, is one example of how organizations boost their visibility and reputation. IOs may also adopt populist rhetoric themselves, presenting their work as a defense of ordinary citizens against corrupt elites. During the eurocrisis, both the IMF and the EU emphasized how their reforms aimed to reduce corruption and protect everyday citizens in Greece, positioning themselves as allies of the public rather than as distant, elite-driven institutions.

IOs often adopt multipronged responses to populist threats. Rather than rely on a single strategy, they combine approaches in order to maximize their effectiveness. For instance, while appeasing populist leaders may preserve engagement, IOs may simultaneously sideline populist constituents to limit domestic blowback to such cooperation. Similarly, covert collaboration with populists can complement public outreach efforts that seek to boost public support for IOs over the long run.

The need for multiple tactics reflects the complexity of the populist threat. IOs often face resistance from multiple populist leaders and must adapt their strategies to suit different contexts. Internal dynamics within IOs also contribute to this variability, as staff, leadership, and nonpopulist member states may have differing priorities and preferred tactics. For example, the IMF has simultaneously provided favorable terms to populists, increased its independence from populist states, and launched public campaigns to build support among domestic audiences, as we explore in subsequent chapters.

While IOs possess a robust defensive toolkit, their ability to employ specific strategies depends on context. Appeasement may be less viable if IOs lack desirable resources to offer or if populist demands conflict with core organizational functions. Similarly, sidelining strategies are more effective when IOs have alternative sources of funding, expertise, or information available to them. Factors like organizational size, funding, and visibility also shape IO responses. Larger, well-resourced IOs have more tools at their disposal, while smaller organizations may struggle to adapt. Visible IOs, such as the WHO during the COVID-19 pandemic or the IMF during economic crises, can more effectively appeal to domestic populations, while less prominent organizations may find it harder to influence public opinion given limited public awareness. These scope conditions are discussed further in the following chapter. We do not test the circumstances under which IOs employ one strategy as compared with another; instead, we expect that IOs employ each method to some degree in order to combat populism. We highlight the general prevalence of each tactic as an essential part of IOs' multilateral toolkit.

1.6. Downstream Consequences

While IOs seek to defend themselves in order to endure populists' attacks, their actions can have far-reaching consequences, reshaping their power, agency, transparency, and legitimacy—and even influencing the trajectory of populism itself. While our analysis primarily focuses on how IOs utilize various defensive strategies, we also consider such implications for global governance. Drawing on existing literature and concrete examples, we highlight how IOs' responses to populist challenges can bolster their resilience but may also amplify the very threats they seek to neutralize.

IOs' defensive strategies often come with trade-offs that can affect their legitimacy and exacerbate the very populism they seek to counter. Populists already perceive IOs as elitist and overreaching, imposing constraints on national sovereignty. IO actions can reinforce these narratives in several ways.

First, engaging with populists behind closed doors to maintain cooperation risks making IOs appear even more opaque and unaccountable, alienating both populists and nonpopulists alike if these covert communications are uncovered.

Second, efforts to engage populists' constituents, such as using populist-friendly rhetoric or emphasizing grassroots benefits, may address transparency concerns but could alienate the IOs' traditional supporters, who may view such tactics as pandering or simplistic. Populist supporters, too, may find this rhetoric inauthentic—IOs are often perceived as untrustworthy when promoting their own brands (Dellmuth and Tallberg 2023).

Third, sidelining populist leaders can validate their criticisms of IOs as elite-dominated bodies that marginalize dissenting voices. By reducing populists' ability to influence policy and access the benefits of membership, sidelining lowers the costs of noncooperation, encouraging further retrenchment.

Fourth, appeasing populist leaders with concessions or reforms may embolden them, providing public victories they can exploit domestically while fueling perceptions among nonpopulist members that the IO is unfairly biased or politically compromised.

Indeed, populism not only fractures IOs internally but also reshapes power dynamics within them. Concessions made to appease populist states—whether through reduced requirements or increased influence—often empower these actors disproportionately. Populists, in turn, can leverage this newfound power to undermine the IO's traditional objectives. For example, populist leaders may weaken enforcement mechanisms, challenge accountability measures, or reduce constraints on member states. Trump's campaign to cripple the WTO's dispute settlement system and African states' resistance to international courts exemplify this trend (see Voeten 2020). By weakening IO autonomy, populists make it easier for states to flout international norms, diminishing the authority of global governance as a whole.

Moreover, in an era of heightened geopolitical competition, IOs' actions to counter populism hold significant implications for the liberal international order. Populists' antagonism toward global governance weakens Western-led institutions and creates openings for revisionist powers like China to assert their influence. During Trump's first presidency, for instance, Chinese president Xi Jinping seized the moment to bolster China's role in the WTO and portray his country as a global leader on climate change after the United States withdrew from the Paris Agreement.[12] These dynamics reveal a dangerous paradox: While IOs work to defend themselves from populist threats, their responses can inadvertently strengthen alternative powers, both from within and beyond the institution.

The cumulative effect of these responses can reshape IOs' standing on the global stage, forcing them to walk a fine line between preserving their authority and risking unintended consequences. While appeasement and reform may preserve status quo levels of engagement, they risk compromising transparency and legitimacy. Conversely, sidelining and confrontation can isolate populist states but may deepen divisions and embolden revisionist powers. Our findings thus underscore both the resilience and fragility of Western-led organizations, as well as the stakes involved in their continued global leadership.

In the concluding chapter, we argue that IOs can mitigate these risks by carefully weighing the costs and benefits of their strategies and striving for a balanced and comprehensive approach. Flexibility and adaptability are crucial

---

12. "Xi Pledges More Openness as China Fulfills WTO Commitments." Xinhua Net, November 5, 2021. https://english.www.gov.cn/news/topnews/202111/04/content_WS6183 dfeec6d0df57f98e4874.html.

if IOs are to endure populist episodes without compromising their legitimacy or fueling further backlash. As *Global Governance Under Fire* demonstrates, IOs possess the tools necessary to survive—but only if they leverage them strategically, judiciously, and with an eye toward long-term stability. By bending to the pressures of populism without breaking, IOs can navigate the turbulence of today's political landscape while safeguarding their role in tomorrow's global governance.

1.7. Contributions

Our work provides a multi-method, unified approach to studying populism and global governance. In doing so, it makes a variety of theoretical and empirical contributions. The book also carries normative implications and offers lessons for practitioners.

1.7.1. Theoretical

This book sheds light on a dimension of international organizations that is often overlooked: their ability to navigate and respond to subversive actors from within. While much of the scholarly focus on IOs has centered on their roles in addressing collective action problems—providing information, reducing transaction costs, and extending time horizons (Keohane 1984; Abbott and Snidal 1998)—these theories generally assume that IOs are coalitions of the willing. In this view, member states join because they see more benefits than costs, and when those benefits diminish, they simply exit. Alternatively, realist accounts dismiss the feasibility of cooperation altogether, offering little explanatory power for the variation in attitudes and behaviors toward IOs that we observe (Grieco 1988; Mearsheimer 1995).

Yet reality is far messier than these accounts imply. Drawing on insights from theories of domestic politics, we argue that IOs, like all institutions, are shaped by competing interests. Some of these actors seek to undermine these organizations from within, driven by ideological opposition or evolving political incentives. Members' preferences and the costs and benefits of participation are not static; they shift over time, producing friction that can lead to inefficiency, underrepresentation, and even hostility (Pratt 2021). At the international level, these dynamics are further complicated by the interplay between state representatives and their domestic constituencies, whose interests often diverge (Putnam 1988).

Existing scholarship has not fully accounted for the presence of hostile actors within IOs. Instead, the literature often assumes that member states act in good faith once they join, with poor outcomes attributed to bureaucratic overreach or isolated instances of noncompliance. These issues are thought to be correctable through internal reforms or punishment mechanisms (Barnett and Finnemore 1999; Autesserre 2014).

We challenge this conventional wisdom by exploring how ideologically driven detractors actively work to undermine IOs from within, reshaping these institutions in profound ways. Far from being passive arenas for state cooperation, IOs are dynamic entities that must grapple with existential threats, including the populist wave that has swept across global politics in recent decades. By highlighting this often-neglected aspect, we contribute to ongoing debates about how political contestation shapes and reshapes organizations (Streeck and Thelen 2005).

Further, our work moves beyond the traditional focus on major geopolitical shifts as drivers of multilateral change (Wallander 2000; Ikenberry 2001). Instead, we examine how continual, incremental political shifts—such as the rise of populist leaders—can fundamentally alter the international environment and the functioning of IOs. We demonstrate that these smaller, persistent pressures are highly consequential in reshaping global governance. In doing so, we extend the literature on how political incentives influence multilateral policymaking (Barnett and Finnemore 1999; Stone 2011; Clark and Dolan 2021), offering new insights into the mechanisms by which IOs adapt, resist, and survive.

While scholars have documented populists' hostility toward IOs and their efforts to dismantle these institutions (Copelovitch and Pevehouse 2019; Voeten 2020, 2021), much of this work portrays IOs as helpless in the face of such challenges. As Dijkstra et al. (2022) note, we are only beginning to understand how IOs respond to existential threats, making this study a timely and necessary contribution to the field. Our research identifies and tests the specific strategies IOs use to defend themselves against the populist onslaught. These strategies range from appeasing populist leaders to sidelining them and engaging directly with their domestic constituents. By exploring these tactics, we offer a more nuanced understanding of how IOs preserve their relevance and authority in an era of mounting challenges.

This book also addresses broader questions about the resilience of IOs and the future of global governance. As populism challenges the foundational principles of the liberal order, IOs are not mere bystanders; they actively resist and adapt to these pressures. However, this resistance comes with trade-offs, raising questions about transparency, legitimacy, and the long-term stability of the international system.

In exploring how IOs navigate such issues, we build on and extend foundational scholarship on the liberal order and its discontents (Borzel and Zürn 2021; Farrell and Newman 2021; Weiss and Wallace 2021). By focusing on the agency of IOs and their ability to pursue their goals even when those goals conflict with member-state preferences (Vaubel 1991; Johnson 2014; Clark and Zucker 2024), we illuminate the practical realities of global governance in an age of upheaval. Ultimately, this work underscores the stakes of understanding IOs not just as facilitators of cooperation, but as actors navigating a turbulent political landscape. By theorizing and testing how IOs defend themselves, we provide a road map for preserving the liberal order in the face of unprecedented threats, offering critical insights into the future of international cooperation.

1.7.2. *Empirical*

This project makes several important empirical contributions, shedding new light on how IOs respond to populist challenges and supplying scholars with valuable data to explore related questions in future research. By documenting how IOs use appeasement and sidelining strategies to counter populists, we reveal the creative and often underappreciated ways these organizations maintain their relevance and authority. To accomplish this, we collected and analyzed several novel datasets.

One such contribution lies in the use of a unique data source: Grays, or written submissions by states filed ahead of IMF board meetings. Secretive interactions between states and IOs are notoriously difficult to study because of their inherent opacity. Yet these submissions provide an unprecedented glimpse into behind-the-scenes diplomacy: Grays remain confidential for years after their initial filing (Carnegie, Clark, and Kaya 2024). Our analysis reveals that populist leaders—despite their public antagonism toward the IMF—engage covertly with the organization more frequently than their nonpopulist counterparts. These findings not only enrich our understanding of populist behavior but also offer a valuable resource for future studies on covert diplomacy in international relations.

We also conducted an original survey experiment on a diverse sample of Americans to examine how IOs might engage skeptical domestic audiences.

Drawing inspiration from real-world IO rhetoric, identified through elite interviews and social media analysis, we tested whether populist-style messaging could sway public opinion toward a hypothetical development IO. The results are striking: IOs can effectively garner support by adopting populist rhetoric, emphasizing their role in helping ordinary people rather than elites. This experiment is paired with new data on IOs' social media strategies, creating a valuable resource for scholars interested in how multilateral institutions navigate public skepticism and build legitimacy among domestic audiences. The findings also open doors for further research on the efficacy of rhetorical strategies in reshaping public perceptions of IOs.

Another key contribution is a dataset on information-sharing agreements between IOs. These agreements, which are especially prevalent among international financial institutions, allow IOs to pool their data and overcome information gaps caused by populist obstruction (Clark 2021, 2025). Our analysis demonstrates that the rise of populism drives IOs to strengthen ties with one another, broadening their access to critical information. Given that each IO draws on a unique blend of data sources—including states, NGOs, private actors, and independent surveillance—these agreements enable organizations to sideline populists and maintain operational capacity. This dataset offers fertile ground for future exploration of the conditions that foster IO collaboration and the consequences of such linkages for global governance.

We also utilize a dataset on the quality and origins of information supplied to IOs (Carnegie, Clark, and Zucker 2024) revealing that populist leaders are significantly less likely to share information compared with their nonpopulist peers. This insight is crucial, as information serves as the lifeblood of IOs, underpinning their ability to function effectively. While much of the existing literature has focused on democracy as a determinant of information sharing (Vreeland, Hollyer, and Rosendorff 2011; Hollyer, Rosendorff, and Vreeland 2018), our data open new avenues for examining additional political factors, such as populism's disruptive role in global governance.

Our analyses rely on a diverse suite of empirical strategies, including descriptive analysis, difference-in-difference designs, text analysis, elite interviews, surveys, and case studies. Interviews with IO officials provided firsthand insights into how populists engage with (or obstruct) these organizations; we include in the appendix a summary table of those we interviewed. Meanwhile, our case studies illustrate the breadth of IOs and populist leaders covered by our theoretical framework, grounding our arguments in real-world contexts. Finally, systematic regression analyses allow us to examine trends across countries and over time, ensuring the robustness of our findings.

By employing this multi-method approach, we demonstrate the generalizability of our framework across diverse IOs and political environments. We hope these data and methodologies will inspire future work on IO resilience, populist disruption, and the broader dynamics of international cooperation. In the concluding chapter, we outline potential directions for future research, emphasizing how our datasets and theoretical contributions can inform the study of populism, IO behavior, and global governance more broadly. By capturing the nuanced interplay between populist actors and multilateral institutions, this project not only advances our understanding of a pressing global issue but also provides tools for scholars to deepen their exploration of these dynamics.

1.7.3. *Practitioners*

Our study examines the defensive measures that IOs deploy to counter populist pressures, holding implications for how IOs can prepare for challenges in the present and future. As populist movements continue to hold sway in diverse political contexts, it is imperative for IOs to strengthen their defenses proactively. We thus offer practical recommendations for policymakers and practitioners committed to preserving and enhancing the role of international institutions. By clarifying the trade-offs of various strategies and proposing a cohesive approach, we offer suggestions to help IOs move toward long-term resilience.

Drawing on the framework of defensive strategies outlined in this book, we argue that IOs should adopt tools from all four categories of responses in concert: sidelining populist leaders, appeasing them, sidelining their constituents, and engaging their constituents. While some strategies are well established in IO playbooks, others have been underutilized, often dismissed as too costly, counterproductive, or unfeasible. However, we contend that a balanced and integrated use of these tools offers the best path forward, providing numerous ideas and examples. Much of this discussion appears in chapter 9.

1.8. Plan of the Book

Chapter 2 develops our theory in detail, introducing our core concepts and deriving our empirical hypotheses. We begin this chapter by defining our main ideas and discussing the conditions under which our theory applies. We lay out the main tenets of populism and explain why populists present a problem for global governance institutions. We then describe the features of IOs that allow them to push back on populist threats, providing specific examples and explaining IOs' options in depth. We discuss the scope conditions, or broad applicability, of the argument and conclude the chapter by deriving our empirical expectations regarding which features IOs adopt to counter populism; these guide the empirical analyses presented in subsequent chapters.

Chapter 3 explores the tactics populists use to undermine IOs. We explain how populists often withhold resources like effort and information as well as engage in toxic communication that can tarnish IOs' reputation and legitimacy. We provide examples of each and demonstrate their prevalence empirically. We show first that populists manipulate information provided to IOs and that their communication is more hostile than that of nonpopulists. We then demonstrate that populists engage less with IOs in public forums than other leaders.

The following four chapters test our theory's predictions regarding specific defensive measures that IOs take to shield themselves from populist attacks: sidelining populists, appeasing populists, sidelining populists' constituents, and appeasing populists' constituents. Chapter 4 analyzes how IOs sideline populists, focusing on the case of information sharing among IOs in particular. Because populists often seek to undermine IOs directly by restricting the flow of information or indirectly by degrading domestic information-collection bureaucracies, we argue that IOs often broaden their information bases by exchanging information with one another. We test our argument using an original dataset of information sharing among IOs that provide development finance to their member states. We show that when IOs face resistance from populist leaders in powerful member states, they sign more and deeper information-sharing agreements with other institutions.

Chapter 5 pivots to a different method IOs employ to combat populist attacks: appeasing populists. In this chapter, we look at how IOs make targeted concessions that benefit populists to mollify them and retain their participation. While a large literature examines when IOs make concessions to allies and friends of leading stakeholders, we analyze when such breaks are awarded to populists. We show that IOs reward members with concessions to prevent them from disengaging and that this keeps more populists in the fold. Pairing statistical analysis using data on the stringency of policy conditionality at the IMF and World Bank with qualitative evidence, we find significant support for our hypotheses. Our findings help make sense of otherwise puzzling instances of breaks given to IO member states.

Chapter 6 examines a third way in which IOs protect themselves from populists: sidelining populists' constituents. We argue that while populists often take aggressive anti-IO stances in public forums, they still desire the benefits of IO membership. Thus, populists are frequently willing to interact with IOs in a behind-the-scenes manner, which allows them to publicly criticize IOs while privately leveraging them to advance their economic and foreign policy agendas. To test our hypothesis, we collected new archival data on states' private participation at the IMF. We find that populists participate more than other types of leaders in these opaque contexts and that their interactions are just as positive in tone as nonpopulists' interactions. This evidence suggests that IOs can increase populist participation by offering covert venues for them to engage, with important implications for institutional design.

In chapter 7, we shift to studying the effects of IO efforts to appease populists' constituents. We focus on how IOs mirror populists' rhetorical style to convince the public that IOs are not distant elites and instead have the people's interests in mind. To test whether such rhetorical tactics work, we ran a survey experiment that manipulates whether a hypothetical development IO uses a populist frame and find that when it does so, people are much more likely to support it. Drawing on interviews with IO officials who worked in particularly contentious states, and extensive data from Twitter/X, we examine an array of cases in which IOs used this proto-populist strategy and show how it can boost support for multilateralism.

Next, chapter 8 provides real-world examples to illustrate how populists undermine IOs in practice, and how IOs respond to these efforts. This chapter serves to illuminate the generalizability of our argument, as we offer cases from a range of IOs, issue areas, and populist countries. In doing so, the chapter shows that populist attacks span the globe and that IOs use remarkably similar strategies to defend themselves across contexts. It also traces the processes through which IOs have battled populist resistance to demonstrate that these strategies can work in practice.

Chapter 9 concludes the book with a discussion of implications for scholars and policymakers, as well as normative considerations that the project raises in terms of transparency, legitimacy, democracy, and equity. We explain how IOs' current strategies may provide reforms and resilience, but they may inadvertently fuel additional resistance. We provide practical recommendations for policymakers and practitioners seeking to preserve the world order. Finally, we delineate the expectations of our framework for the future of global governance and the liberal international order that undergirds it.

2

Theory

THIS BOOK delves into a pressing question for global governance: How do IOs respond to populist challenges, and what are the broader implications of their actions? In addressing this question, we tackle other theoretically significant puzzles, such as why some states receive special concessions from IOs while others are held to strict standards, why IOs sometimes collaborate but at other times compete, and how they navigate the balance between transparency and secrecy. We also explore when and why IOs reach out to domestic audiences and the messages they choose to communicate.

At the heart of our analysis lies a simple yet critical assertion: IOs are not merely passive players in the international arena. Instead, they are strategic agents that actively shape global governance, especially when confronted with existential threats like populism. By focusing on IOs' capacity to push back against opposition, we reveal how these institutions defend their mandates, adapt to challenges, and evolve to meet the demands of a shifting global landscape.

While IOs may use these strategies to counter other adversarial actors, populists present a particularly formidable and sustained challenge. As discussed in the introduction, populism poses a credible, large-scale threat to IOs because of its ideological opposition to global governance and its ability to mobilize domestic support. Unlike transient or isolated challenges, populism represents a structural challenge to the liberal international order. Populist leaders often frame IOs as elitist and out of touch, portraying them as threats to national sovereignty. These criticisms resonate with domestic audiences, undermining IOs' legitimacy and effectiveness.

In response, IOs face a range of strategic choices. They must decide how to counter populist opposition while maintaining their credibility and relevance. This book theorizes the menu of options available to IOs, from appeasing populists through concessions to sidelining them and engaging directly with their domestic constituents. We examine how IOs formulate these responses, the decision makers involved, and the implications of these strategies for global governance. We also outline the empirical strategy we adopt in the following chapters to assess the theory and conclude with a description of the international finance arena in which we conduct many of our statistical tests.

2.1. Defining Populism: Understanding the Challenge to IOs

To build a unified theory, it is essential to first define our key concept: populism. While scholars have long debated its precise contours, recent literature coalesces around two central ideas. First, populists believe a nation's "true people" are locked in perpetual conflict with outsiders, including establishment elites. Second, populists assert that nothing should constrain the will of these "true people" (Mudde and Rovira Kaltwasser 2017). These principles form the backbone of the populist worldview and underpin the challenges they pose to IOs.

Populism is widely regarded as a "thin-centered ideology" (Mudde and Rovira Kaltwasser 2017; Busby, Gubler, and Hawkins 2019) because, unlike more comprehensive worldviews (e.g., liberalism or fascism), it is compatible with other belief systems. As such, populism often fuses with other ideologies, broadening its appeal and impact. On the right, it aligns with nativism, defining the "true people" in ethnic or racial terms and targeting immigrants or minorities as threats to national identity (Copelovitch and Pevehouse 2019). On the left, populism frequently adopts socialist overtones, framing the "true people" as economically disadvantaged groups locked in a struggle against wealthy elites (Copelovitch and Pevehouse 2019).

This ideological flexibility allows populism to thrive across a range of political regimes, from established democracies to authoritarian systems. Leaders as diverse as Venezuela's Hugo Chávez, the United States' Donald Trump, and Turkey's Recep Tayyip Erdoğan exemplify populism's adaptability. Often, populists come to power through democratic means, only to implement illiberal reforms once in office, as seen in the leadership of Brazil's Jair Bolsonaro and Hungary's Viktor Orbán.

Central to populism is a deep distrust of elites—often including scientists, technocrats, and bureaucrats—who are seen as out of touch with the experiences and priorities of ordinary people (Carnegie, Clark, and Zucker 2024). Populists challenge these experts' authority to "formulate truth claims," prioritizing practical knowledge and lived experience over formal education and specialized expertise (Rigney 1991, 447). This skepticism often extends to international bodies, like the United Nations, World Trade Organization, and International Criminal Court, which populists accuse of using expertise as a tool for exploitation (Brewer 2016).

This anti-elite sentiment resonates strongly with populist constituents. Supporters often feel neglected by traditional governance structures and turn to populist leaders as champions of their concerns (Rico, Guinjoan, and Anduiza 2017). Economic anxiety, perceived loss of status, and frustrations over immigration frequently fuel this alignment (Malhotra, Margalit, and Mo 2013; Baccini and Weymouth 2021; Ballard-Rosa et al. 2021; Broz, Frieden, and Weymouth 2021). These grievances, coupled with a distrust of expert authorities, leave populist voters particularly susceptible to conspiracy theories and misinformation (Oliver and Wood 2014; Oliver and Rahn 2016). Populist leaders exploit these tendencies, manipulating narratives and denying inconvenient facts to strengthen their appeal.

Populists' opposition to elites takes on a special significance when it comes to IOs, which are often staffed by the very technocrats and experts they vilify. For populist leaders, IOs represent not only a repository of elite influence but also a direct threat to national sovereignty. These leaders often frame IOs as meddling institutions that impose foreign agendas and undermine the will of their domestic constituencies. By attacking global elites, populists position themselves as the authentic voice of ordinary citizens, amplifying their appeal at home (Wajner 2022).

Populists' disdain for IOs is further fueled by the constraints these institutions place on their actions. IOs often enforce rules that limit leaders' ability to implement their agendas or govern unilaterally (Vreeland 1999; Drezner 2017). These restrictions can be deeply frustrating for populists, who wish to forcefully assert their sovereignty. When IO mandates conflict with domestic priorities, populists blame these institutions for stifling progress and alienating their constituents. This narrative resonates with populist supporters, who already harbor resentment toward elites and internationalism. As Taggart (2000) puts it, "internationalism and cosmopolitanism are anathema to populists."

This antagonism toward IOs has far-reaching implications for global governance. By rejecting the legitimacy of international norms and institutions, populists challenge the foundations of multilateral cooperation. As they erode public trust in IOs, populist leaders create opportunities for nationalistic policies to flourish, often at the expense of collective action on critical global issues such as climate change, public health, and economic stability.

2.2. Populist Tactics to Undermine IOs

Populists often resent IOs' elite-driven and constraining nature, viewing them as obstacles to their vision of direct representation of "the people." In response, populist leaders frequently seek to undermine IOs' authority and legitimacy. To do so, they draw from a diverse arsenal of rhetorical and material tactics, each designed to disrupt the functioning of these institutions and either weaken their standing on the global stage or operate more in line with populists' agendas.

As we previewed in the opening chapter, populists target IOs by withholding critical resources—such as effort, information, and funding—and engaging in toxic communication strategies that sow discord and erode organizational cohesion. These methods are deliberately crafted to reduce IOs' effectiveness and legitimacy, making it harder for them to carry out their mandates. In this chapter, we delve deeper into these subversive strategies, unpacking how populist leaders deploy them to advance their agendas.

Our account focuses on what we identify as the most prevalent and impactful tactics in the populist playbook. While not exhaustive, these strategies illustrate the breadth and depth of populist opposition to IOs. From calculated noncompliance to the strategic withholding of resources, populist leaders employ a range of approaches that challenge IOs' ability to govern effectively. These strategies are summarized in table 2.1.

However, this chapter is not solely about populists' actions; we also connect these tactics to the broader consequences they have for the international system. Chapter 3 builds on this foundation by presenting empirical tests that support the patterns and mechanisms outlined here. Yet our primary focus remains on IOs' responses to these attacks—how they can adapt, counter, and ultimately endure. By examining the interplay between populist subversion and IO resilience, we aim to illuminate the lasting impact of populism on global governance.

2.2.1. Exit

Few actions demonstrate dissatisfaction with IOs more dramatically than a state's decision to exit. Since World War II, there have been more than 200 cases of IO withdrawal, and this trend has accelerated in recent years, fueled

TABLE 2.1. Populist tactics to undermine IOs

Tactic	Examples
Exit	• US withdrawal from the Paris Agreement during Trump's first presidency. • Brexit and its potential domino effect on the EU. • Greece's near-departure from the Eurozone during the Eurocrisis.
Creating competitor IOs	• Establishment of the Asian Infrastructure Investment Bank (AIIB) as an alternative to the World Bank. • Creation of regional organizations like the Visegrád Group (V4) and the Bolivarian Alliance for the Peoples of Our America (ALBA). • Use of rival IOs for symbolic politics, as seen with UNASUR.
Cutting funds	• Trump withholding funding from NATO, WHO, UNHCR, and UNESCO. • US Congress delaying contributions to the World Bank and United Nations. • Freezing of funding to UNRWA by the US and European states.
Effort withholding	• Populist states ignoring WTO rulings or skipping IMF and World Bank Board meetings. • Refusal to comply with IO regulations or norms, undermining collaboration.
Information manipulation	• Withholding or falsifying economic data critical for IMF assessments. • Erosion of domestic data collection mechanisms under populist regimes. • Spreading misinformation about IOs to fuel public mistrust.
Co-optation	• Appointment of David Malpass to lead the World Bank, deprioritizing climate initiatives. • Use of WTO national security exceptions to impose tariffs, as seen under Trump. • Delegates from rights-abusing states co-opting human rights organizations.
Toxic communication	• Scapegoating IOs through speeches, tweets, and campaign slogans. • Greece's Syriza party criticizing the IMF during elections but negotiating with it in power. • Amplification of conspiracy theories to undermine IO credibility.

by the rise of populist politics (von Borzyskowski and Vabulas 2019b). Exiting an IO is not a casual decision; most institutions establish formal procedures that states must follow, including notifying other members and observing a probational waiting period—typically at least a year—before completing the process (Copelovitch and Putnam 2014). The United States encountered such a waiting period when exiting the Paris Agreement during Donald Trump's first term as president. Exit is also costly, sometimes leading to IO death (von Borzyskowski and Vabulas 2024b).

Given its costliness, even the mere threat of withdrawal can serve as a powerful coercive tool. These threats are not idle; they often create significant bargaining leverage for leaders, forcing IOs to make concessions to retain their participation (Clark 2022). Donald Trump, for instance, frequently threatened to leave major institutions such as NATO and the WTO, which elicited proposed reforms and benefits from these institutions, as we detail in our case studies.

When a state publicly considers exiting, it may raise doubts about the organization's mission, effectiveness, and cohesion. The impact of such threats often hinges on their credibility, and populists' threats may be especially credible—their ideological and electoral motivations support disengagement from IOs, reducing the perceived costs of withdrawal and making their threats more destabilizing.

Despite their rhetorical fervor, however, populist exits from IOs are relatively rare because the costs of withdrawal are substantial. For the departing state, the process is typically protracted and politically contentious, drawing significant ire from other members. These exits are not isolated events—they carry the risk of a contagion effect, where the departure of one state inspires others to follow. This fear loomed large during Britain's exit from the EU and Greece's near-departure from the eurozone during the eurocrisis, as American and European officials worried about a domino effect (Clark 2025).

Leaving an IO also comes with immediate losses. States forfeit access to the economic, security, and informational benefits that membership provides (Keohane 1984; Davis 2023). IOs serve as hubs for negotiation, socialization, and intelligence sharing, and departing members lose their influence over these processes.[1] This absence from decision making can result in policy outcomes that diverge even further from the departing state's interests, leaving

---

1. Even the ability to set the deliberative agenda carries significant benefits (Arias 2022; Arias, Clark, and Kaya 2024).

them with little recourse to advocate for their positions or those of their allies (Hirschman 2004).

Further complicating the calculus, exit often requires undoing costly commitments made upon joining the institution. IO membership frequently demands policy adjustments to meet accession criteria, as illustrated by China's liberalization to join the WTO in 2001. These investments lose value upon departure, and rejoining the IO later would likely require additional concessions because countries often shirk their multilateral commitments over time. Moreover, existing members may exploit the re-entry process to extract more favorable terms or block re-admission altogether for political or security reasons (Davis and Pratt 2020; Davis 2023).

The repercussions of exit extend far beyond the departing state; they can also damage an IO's stability and legitimacy. When a powerful state or even a coalition of smaller states withdraws, the institution risks losing critical financial and informational resources, potentially crippling its ability to fulfill its mandate (Broz 2008; von Borzyskowski and Vabulas 2024b). Staff and management structures may falter as IOs rely heavily on powerful member states to staff their secretariats and host their headquarters (Kilby 2013; Novosad and Werker 2019; Parízek 2017), leaving the IO vulnerable to irrelevance or even collapse (Gray 2018).

2.2.2. Creating Competitor IOs

Leaders dissatisfied with existing IOs have increasingly turned to an alternative to exit: creating rival institutions or aligning with alternative organizations that better suit their preferences. In an era of IO proliferation, states now have a growing menu of options (Alter and Meunier 2009; Pratt 2021), enabling populists to participate in IOs whose rules, norms, or memberships align most closely with their ideological leanings. This strategy allows them to sidestep IOs they perceive as elitist or overly constraining.

However, establishing a new IO is no small feat. It requires immense financial resources, political will, and the ability to recruit a critical mass of member states. Thus, states often first try to reform an IO to suit their needs rather than create a new one (Jupille, Mattli, and Snidal 2013). Building institutional credibility is also a steep hurdle—one that involves securing the legitimacy necessary to ensure compliance from member states (Clark and Pratt 2024).[2]

---

2. See also Freeman, Carroll, and Hannan (1983) on the "liability of newness."

These challenges are particularly pronounced in issue areas with high barriers to entry, such as emergency financing, which demands substantial reserves of financial capital and expertise (Lipscy 2015, 2017). Not surprisingly, many successful IOs have emerged in the aftermath of crises, when systemic shocks created the political space for new multilateral arrangements to take root (Ikenberry 2001).

Even when new IOs are successfully launched, they often pale in influence compared with their established counterparts, which have spent decades cultivating resources, expertise, and trust among states. For example, despite the existence of numerous regional alternatives to the IMF, countries facing financial crises often turn to the Fund because of its unparalleled resources and technical know-how (Henning 2011). Similarly, some so-called challenger IOs mirror the structures of existing institutions, making them less true alternatives and more complementary bodies. The Chinese-led Asian Infrastructure Investment Bank, for instance, shares notable similarities with the World Bank and even co-finances development projects alongside it (Clark 2021, 2025).

Yet not all challenger-led IOs aspire to wield the same level of influence as traditional institutions. Populists often prioritize IOs that reinforce their nationalist agendas and grant them more autonomy rather than those that demand stringent compliance or oversight. These alternative IOs frequently act as platforms for symbolic politics—forums for defiant speeches, elaborate ceremonies, and other displays of leadership that boost domestic rather than international legitimacy.

Examples of such populist-driven IOs include the Visegrád Group (V4), a loose alliance of Hungary, Slovakia, Poland, and the Czech Republic; the Bolivarian Alliance for the Peoples of Our America (ALBA), championed by Venezuela's Hugo Chávez; and the Union of South American Nations (UNASUR). These organizations often function less as robust multilateral entities and more as vehicles for populist leaders to advance their national interests and criticize Western-led institutions (Söderbaum, Spandler, and Pacciardi 2021).

From the perspective of established IOs, the rise of rival institutions poses significant risks. Competition among IOs fragments the international system, forcing established organizations to offer more favorable terms to retain member states. This dynamic undermines their leverage, making it harder for them to enforce rules and achieve their policy goals. In some cases, it leads to a race to the bottom, with IOs prioritizing membership retention over long-term efficacy (Busch 2007; Alter and Meunier 2009; Davis 2009; Clark 2022).

In short, state participation is the lifeblood of IOs. Membership provides critical financial resources, information, and legitimacy—without which IOs struggle to function as effective governance actors. The emergence of alternative IOs disrupts this delicate ecosystem, allowing states to shop for institutions that best suit their interests and ideologies. This is particularly true when rival IOs are spearheaded by populists, whose goals often clash with those of traditional, Western-led organizations.

Competition among IOs is most intense when leading member states in each organization are ideologically or geopolitically unaligned (Clark 2025). For example, populist-led IOs frequently position themselves as counterweights to Western institutions, reinforcing divides between global governance models. This divergence adds another layer of complexity to an already fragmented international landscape, challenging the ability of IOs to act cohesively in addressing global issues.

The proliferation of rival institutions led by populists underscores the challenges facing established IOs in maintaining their relevance and authority. While these alternative IOs may lack the resources or influence of their more entrenched counterparts, their very existence shifts the balance of power, creating new fault lines in the international order. For traditional IOs, navigating this competitive terrain requires a careful balance of reform, strategic engagement, and resilience to counter the populist-driven reshaping of global governance.

2.2.3. Cutting Funds

One of the most impactful ways populist leaders can weaken IOs is by cutting their funding. This tactic, whether executed through outright refusal to make payments or through strategic delays, severely undermines an IO's operations. The 2024 decision by the United States and several European states to freeze funding to UNRWA (United Nations Relief and Works Agency for Palestine Refugees) serves as a stark example of how destabilizing such actions can be.[3]

For most IOs, member-provided funding is the vast majority of their budgets, underpinning nearly every activity, from operational costs to on-the-ground missions. While some organizations benefit from private sector contributions or returns on investments, this nonstate financing typically accounts for a small fraction of their overall budgets. Contributions from

---

3. Rob Merrick, "US Isolated Over UNRWA Funding Freeze After UK Restores Support." Devex, July 19, 2024.

member states are often structured in one of three ways: voluntary (as in the World Health Organization), formula-based (as in the IMF and World Bank), or a hybrid of the two. Regardless of the system, the largest financial contributors tend to be the world's most powerful countries, making the loss of their support especially devastating.

The United States, for instance, has a long history of using funding as leverage to shape IO policies, with Congress frequently holding up contributions to the World Bank and United Nations to influence their agendas (Nielson and Tierney 2003; Broz 2008; Novosad and Werker 2019). President Donald Trump escalated this approach during his first term in office, withholding funds from NATO, the WHO, UNHCR, and UNESCO to pressure these organizations into adopting more favorable policies. By cutting funding, populist leaders achieve a dual political victory: redirecting resources to domestic causes while simultaneously undermining what they often characterize as unaccountable global institutions.

This tactic is particularly advantageous for populists because it is both reversible and strategic. Withholding funds can coerce IOs into granting concessions without severing ties entirely, allowing populist states to continue benefiting from the organization's operations. Many IOs, such as the United Nations, have mechanisms that prevent immediate penalties for nonpayment; voting power or membership privileges are suspended only after arrears accumulate for years. This leeway gives populists a prolonged window to manipulate the situation to their advantage.

When funding is abruptly withdrawn, the consequences for IOs can be severe, especially for those with extensive operations, large secretariats, or numerous field missions. These organizations depend on member contributions to pay staff, equip field agents, fund programs, and deliver aid or loans. While some IOs, like the World Bank, generate revenue through interest on loans to middle-income countries, this is often insufficient to sustain concessional programs or high-risk projects. For example, the World Bank's International Development Association (IDA), which provides concessional loans to the world's poorest countries, relies heavily on periodic replenishments from member states. Threats to this funding, such as those historically issued by the US Congress, have triggered internal crises, disrupted operations, and raised doubts about the organization's reliability and legitimacy (Nielson and Tierney 2003).

The cascading effects of budget cuts can include program suspension, staff layoffs, and delays in critical initiatives, particularly in organizations already stretched thin by their mandates. For instance, while some IOs manage to buffer short-term financial shocks through investment income, these reserves are rarely sufficient for long-term purposes. This fragility underscores how vital consistent funding is to the survival of IOs, especially those tasked with responding to crises or providing essential services.

Populists' deliberate use of funding as a political weapon creates ripple effects that extend beyond the immediate fiscal challenges. Large-scale funding cuts undermine IOs' legitimacy by casting doubt on their stability and their ability to fulfill their mandates. When powerful states disrupt their financial commitments, they send a signal to other member states, potentially encouraging further noncompliance; if the richest states in the international system are unwilling to spare funding to IOs, why should smaller states? The resulting instability risks creating a contagion effect, where IOs become hollowed-out shells incapable of carrying out their missions effectively.

2.2.4. *Effort Withholding*

Scholars have long studied the factors driving noncompliance with IOs, from domestic political dynamics (Findley, Nielson, and Sharman 2014) to the specifics of treaty design (Downs, Rocke, and Barsoom 1996). Yet the role of populism in shaping compliance with international commitments has received far less attention. Populist leaders often adopt an antagonistic stance toward global governance, reducing their cooperation with IOs in ways that disrupt institutional effectiveness.

Noncompliance by populists can take many forms, from ignoring rules and norms to skipping critical meetings. IOs rely on members to adhere to established regulations, with mechanisms in place to address violations. For example, states that break WTO rules or flout ICSID decisions may face dispute-resolution proceedings and even economic retaliation. Rather than back down, however, populists often escalate these conflicts, refusing to abide by rulings, thus further undermining the credibility of the IOs involved.

Populist noncompliance extends beyond the legal realm to the symbolic. Leaders may refuse to attend IO meetings or send lower-level representatives, signaling their disdain for these institutions. At organizations like the IMF and World Bank, board meetings are essential for approving programs, conducting surveillance, and shaping institutional agendas (Arias, Clark, and Kaya 2024). The absence of high-ranking officials diminishes the scope of collaboration and reduces IOs' ability to carry out their mandates (Frieden 2021).

Noncompliance is an appealing tactic for populists because it is easy to implement and offers a platform to broadcast their opposition to global elites. Yet this approach is not without costs. IOs often impose sanctions, initiate litigation, or cut off access to benefits for noncompliant states (Hafner-Burton 2008). At the IMF, for example, loans are disbursed in tranches, and further disbursements are withheld when states fail to meet conditionality requirements. This can lead to economic fallout and trigger domestic backlash from constituencies reliant on IO benefits.

IOs also face broader risks when powerful states refuse to comply. Noncompliance by influential members can create a ripple effect, encouraging other states to disregard rules and jeopardizing the IO's legitimacy and stability (Cialdini and Goldstein 2004; Carnegie and Carson 2020). The problem becomes especially acute when IOs rely on unanimous agreement to advance their agendas or when noncompliers hold pivotal positions within the organization. In such cases, IOs may find themselves paralyzed, unable to enforce rules or fulfill their missions effectively.

2.2.5.   *Information Manipulation*

Information is a crucial resource that states provide to IOs, and populists can wield it effectively to undermine them. The WHO, for instance, requires comprehensive data on disease outbreaks in order to coordinate global responses (Ge 2022). Similarly, the International Monetary Fund relies on state-provided economic data to forecast systemic risks, while the International Atomic Energy Agency depends on insights into nuclear programs to enforce nonproliferation agreements. The absence of reliable information can cripple global efforts to address trade flows, human-rights violations, health crises, and nuclear compliance, diminishing IOs' ability to deliver on their missions (Carnegie and Carson 2020).

Although IOs employ tools like surveillance technologies, open-source data, and on-the-ground inspections to collect information, their capabilities are often constrained. The IAEA sends inspectors to nuclear sites, and the European Commission monitors elections for fairness (Kelley 2009), but such efforts rarely cover the full spectrum of data needed. Member states frequently resist empowering IOs with greater independent capacity, fearing a loss of sovereignty or an expansion of IO authority into unintended areas (Barnett and Finnemore 1999). States may allow election monitors to be present only at specific polling stations—for example, while pursuing subversion elsewhere (Kelley 2012). As a result, IOs are typically left dependent on the willingness of member states to share critical information.

This dependence gives populists a unique opportunity to undermine IOs. Populist leaders may deliberately withhold data, provide false or incomplete information, or weaken domestic mechanisms for data collection (Giacalone and Knouse 1990; Serenko 2019). For example, if a state halts the publication of economic statistics or dismisses independent experts, the quality of information flowing to IOs deteriorates. By eroding the information pipeline, populists can hobble IOs' ability to function effectively.

Populists can further distort IO-generated data to fit their narratives, selectively presenting findings or simplifying complex issues for political gain (Ebrahim 2002). They often challenge the expertise and authority of the professionals who inform IO decisions, framing them as out-of-touch elites who disregard the will of the people. By questioning IOs' credibility, populists discredit the very foundations of their operations.

In more aggressive cases, populists may spread misinformation about IOs to sow public mistrust. They can amplify conspiracy theories suggesting that IOs operate against national interests or secretly conspire with global elites—extreme examples of scapegoating (Handlin, Kaya, and Günaydin 2023). Highlighting perceived failures while conveniently ignoring successes allows populists to paint IOs as ineffective or even harmful. By exploiting gaps in public understanding and promoting sensationalized narratives, they can erode domestic support for international cooperation.

This strategy is particularly appealing to populists because it allows them to control the narrative. They position themselves as defenders of sovereignty and champions of ordinary citizens while casting IOs as tools by and for a disconnected elite (Copelovitch and Pevehouse 2019). Even when IO initiatives demonstrably benefit a country, populists may frame those benefits as accruing only to domestic elites, or may take credit for generating the benefits themselves, further undermining IOs' legitimacy.

For IOs, the consequences of this information warfare can be dire. Without reliable input from member states, IOs face challenges in achieving their mandates. When their credibility is publicly tarnished, they may struggle to rebuild trust, even if a populist leader is eventually replaced. IOs thus face incentives to ensure the reliable transmission of key data and documents from member states.

2.2.6.   Co-optation

Populists don't just challenge IOs from the outside—they can infiltrate and corrupt them from within, reshaping their objectives to serve their own interests. Co-optation occurs when populist leaders strategically appoint loyalists or like-minded individuals to key positions within IOs, effectively steering these institutions away from their original mandates, or use their influence over IOs to do so themselves. This strategy, while sometimes subtle and difficult to detect when it occurs, can erode IOs' foundations and compromise their legitimacy.

One way populists infiltrate IOs is by staffing them with representatives who resist or actively undermine IOs' missions. For example, countries with poor human-rights records have placed delegates in human-rights organizations, turning watchdogs into lapdogs and diluting their ability to promote global accountability (Hafner-Burton 2012). Similarly, intelligence agencies have leveraged IOs to gain access to sensitive information. The Soviet Union famously exploited its position at the UN to gather intelligence on the United States, while more recently China and Russia have been accused of leveraging their access to the EU and NATO headquarters to obtain confidential data (Bosco 2012). Former Polish prime minister Mateusz Morawiecki has similarly espoused a desire to join forces with other far-right parties across Europe in his role as president of the European Conservatives and Reformists as a means of enforcing a more right-wing agenda in the EU.[4]

Populists also exploit IOs' rules and procedures to their advantage. While IOs often include escape clauses or exemptions for extraordinary circumstances, populists may misuse these loopholes during routine periods to sidestep organizational constraints. For example, Donald Trump in his first term invoked a national security exception under WTO rules to impose higher tariffs, a move that many feared would set a dangerous precedent for other members to follow suit.[5] This type of strategic rule-bending undermines trust in IO governance and encourages other states to defect as well, destabilizing the global rules-based order.

Another form of co-optation occurs when populists install allies at the helm of IOs to align their agendas with national interests. Donald Trump's

---

4. Max Griera, "Morawiecki to Be Elected ECR Party President." *Politico.* January 13, 2024.

5. Krzysztof Pelc, "The US Broke a Global Trade Taboo. But Here's Why the US Measures May Be Legal." *Washington Post.* Monkey Cage. June 2018.

appointment of David Malpass as president of the World Bank raised concerns about the institution's independence. Malpass, a vocal critic of multilateralism, sought to limit interest-generating loans to middle-income states like China and India. He also deprioritized climate change initiatives, scaling back on essential projects and staffing that could have advanced global environmental goals.[6] This pattern of behavior is not isolated; populists like Hungary's Viktor Orbán have used similar tactics to nudge institutions like the European Union in illiberal directions.

While larger powers have the resources and influence to co-opt IOs, even smaller states can find ways to punch above their weight. Institutional features like rotating leadership positions or rules that make smaller states pivotal actors in decision making can amplify their influence. For instance, weaker states often gain significant sway when elected to the UN Security Council or chosen to represent constituencies at the IMF. However, smaller states generally lack the ability to dominate IOs on the same scale as global powers.

The impact of co-optation on IOs can be profound, skewing institutional outputs toward the narrow agendas of populist states and eroding the trust of other members and external stakeholders. IOs may lose credibility as neutral arbiters, making it harder to attract funding, support, and cooperation. The process of identifying and reversing the damage caused by such internal subversion is often slow and fraught, leaving IOs bogged down in inefficiency and discord.

2.2.7. Toxic Communication

Populists can wield yet another powerful, cost-effective weapon in their battle against IOs: rhetoric. By scapegoating IOs for unpopular policies or domestic challenges, populist leaders shift blame and stoke public discontent. This strategy, deployed through speeches, tweets, and campaign slogans, often paints IOs as meddling elites disconnected from the needs of ordinary citizens (Vreeland 1999; Etter, Ravasi, and Colleoni 2019). Such rhetoric doesn't just deflect responsibility—it can make IOs more visible to the public and amplify dissatisfaction with their actions (Copelovitch and Pevehouse 2019; Dellmuth and Tallberg 2023).

For populists, the appeal of rhetorical attacks lies in their simplicity and efficiency. Unlike the labor-intensive processes of cutting funding or creating

6. "World Bank Under Fire for Being 'Missing in Action' on Climate Change." *Financial Times.* December 13, 2021.

alternative organizations, a scathing remark about an IO during a rally or in a viral social media post can be executed with minimal preparation and resources. These attacks allow populist leaders to score domestic political points by presenting themselves as champions of sovereignty and resistance to international elites, all while continuing to enjoy the benefits of IO membership.

Though less costly than many other weapons at their disposal, the issuance of hostile rhetoric can still be risky. If a populist's rhetoric contradicts their actions—such as cooperating with an IO while publicly criticizing it—their constituents may perceive such inconsistency as a breach of trust. This tension was starkly evident in the case of Greece's Syriza Party, which railed against the IMF during its election campaign only to enter negotiations with the Fund once in power (Henning 2017). Such mismatches between rhetoric and policy can erode leaders' credibility, exposing them to backlash from their base.

From the perspective of IOs, rhetorical attacks can inflict significant harm, though less so than when leaders cut off the flow of funds or information. Public trust is a cornerstone of an IO's ability to function effectively, as many organizations depend on a favorable public mood to implement programs and enforce agreements (Milner and Tingley 2012; Brutger and Clark 2022). Anti-IO rhetoric can sow skepticism among the public, undermining the legitimacy these institutions need to operate. Public backlash, fueled by populist messaging, can disrupt program implementation, delay negotiations, and hinder compliance with IO directives. If rhetorical attacks continue to gain traction, IOs may find themselves increasingly hamstrung, unable to enforce their mandates or garner the backing necessary to address global challenges effectively (Hurd 1999; Tallberg and Zürn 2019; Dellmuth and Tallberg 2023).

2.3.   How IOs Fight Back

In the face of populist attacks, IOs are far from passive bystanders—they fight back. When confronted by populists within their ranks, IOs deploy a diverse arsenal of strategies, pursuing four primary options that can be employed individually or in tandem: appeasing populists, sidelining populists, appeasing populists' constituents, and sidelining populists' constituents. While these strategies were introduced briefly in the book's opening chapter, we now delve into each in greater detail, exploring how IOs implement these measures, the conditions that make them feasible, and the potential normative and practical trade-offs they entail.

IOs are typically reactive, addressing populist threats only after they materialize, rather than preemptively adjusting their operations. Institutional inertia, or status quo bias, often keeps reforms at bay until organizations face significant disruptions. Such path dependence has long been noted in scholarly work that highlights how entrenched rules and routines make IOs (and institutions more generally) resistant to change (Bennett and Elman 2006; Page 2006; Kaya 2015). However, crises like those posed by populist leadership can serve as catalysts for adaptation, forcing IOs to evolve in response to threats and reshaping global governance in the process (Krasner 1976; Wallander 2000).

This reactive tendency underscores the need for IOs to weigh their options carefully once they decide to confront populists. Their strategies must account for the severity and credibility of the populist threat, balancing the urgency of immediate action with the long-term implications for their legitimacy and effectiveness.

The bulk of our evidence lies in four empirical chapters, each systematically examining how IOs apply these strategies to counter populists. By testing the prevalence and effectiveness of these tactics, we illuminate the broader implications of populism for global governance. These chapters offer a comprehensive view of IOs' adaptive responses, helping us draw robust conclusions about how populism reshapes international institutions and the rules-based order they uphold.

Through this analysis, we seek to demonstrate that IOs are strategic agents capable of navigating existential threats. Their ability to deploy tailored responses to populist challenges offers crucial insights into the resilience and adaptability of global governance in an era of rising political instability.

2.3.1.   Appeasing Populists

Faced with populist threats, IOs may decide that appeasement is the path of least resistance. By accommodating populists' demands (within reason) and offering tangible or symbolic concessions, IOs can defuse antagonism and ensure continued participation. This approach allows populists to claim victories—both to their domestic audiences and on the global stage—potentially easing tensions and enabling the IO to carry out its work.

Appeasement operates on a simple premise: If populists are given extra benefits or their grievances are addressed, they may dial back their opposition. While populists may harbor general hostility toward IOs, they are often especially antagonistic toward institutions that appear rigid or unresponsive.

Meeting their demands, even partially, can help IOs avoid becoming ongoing targets of populist ire. It may also offer populists an opportunity to portray themselves as champions of their people, extracting favorable outcomes from allegedly unyielding international elites.

IOs have two main levers for appeasing populists: increasing the benefits of membership and decreasing its costs. These tactics leverage the fundamental logic of international cooperation, wherein states weigh the costs and benefits of participation when deciding whether to engage with multilateral institutions (Keohane 1984).

To increase the benefits provided, IOs might offer populists greater formal or informal influence, such as key appointments, larger voting shares, or the ability to shape agendas. Financial incentives like increased lending or technical assistance are another powerful draw. Prestige also plays a role; populists may gain symbolic victories by hosting IO events, delivering speeches in high-profile forums, or receiving favorable classifications.

To reduce costs, IOs might lower the barriers to membership by waiving dues, overlooking rule violations, or turning a blind eye to controversial policies. For instance, dispute-settlement bodies might decline to rule against a populist state, or human-rights institutions might ignore transgressions to avoid conflict (Busch and Pelc 2010; Voeten 2021). Narrowing the scope of obligations by demanding less of members in general has also proven effective in placating resistance.

Importantly, appeasement need not mean major concessions. IOs often adopt symbolic or low-cost measures to address populist grievances without undermining the IOs' core missions. Selective appeasement can involve giving populists just enough to quiet dissent while preserving institutional integrity. For instance, IOs might promise reforms but delay implementation, gambling that a populist leader will leave office before the changes take effect. NATO's symbolic increases in member contributions to appease Donald Trump during his first term—without granting him deeper concessions—exemplify this approach.

Some IOs also use appeasement tactically, providing incremental benefits over time rather than all at once. This creates leverage: If populists continue to escalate their attacks, IOs can withhold further incentives, mitigating the risk of outright extortion. Changes to vote shares in international financial institutions often follow such a pattern (Carnegie and Clark 2023).

Examples of IO appeasement are widespread. The IMF has tailored loan packages for populist leaders, often imposing fewer conditions than on nonpopulist counterparts, as we show in chapter 5. The EU, meanwhile, has tempered its policies to address Viktor Orbán's resistance to liberalization. In other cases, IOs have adjusted their mandates to gain buy-in from skeptical states—examples include the International Energy Agency's inclusion of environmental priorities and the OECD's pivot from addressing tax havens to fostering tax cooperation (Bonucci et al. 2022).

However, despite its appeal, appeasement is not always a viable strategy. Populists with deeply entrenched ideological opposition to multilateralism may reject even generous concessions. Simultaneously appeasing multiple oppositional states can overwhelm an IO's resources and spark discontent among other members, as seen in EU budget negotiations where too many leaders demanded too much (Sadeh, Raskin, and Rubinson 2022). Institutional rules might also constrain IOs' flexibility to appease, and populist leaders constrained by their domestic audiences may find it politically costly to cooperate with an IO, regardless of incentives.

Even when appeasement works, there's no guarantee that populists will play fair. They may accept the concessions only to continue their hostile actions, leaving IOs worse off. In these cases, providing incremental benefits over time can act as a safeguard, ensuring that populists have something to lose if they escalate tensions. Coupling benefits with clear conditions mitigates the risk of future defection.

Granting concessions to populists can also raise serious ethical and reputational questions, with critics accusing IOs of compromising their principles to buy off adversaries. When benefits appear to reward bad behavior, IOs may face accusations of corruption, unfairness, or cowardice. For example, overlooking human rights abuses to placate populists could undermine an IO's credibility as a human-rights authority.

Appeasement may also embolden populist leaders, who can tout concessions as political victories, further solidifying their power domestically. This dynamic risks alienating nonpopulist members and undermining the IO's legitimacy among broader audiences (Hurd 1999; Tallberg and Zürn 2019). It may also encourage pushback by other countries that are skeptical of institutional rules and norms.

Appeasement thus offers IOs a pragmatic way to address some populist challenges. By carefully calibrating concessions, IOs can maintain their operations while minimizing damage to their core missions. However, this strategy requires precision, transparency, and foresight to avoid empowering populists or compromising institutional integrity.

2.3.2.   *Sidelining Populists*

In the face of populist resistance, IOs may find their best course of action is working around rather than directly confronting populist leaders. By reducing interactions with populists and thereby minimizing their influence, IOs can create a buffer, allowing operations to continue with less interference. Interestingly, populists may also welcome a reduced role, avoiding the scrutiny or commitments that come with active participation. This mutual disengagement enables IOs to maintain formal ties with populist-led states, keeping the door open for renewed collaboration if leadership changes.

Sidelining can range from overt measures, like imposing sanctions or suspending memberships to more subtle tactics, such as limiting invitations to key meetings or withholding communication. Sanctions and suspensions are not new; they are often shaped by geopolitical considerations, such as the intransigent countries' closeness to powerful stakeholders (von Borzyskowski and Vabulas 2019a). These actions aim to bring populists back into compliance, deter other states from undertaking similar behavior, or garner support from nonpopulist allies, NGOs, or domestic constituencies.

On a subtler level, IOs can isolate populists by engaging only selectively with them. This mirrors domestic strategies where nonpopulist political parties marginalize populists by excluding them from coalitions or alliances (Akkerman and Rooduijn 2015). Such approaches can also complement appeasement strategies, offering populists benefits for cooperation while exacting costs for defiance.

IOs can sideline populists in several specific ways. First, they can strengthen their internal capabilities. This might include investing in new surveillance technologies, expanding on-the-ground inspections, or refining open-source intelligence analysis. Hiring additional experts or retraining existing staff can also help IOs fill informational gaps left by uncooperative states.

Second, IOs can shift their priorities, reallocating resources to areas where they are less dependent on populist input. By narrowing their focus to tasks that require minimal engagement from resistant members, IOs can continue their operations with fewer disruptions. This flexibility allows IOs to pivot back to broader mandates once populist pressures subside. Such circumspection is a common institutional reaction to member resistance (Busch and Pelc 2010).

Third, IOs can diversify their partnerships, seeking support from alternative sources such as nonpopulist states, NGOs, or other international institutions. For example, co-financing agreements and data-sharing partnerships between IOs can help fill resource and information voids (Clark 2025). NGOs, with their extensive networks and local knowledge, can also provide critical inputs when state cooperation wanes; NGOs are plentiful in global development and environmental research in particular (Bush and Hadden 2019; Hadden and Bush 2020).

Several historical cases highlight the effectiveness of sidelining populists. During Donald Trump's first term, for instance, the Paris Agreement persisted despite US withdrawal, as other nations stepped up to fill the leadership void. Similarly, when Trump cut funding to the UN agency for Palestinian refugees, European and Persian Gulf states increased their contributions to mitigate the impact.[7] The WTO offers another example: When populist leaders blocked its agenda, the director-general sidelined these actors by negotiating around them and removing them from key positions.[8] States that desired continued cooperation also created the Multi-Party Interim Appeal Arbitration Arrangement (MPIA) to hear interstate disputes despite the unwillingness of the United States to confirm judges to the WTO's appellate body, and the MPIA has been effective at deterring breaches of WTO rules (Pelc 2024).

However, while sidelining offers a practical way to navigate populist resistance, it also has limitations. For one, this strategy risks angering populist leaders through exclusion, potentially prompting them to escalate their opposition. They might lobby other states to join their boycott, amplify noncompliance, or even withdraw entirely, leading to broader instability within the IO.

Moreover, some member states may resist efforts to sideline populists, fearing that the IO might become too independent of or unaccountable to member states. Populists may also hold critical resources, such as unique information (e.g., in the security arena) or substantial funding, that are not easily replaced by other sources. For example, when powerful states like the United States are led by populists, their absence can leave significant gaps in IO operations, funding, information, and moral leadership. Without these contributions, cooperation and momentum may stall.

Sidelining populists also raises normative and legitimacy concerns. Excluding certain states from decision-making processes could reinforce accusations

---

7. Amanda Shendruk and Zachary Rosenthal, "Funding the United Nations: What Impact Do US Contributions Have on UN Agencies and Programs?" *Council on Foreign Relations.* 2021. https://on.cfr.org/3D6KPMW.

8. Interview with WTO official, October 2022.

of a "democratic deficit" in global governance (Dahl 1999), wherein IOs are perceived as serving elite interests rather than the broader international community. This perception may alienate not only populist leaders but also their domestic constituencies, fueling further backlash against IOs. Critics might also accuse IOs of overstepping their mandates, acting unilaterally, or wielding disproportionate power. Such perceptions can undermine the trust and credibility necessary for IOs to function effectively, creating long-term challenges even if short-term goals are achieved.

Sidelining can therefore be a valuable tool for IOs, allowing them to navigate the complexities of populist resistance. However, sidelining's success depends on careful calibration. Overuse or misuse can backfire, exacerbating tensions or diminishing an IO's legitimacy.

2.3.3. *Appeasing Populists' Constituents*

In addition to directly engaging with populist leaders, IOs can take a more indirect approach by appealing to the public—the very constituents populist leaders rely on for their power. By making international cooperation salient and cultivating a favorable image among citizens, IOs can soften public opposition to international cooperation, potentially reducing domestic pressure on populist leaders to resist IO engagement.

IOs have a range of tools to connect with citizens and highlight the tangible benefits they provide. Social media, press releases, and partnerships with local media outlets allow IOs to publicize their contributions, such as development aid, infrastructure development, disaster relief, or economic assistance. By branding their aid and assistance programs with their names and logos—think of the UN's iconic blue helmets during peacekeeping missions or UNICEF-branded supplies—IOs ensure that recipients recognize the source of the support (Dietrich and Winters 2015; Cruz and Schneider 2017). Such visibility reinforces the idea that IOs are working in citizens' interests, potentially alleviating economic anxieties that fuel populism.

Direct engagement is another avenue. During technical assistance missions or on-the-ground inspections, IOs like the IMF often send representatives to communicate and build trust with local communities, explaining their initiatives and showcasing their impact. For example, when the WTO provides technical assistance, it often pairs the effort with community-focused events, including social gatherings and talks aimed at demystifying its role and benefits. Similarly, the IMF's resident representatives engage with citizens and policymakers during Article IV surveillance missions (Clark and Zucker 2024), helping to humanize the organization's work.

In some cases, IOs go a step further by adopting anti-elite rhetoric to connect with skeptical audiences. By emphasizing their role in helping "the true people," IOs can tap into populist narratives that resonate with citizens. The IMF's outreach in Greece during the 2010–2014 debt crisis is a notable example, as it framed its interventions as efforts to curb corruption and empower ordinary citizens against entrenched elites. Other IOs, like the WTO, have centralized their communication strategies to better reach skeptical populations, ensuring that their messaging is consistent, accessible, and relatable (Ecker-Ehrhardt 2018b).

While appealing directly to populists' constituents is a promising strategy, it is not without its challenges. In democracies, public opinion on international issues tends to be shaped by domestic opinion leaders rather than by grassroots movements. Foreign policy topics like trade and global governance often have low salience among voters (Guisinger 2009; Guisinger and Saunders 2017), making such issues unlikely to sway electoral outcomes and voters unlikely to hold populist leaders accountable for their decisions in these areas. In authoritarian regimes, citizen influence on leadership can be even more limited, though there are exceptions where public opinion shapes policy decisions (Weiss 2013).

IOs may also face obstacles in reaching constituents because of low awareness of their existence or work. Surveys indicate that many citizens, particularly in countries like the United States, have little knowledge of IOs or their roles in global governance (Brutger and Clark 2022). Without established communication channels, IOs may struggle to reach or resonate with the public. Additionally, citizens might view IO outreach efforts as insincere or manipulative (Dellmuth and Tallberg 2023), particularly if messaging is perceived as overly simplistic or disconnected from local realities. Such perceptions could backfire, reinforcing populist narratives that paint IOs as out of touch.

Efforts to sway public opinion can carry unintended consequences. Branding aid or assistance with an IO's name, for instance, might undermine a government's legitimacy by overshadowing its role in providing public goods. In fragile or weak regimes, this could exacerbate instability or even provoke backlash from leaders. Similarly, adopting populist rhetoric to appeal to citizens can alienate IOs' core constituencies, such as educated elites, who may view such messaging as disingenuous or pandering. If perceived as shaming or undermining a country's leadership, these actions could trigger a rally-'round-the-flag effect, bolstering public support for populists and intensifying opposition to IOs.

IOs thus must demonstrate their value in ways that resonate with the public while avoiding actions that could exacerbate tensions or erode trust. Effective communication, visible contributions to public welfare, and culturally sensitive outreach can help IOs walk this tightrope. However, they must remain mindful of the potential risks and limitations of this approach, tailoring their strategies to the unique political and social contexts they operate in.

2.3.4.   Sidelining Populists' Constituents

A final approach available to IOs is to sideline the constituents of populist leaders, either by empowering nonpopulist domestic actors or by keeping the public unaware of the IOs' interactions with populist leaders. While this strategy can be effective under certain conditions, it also raises significant normative and practical concerns.

One method of sidelining populists' constituents is to actively shift the domestic balance of power in favor of nonpopulist groups. IOs can amplify the voices of nonpopulists or incentivize voters to support nonpopulist leaders by offering tangible benefits. For example, the European Union presented Polish voters with a stark choice, promising significant agricultural subsidies if a nonpopulist government were elected (Csehi and Zgut 2021). These strategies aim to marginalize populist leaders by reducing their domestic appeal and creating incentives for citizens to back alternative political figures.

Another tactic is to circumvent populists' constituents by engaging in covert interactions with populist leaders. Leaders often face electoral punishment for inconsistencies between their rhetoric and actions (Tomz 2007). Publicly criticizing IOs while privately cooperating with them can damage populists' credibility. To avoid this, IOs can offer secure, confidential avenues for communication and negotiation. For instance, the IMF uses private discussions at executive board meetings, where states' submissions are archived and kept secret for five to seven years before being released to the public (Carnegie, Clark, and Kaya 2024). Such measures allow populists to engage constructively without risking domestic backlash.

Similarly, IOs can handle rule violations discretely, opting not to publicize infractions. Institutions like the International Atomic Energy Agency (IAEA) and the WTO often discover violations but carefully weigh whether to disclose them. Public exposure might enforce norms but could also provoke backlash among populists' constituents, who often view IOs as illegitimate constraints on sovereignty. By addressing violations privately, IOs can preserve relations with populists while avoiding inflaming anti-IO sentiment.

Examples of covert interactions abound in the international system. The WTO historically conducted private negotiations in its "green room," while the Bank for International Settlements has long operated under a veil of secrecy (Carnegie and Carson 2020). Similarly, the IMF's approach to behind-the-scenes communication enables sensitive discussions without risking public fallout.

However, sidelining populists' constituents can also have downsides. If populists oppose IOs for ideological reasons, rather than because of constituent pressure, sidelining efforts may fail to change their behavior or result in cooperation. Additionally, this strategy depends heavily on the IO's ability to prevent leaks and press coverage of populist–IO interactions. Populist leaders are unlikely to engage secretly if they suspect that the information might eventually be exposed, thereby jeopardizing their domestic standing. Of course, such concerns are more dire when IOs are salient domestically and thus likely to provoke a strong reaction among the public.

The use of secrecy also raises significant normative concerns. Transparency is often considered a cornerstone of good governance (Besley and Burgess 2002), and increasing secrecy in IOs could invite accusations of hypocrisy and corruption. Many IOs advocate for greater transparency among their member states (Hollyer, Rosendorff, and Vreeland 2014), and adopting secretive practices themselves risks undermining the IOs' credibility and legitimacy.

Furthermore, secrecy can inadvertently reduce democratic accountability. When citizens are unaware of their government's interactions with IOs, they lose an essential channel for holding both domestic leaders and IOs accountable (Hirose et al. 2024; Clark, Dolan, and Zeitz 2025). While secrecy may keep populist states engaged with IOs, it also diminishes the ability of constituents to influence or understand global governance processes.

An additional risk is that secrecy can empower populists to continue their public attacks on IOs while privately benefiting from their operations. By obscuring the benefits that IOs provide, this approach allows populist leaders to perpetuate misleading narratives about the role and value of IOs, thereby deepening public distrust. Over time, this dynamic can erode public understanding of the importance of IOs and further entrench populist influence even as populist leaders accrue material benefits from IOs.

Sidelining populists' constituents is therefore a complex yet often effective strategy. IOs should weigh the benefits of retaining populist participation against the risks of reduced transparency, weakened public accountability, and potential backlash. To mitigate these risks, IOs could consider pairing this approach with targeted public outreach efforts, ensuring that the broader public understands the value of their work without their directly confronting populist leaders.

2.4.   Microfoundations: Actors and Incentives

The dynamics underlying why IOs choose to appease or sideline populists and their constituents are deeply rooted in a web of institutional, psychological, and strategic incentives. These microfoundations can be understood by examining the motivations and pressures faced by the key actors involved: populist leaders, IO leaders, IO bureaucrats, domestic publics, and nonpopulist leaders. By exploring these actors and their incentives, we can better grasp how and why IOs craft their responses to populist pressures.

2.4.1.   Populist Leaders

Populist leaders are, at their core, politicians and thus prioritize staying in power. To achieve this, they must satisfy a range of stakeholders, from their voter base to influential elites and lobbying groups (Grossman and Helpman 1994). These competing demands create a balancing act, especially when it comes to populist leaders' relationship with IOs.

Populists derive much of their appeal from their anti-elite rhetoric, positioning themselves as champions of "the people" against perceived globalist elites. Publicly opposing IOs, which are often seen as bastions of elite power, serves as a potent signal of their commitment to this narrative. For populist leaders, taking high-profile stances against IOs—whether through fiery speeches, dramatic walkouts, or cutting off resources—reinforces their populist credentials and keeps their constituents engaged and energized.

However, populists must also grapple with the tangible benefits IOs provide. From economic assistance to security cooperation, IOs offer resources that can bolster a country's performance—a crucial metric for any leader's popularity. This creates a tension: While shunning IOs may please voters, failing to deliver on economic growth or national stability can erode public support.

Beyond their voter base, populists must also navigate the interests of domestic elites and lobbyists, who play a key role in shaping policies and funding campaigns. Many of these groups have stakes in the very policies IOs promote—such as infrastructure investments tied to aid packages or tariff arrangements negotiated through multilateral agreements. For instance, private companies often implement IO lending projects, profiting from contracts and partnerships with these institutions (Malik and Stone 2018). They similarly may have a heavy hand in trade deals and tariff negotiations (Kim 2017).

However, the relationship with elite interests can cut both ways. For populists like Donald Trump or Jair Bolsonaro, whose platforms include environmental deregulation, conflicts with environmentally focused IOs may be not only expected but strategic. For such leaders, aligning with business interests that oppose IO agendas—such as those advocating for fossil fuel expansion—can further their political goals while undermining the IOs' authority.

Populists' opposition to IOs is not merely performative. Instead, it often stems from deeply held beliefs. Many populist leaders are ideologically predisposed to distrust elite-driven institutions, viewing them as threats to national sovereignty and the will of the people. These beliefs may be shaped by personal backgrounds, political experiences, or broader worldviews, consistent with biographical approaches in international relations (Krcmaric, Nelson, and Roberts 2020).

For instance, a populist leader with a history of nationalist advocacy may harbor genuine disdain for the constraints imposed by IOs, such as trade rules or human-rights norms. These ideological convictions can make their opposition to IOs more resolute, driving them to resist both public cooperation and private engagement.

When deciding whether and how to oppose IOs, populists weigh the costs and benefits of their policy choices through a multifaceted lens. If populists view anti-IO rhetoric primarily as a tool to energize their base, they are likely to stage high-profile confrontations with IOs. This may involve public denunciations or symbolic acts of defiance, paired with quiet cooperation behind closed doors to avoid sacrificing the tangible benefits of IO membership. For ideologically driven populists, opposition runs deeper. These leaders resist IOs both publicly and privately, even at the expense of losing access to IO resources. Their resistance is less about strategic calculation and more about aligning their actions with their convictions.

In both cases, cooperation with IOs occurs only when the perceived benefits, whether material, political, or ideological, outweigh the costs. For IOs, understanding these motivations is critical to crafting effective strategies for navigating populist challenges, whether through appeasement, sidelining, or a combination of the two.

2.4.2.   IO Leaders and Bureaucrats

We argue that IO leaders and bureaucrats possess significant agency in the face of populist challenges. Their careers and the viability of their institutions depend on maintaining the robustness and legitimacy of the IOs they serve (Gray 2018; Tallberg and Zürn 2019). When populist leaders challenge these institutions, IO staff and leaders must adapt to threats while safeguarding the organization's core mission and long-term survival.

For IO bureaucrats, the stakes are personal as well as institutional. Their professional reputations hinge on their ability to deliver results, and populist resistance threatens to derail this. If IOs falter as a result of insufficient financial or informational inputs from member states, staff may face performance penalties, layoffs, or pay cuts (Heinzel and Liese 2021). These public servants are thus incentivized to ensure that their organizations not only persist but thrive.

Yet bureaucrats are not simply careerists. Over time, they become deeply embedded in their institutions, shaped by organizational routines, norms, and decision-making processes. This engenders path dependence that makes them resistant to sweeping change, even in the face of populist threats. Rather than pursuing radical reforms, bureaucrats often take a pragmatic approach, neutralizing populist challenges through appeasement on peripheral issues or by working around them. These strategies enable IOs to maintain their core functions and long-term objectives while projecting an image of flexibility. They are also consistent with documented patterns of incremental reform in IOs (Kaya 2015; Carnegie and Clark 2023).

When confronted with disruptive populist leaders, bureaucrats often prioritize minimizing losses (Kahneman and Tversky 1979). Cognitive biases may steer decision making toward strategies like appeasement or sidelining, which mitigate immediate risks but can sometimes erode institutional norms or integrity. These approaches are seen as the lesser of two evils, preserving the IO's operations in the short term while avoiding more severe disruptions.

IO bureaucrats have access to the tools to counter populist pressures that we have described. For example, they can appease populists by tailoring conditions on loans, adjusting technical assistance programs, or prioritizing populists' concerns on organizational agendas. Judges, for example, may decline to rule against populist states to avoid escalation, while other staff might overlook rule violations.

They can also sideline populists by working creatively around uncooperative leaders, forming partnerships with other institutions, deepening ties with nonpopulist actors, or redirecting resources to initiatives less reliant on populist input. Bureaucrats can further sideline constituents by increasing reliance on secrecy mechanisms to shield IO operations from populist scrutiny or public backlash. Finally, they can appease constituents through their control of social media and public communication, which allows them to highlight the tangible benefits of IOs to win over skeptical domestic audiences.

Leaders of IOs face even greater visibility and accountability. As the public faces of their institutions, they are judged on their ability to navigate crises and achieve organizational mandates. Successful leadership can pave the way for future opportunities in domestic or international politics, further incentivizing leaders to thwart populist resistance.

Institutional leaders can pursue many of the same strategies of bureaucrats, though their influence over policymaking varies across institutions. In many cases, organizational leaders are figureheads with significant agenda-setting authority: They can instruct managers and bureaucrats to pursue certain initiatives or emphasize specific policy areas (Copelovitch and Rickard 2021). They may also publicly praise or criticize certain countries and governments—for example, NATO head Jens Stoltenberg credited Trump for pushing other NATO members to increase defense spending. While substantial changes to voting shares or institutional leadership positions typically require member state assent, leaders can sometimes dole out targeted benefits (e.g., encouraging staff to provide larger loans to certain countries) to appease populists, and they can forge cooperative agreements with other institutions as a part of a sidelining strategy. Finally, they can sideline constituents by increasing secrecy, establishing confidential channels to engage with populist states.

A complicating factor is the risk of IOs' being co-opted by populists. When populist leaders come to power, they often attempt to install skeptics or loyalists in key IO positions, potentially undermining resistance from within (Bellodi, Morelli, and Vannoni 2024). For example, Donald Trump during his first term appointed David Malpass—an outspoken critic of large financial outlays from IOs—as the head of the World Bank, signaling an intent to reshape the institution's agenda.

Complete bureaucratic overhauls, however, are rare. Populists may lack the political capital or institutional authority to dismantle entrenched IO structures. Moreover, the time and energy required for such efforts can deter even the most determined leaders. As a result, populists often focus on placing allies in high-profile leadership roles while leaving much of the bureaucracy intact. This partial co-optation underscores the resilience of IOs but also highlights the challenges they face in maintaining independence and integrity.

2.4.3.   *Domestic Publics*

We conceptualize domestic publics as individuals with preferences over policies and leaders, though we remain neutral on the origins of these preferences. Decades of research demonstrate that people often develop deep partisan attachments (Green, Palmquist, and Schickler 2002) that frequently guide their approval (or disapproval) of policies and institutions, including IOs (Schlipphak, Meiners, and Kiratli 2022). These attachments mean that political leaders and other elites wield considerable influence over public attitudes toward IOs, shaping narratives that either bolster or undermine support.

However, public opinion isn't solely a reflection of elite cues. Citizens' views can evolve independently, driven by personal experiences, new information, or major events. Leaders, even those with strong support, are not immune to losing public favor as a result of scandals, perceived betrayals, or failure to deliver on promises. In democracies, this risk is particularly acute, as leaders who fail to maintain public backing can be ousted at the ballot box. But even in nondemocratic regimes, public opinion matters; authoritarian leaders often rely on public perception to legitimize their rule and quell dissent. In both cases, citizens act as a check on leaders' behavior, constraining their actions when public preferences are strongly felt.

Citizens also play a critical role in shaping the fortunes of IOs. Unlike states, IOs lack territory or military power; they derive much of their legitimacy and influence from public perception (Hurd 1999; Buchanan and Keohane 2006). When citizens lose faith in an IO, the institution's ability to enact meaningful change or fulfill its mission may be severely undermined. This makes public support a cornerstone of IOs' operational viability. Additionally, because public opinion can shape leaders' actions, IOs must be attuned to how they are perceived by domestic audiences.

That said, citizens often think very little about IOs in their day-to-day lives (at least in highly developed contexts; see Dolan and Milner 2023). For many,

IOs exist on the periphery, overshadowed by the immediacy of personal and local concerns. However, during moments of heightened salience—such as financial crises, pandemics, wars, or other major global shocks—public attention shifts sharply toward these institutions. In such periods, IOs become prominent actors in the public consciousness, as their decisions directly affect citizens' lives and dominate news cycles. These moments of visibility can be both an opportunity and a challenge: Public opinion becomes a critical factor in determining whether IOs are perceived as trustworthy stewards of global governance or as dominated by out-of-touch elites. For IOs, maintaining favorable public opinion during such high-stakes moments is essential to safeguarding their legitimacy and effectiveness (Dellmuth and Tallberg 2023).

2.4.4. *Nonpopulist Leaders*

Nonpopulist leaders of IO member states share a fundamental incentive with their populist counterparts—namely, the drive to retain power. This requires maintaining the support of constituents and interest groups while navigating their own ideological beliefs. However, nonpopulists are generally more inclined than populists to engage constructively with IOs and leverage the substantive benefits these institutions provide. Many nonpopulist leaders view international cooperation as a cornerstone of their governance philosophy, aligning with the missions of global institutions like the WTO, World Bank, IMF, and UN, which rely on the participation and buy-in of nearly all states in the international system. Nonpopulist leaders also suffer fewer political costs than populists from meaningful engagement with IOs.

For nonpopulist leaders, the stakes can be high when it comes to the functionality of IOs. These institutions provide critical platforms for influencing international policymaking, enabling leaders to amplify their voices on the global stage. Beyond policymaking, IOs deliver tangible benefits, such as financial aid, favorable trade terms, and enhanced security measures. Without well-functioning IOs, nonpopulist leaders risk losing these advantages, which can weaken their domestic standing and international clout. While not all nonpopulist leaders fully support IOs, their critiques of IOs are often targeted to specific institutions and are not as widespread or programmatic as those of populist leaders.

Recognizing the importance of strong IOs, nonpopulist leaders often play an active role in insulating these institutions against populist threats. Whether by directly engaging in strategies to counter populist resistance or by supporting bureaucrats and IO leaders in their efforts, nonpopulist leaders aim to safeguard the integrity and effectiveness of global governance. In doing so, they help ensure that IOs remain resilient actors capable of advancing international cooperation in an increasingly polarized world. However, this does not mean they support all strategies IOs undertake to keep populist leaders in the fold. They may, for example, oppose attempts to appease populist leaders by redistributing voting shares or issuing large loans. Such steps can invoke fairness concerns.

2.5. Scope Conditions

Populists frequently target IOs with hostility, and as we demonstrate throughout this book, IOs respond with a repertoire of strategies to counter these challenges. These responses highlight a surprising resilience on the part of IOs, helping to explain why these institutions have persisted through turbulent times. However, the effectiveness and applicability of these strategies are not universal; they depend on a range of conditions tied to the characteristics of both IOs and the populist threats they face. Here, we outline the key scope conditions that shape whether and how IOs can respond to threats to their writ.

First, populists do not consider all IOs equal. Their ideology, which is deeply skeptical of elites and resistant to constraints on national sovereignty, predisposes populists to view certain IOs with particular antagonism. IOs that employ international, expert bureaucrats, have sprawling bureaucracies, and intrude deeply into domestic affairs are more likely to attract populist ire.

Institutions such as the EU, WTO, UN, NATO, IMF, and World Bank fit this profile. These organizations are often staffed by highly educated economists, lawyers, and bureaucrats, many of whom are Western-trained and whose policy preferences frequently diverge from those of populist leaders (Nelson 2017; Clark and Dolan 2021). In contrast, smaller regional IOs, which tend to have less stringent rules, more local staffing, and symbolic rather than enforcement-focused mandates, are less likely to provoke populist opposition. Regional financial arrangements, for example, offer small loans with significantly fewer strings than those of the IMF (Clark 2022). These smaller organizations often allow populists to opt out of initiatives and operate with limited enforcement mechanisms, making them less threatening and more accommodating.

Further, not all populist states pose equal threats to IOs. Powerful countries like the United States or the UK, when led by populist leaders, can significantly destabilize IOs. Their contributions to funding, staffing, and institutional legitimacy are critical, giving these states disproportionate influence. IOs are thus more likely to employ costly strategies when dealing with powerful populist states.

Smaller or less wealthy populist states, while less independently threatening, can still wield meaningful influence. They may strategically align with other populist states or exploit IO decision-making rules—such as unanimity requirements—to amplify their impact. In issue areas with negative externalities, such as trade or environmental compliance, even small states' defections can trigger cascading noncompliance, forcing IOs to act (Barrett 2003).

Our theory also carries strategy-specific scope conditions. When it comes to sidelining populist leaders, this strategy is most effective when IOs have alternative resources available to replace what populists might withhold. For instance, if a populist state cuts funding or refuses to provide critical data, IOs can mitigate the impact by seeking support from other member states, NGOs, or private sector entities. However, this approach works best when the IO has sufficient financial and informational independence.

Appeasing populist leaders is possible when IOs can offer targeted benefits to populist states. These benefits may include increased voting shares, financial assistance, or exemptions from stringent rules. IOs with more resources and leverage, such as weighted voting mechanisms or robust financial tools, are better positioned to implement this strategy. However, the effectiveness of appeasement depends on the populist state's willingness to accept these benefits and reduce its opposition.

Sidelining populist constituents often requires IOs to operate through covert channels or shield interactions from public scrutiny. IOs like the WTO and the IMF, which have well-established avenues for confidential communication, are particularly suited to this approach. However, secrecy is effective only if populists have an interest in engaging with the IO and if the IO can credibly ensure that these interactions remain hidden from domestic audiences.

Appeasing populist constituents is more feasible for IOs with strong public-facing communication strategies, such as active social media accounts or branded aid initiatives. Newer or less well-known IOs may find it easier to sway public opinion, as they face fewer entrenched perceptions. Public outreach is particularly critical for IOs that rely on public support to achieve their mandates, such as international financial institutions during crises.

Thus, while the strategies outlined in this book demonstrate IOs' adaptability, their efficacy varies depending on institutional resources, the nature of the populist threat, and the broader political context. Powerful IOs with extensive resources and established communication channels are better equipped to counter populist challenges, while smaller or more resource-constrained organizations may struggle.

2.6.   International Finance

Our empirical analyses span a broad range of IOs with diverse mandates, operating across various substantive issue areas, time periods, and global regions. However, we pay special attention to international finance, a domain dominated by institutions that focus on concessional development financing and emergency lending. This concentrated focus allows for systematic comparisons across our empirical analyses and provides a foundation for engaging deeply with the extensive scholarly literature examining IOs in this realm (Stone 2011; Schneider and Tobin 2016; Lipscy 2017; Pratt 2021).

IFIs, such as the World Bank and the IMF, are particularly well suited for analysis because of their high levels of transparency. This openness enables the collection of rich datasets that may not be available for other types of IOs. Additionally, these institutions are among the oldest and most influential actors in the global arena and liberal international order, making them ideal case studies for understanding how IOs operate under pressure and how they respond to populist threats.

Given the centrality of the World Bank and IMF to global development, we provide an overview of their purposes, operations, and vulnerabilities to populist challenges. These institutions are key players in delivering aid, facilitating structural reforms, and responding to financial crises. Their high-profile roles often make them lightning rods for populist criticism, particularly because their conditionality programs and governance structures are frequently framed as emblematic of elite international control. As such, these IOs feature prominently in our analyses, offering a rich lens through which to study the broader implications of populist–IO interactions.

2.6.1.   The IMF

The IMF, established in 1944 at the Bretton Woods Conference, stands as one of the pillars of the global financial architecture. With nearly universal membership, the IMF is tasked with ensuring stability in the international monetary system and preventing economic crises. Armed with a lending capacity of up to $1 trillion, the Fund plays a pivotal role in global economic governance.

Headquartered in Washington, DC, the IMF operates with a robust structure that reflects its international reach. Its approximately 2,700 staff members hail from 150 countries, contributing to a diverse and dynamic institutional culture. Governance is anchored by a twenty-four-member Executive Board, which oversees the IMF's daily activities. Each member country is represented by an executive director, while the Board of Governors—comprising one governor per member country, typically a high-ranking official from the central bank or finance ministry—provides strategic oversight. The managing director, traditionally a European, leads the institution, supported by an American deputy in a well-established transatlantic arrangement.

The IMF's core responsibilities include monitoring global and regional economic trends through its surveillance function and offering tailored economic advice to member states. The Fund publishes a wide range of technical reports, including assessments of economic progress and forecasts of global and regional outlooks. In times of economic distress, the IMF extends lifelines to countries facing balance-of-payments crises, designing loan programs that are often contingent on policy adjustments to address underlying economic challenges. Beyond lending, the Fund offers technical assistance and capacity-building initiatives, such as advising on exchange-rate management, reforming banking systems, or modernizing tax structures.

The IMF's operations are financed primarily through member quotas, contributions that reflect each member's relative economic power and influence. These quotas determine voting power within the organization, with the United States maintaining a dominant position, holding around 16 percent of the vote share that grants it veto power over key decisions, including amendments to the Articles of Agreement. While decisions are frequently reached by consensus, formal voting remains an essential part of the governance process.

To bolster its resources, the IMF engages in multilateral and bilateral borrowing agreements and often co-finances programs alongside peer institutions such as the European Stability Mechanism and the Eurasian Fund for Stabilization and Development. This collaborative approach underscores the IMF's centrality in a networked global economic system, enabling it to respond effectively to diverse challenges in an ever-changing world.

2.6.2.   The World Bank

The World Bank, born alongside the IMF at the Bretton Woods Conference in 1944, is another cornerstone of the global financial system. Often collaborating closely with the Fund, the Bank shares many structural similarities but pursues a distinct mission centered on fostering economic development and reducing poverty worldwide.

Like the IMF, the World Bank boasts near-universal membership, with nearly all countries represented on its Board of Governors. This governing body, composed of finance or development ministers from member states, delegates the institution's daily operations to a twenty-five-member executive board. At the helm of the Bank is its president, traditionally an American, reflecting the United States' significant influence within the institution.

The World Bank Group comprises five distinct entities, but this discussion focuses on its two primary arms: the International Bank for Reconstruction and Development (IBRD) and the International Development Association (IDA). Together, these entities cater to countries at different stages of development. The IDA supports low-income nations through interest-free loans and grants, addressing critical needs such as infrastructure, education, and health care. The IBRD, on the other hand, provides nonconcessional loans primarily to middle-income countries. The Bank finances these loans by borrowing from private markets, leveraging its top-tier credit rating—a reflection of its backing by major creditworthy governments—to secure favorable terms. Interest income from IBRD loans is then channeled to bolster the IDA's concessional lending capabilities.

The World Bank's operations are intricately tied to its members' financial contributions. Wealthy countries fund IDA programs, with the United States playing a pivotal role; American congressional approval is required to replenish the IDA budget every three years. This dependence underscores US influence, both formally, through veto power over key decisions, and informally, through the Bank's headquarters in Washington, DC, and its sway in hiring decisions.

Beyond its lending activities, the World Bank complements the IMF's work in monitoring global economic conditions. The two institutions collaborate on reports such as the Financial Sector Assessment Programs (FSAPs), which evaluate countries' financial health and resilience. This partnership highlights their shared commitment to global economic stability and development.

In sum, the World Bank serves as a vital player in advancing global development goals, leveraging its financial expertise, credit strength, and collaborative networks to assist nations at every stage of economic growth. With its unique blend of concessional and nonconcessional lending, the Bank remains a critical institution for fostering economic progress and addressing the world's most pressing challenges.

2.6.3.   Additional IFIs

A variety of other funds and development banks exist in this space, many of which are regionally focused. For example, regional financing arrangements include the Latin American Reserve Fund, the Arab Monetary Fund, and the European Stability Mechanism. Meanwhile, regional development banks include the AIIB, Asian Development Bank, African Development Bank, and Islamic Development Bank. Table 2.2 includes a complete list of the IOs that fall into the development and emergency-lending categories.

Many of these organizations operate similarly to the World Bank and IMF, though they tend to be headquartered in the region they operate in and are led by a large regional government. They often specialize in particular areas of development; for instance, the Asian Development Bank possesses significant expertise in geothermal infrastructure projects that the World Bank and other regional IOs may lack. Their budgets and bureaucracies are relatively smaller than the Bretton Woods institutions, and they tend to attach fewer conditions to their assistance, making them attractive outside options for skeptics of the IMF and World Bank.

2.6.4.   The Populist Threat for International Finance

Populist-led donor and recipient nations frequently clash with the IFIs that oversee these spaces. While recipient countries value the financial aid and technical expertise provided by institutions like the IMF and World Bank, the loans often come with strings attached in the form of explicit or implicit conditions. These requirements can be burdensome for any government to implement (Clark 2022). However, populist leaders often find them particularly objectionable, as they directly infringe on national sovereignty. Similarly, populists frequently reject the technical advice proffered by IFIs, viewing it as the product of detached elites and technocrats, often from foreign backgrounds, who do not represent the interests or identities of the populist state.

TABLE 2.2. List of international financial institutions

Institution	Date	Members
International Bank for Reconstruction and Development (IBRD)	1944	189
Council of Europe Development Bank (CEB)	1956	41
European Investment Bank (EIB)	1958	27
Inter-American Development Bank (IADB)	1959	48
Central American Bank for Economic Integration (CABEI)	1960	14
African Development Bank (AfDB)	1965	80
Asian Development Bank (ADB)	1966	68
East African Development Bank (EADB)	1967	4
Arab Fund for Economic and Social Development (AFESD)	1968	21
Andean Development Corporation (CAF)	1968	18
Caribbean Development Bank (CDB)	1970	27
Islamic Development Bank (IsDB)	1973	57
West African Development Bank (BOAD)	1973	8
Development Bank of the Central African States (BDEAC)	1975	6
Arab Bank for Economic Development in Africa (BADEA)	1975	11
Arab Monetary Fund (AMF)	1976	22
Development Bank of the Great Lakes States (BDEGL)	1976	3
OPEC Fund for International Development (OFID)	1976	12
Nordic Investment Bank (NIB)	1976	8
International Fund for Agricultural Development (IFAD)	1977	177
Latin American Reserve Fund (FLAR)	1978	7
Eastern and Southern African Trade and Development Bank (TDB)	1985	22
Nordic Development Fund (NDF)	1989	5
European Bank for Reconstruction and Development (EBRD)	1991	69
Black Sea Trade and Development Bank (BSTDB)	1992	11
North American Development Bank (NADB)	1993	2
Chiang Mai Initiative (CMI)	2000	13
EU Balance of Payments Assistance Facility (EU BoP)	2002	9
Economic Cooperation Organization Trade and Development Bank (ETDB)	2005	10
Eurasian Development Bank (EDB)	2006	6

Continued on next page

TABLE 2.2. (*continued*)

Institution	Date	Members
Eurasian Fund for Stabilization and Development (EFSD)	2009	6
European Stability Mechanism (ESM, formerly EFSF)	2010	19
European Financial Stabilization Mechanism (EFSM)	2010	27
New Development Bank (NDB)	2013	5
BRICS Contingent Reserve Arrangement (CRA)	2014	5
Asian Infrastructure Investment Bank (AIIB)	2015	75

Note: The membership data are accurate as of February 2020 and include only shareholding members of each institution where applicable; see Clark (2025).

Historical examples illustrate how IFIs' policy interventions can inadvertently fuel populist uprisings. In Europe, austerity measures imposed by the IMF and the EU during the eurocrisis ignited a wave of populist fervor in countries like Greece and Spain, where anti-establishment parties had gained significant traction. Similarly, in Latin America, leaders such as Evo Morales in Bolivia, Rafael Correa in Ecuador, and Hugo Chávez in Venezuela rode to power on a backlash against establishment politicians who advocated compliance with international institutions' demands. These leaders positioned themselves as defenders of national dignity against external economic dictates, leveraging public discontent to consolidate their political platforms and often implementing anti-democratic reforms in the process (see Meyerrose 2020).

On the donor side, populist-led states often harbor a deep-seated aversion to foreign aid and the financial contributions mandated by IFIs. For example, Trump's administration voiced repeated grievances over the substantial financial commitments required by NATO and various UN bodies, reflecting a broader, populist skepticism of multilateral institutions that demand significant fiscal outflows. Trump was especially averse to the World Bank's lending to middle-income countries like China and India, culminating in the appointment of David Malpass as president of the institution.

This resistance to IFIs manifests not only in financial reluctance but also in the withholding of critical information. For IFIs, data are a vital currency—they rely on accurate and timely information to craft expert recommendations and policy prescriptions. As we explore statistically in chapter 3, populist leaders are often hesitant to share such information, and this reticence can undermine the institutions' ability to function effectively.

In some cases, populist frustration drives the creation of alternative institutions that better align with their preferences and impose fewer demands on their members (Pratt 2021). These competitor organizations allow populist leaders to reduce their reliance on traditional IFIs or, in extreme cases, to withdraw entirely (von Borzyskowski and Vabulas 2019b). This exit option is particularly feasible in the development area, given the proliferation of organizations operating in this space (Lipscy 2015).

Ultimately, both populist-led donor and recipient states have strong incentives to distance themselves from IFIs. For donors, the financial burdens and perceived inefficiencies of these institutions fuel opposition, while recipients reject the sovereignty constraints and technocratic influence associated with IFI engagement. Together, these dynamics threaten to erode the effectiveness and legitimacy of IFIs, posing significant challenges to their operations and their broader role in global governance.

2.7. Conclusion

Our theoretical framework forms the foundation of our central hypotheses: When populists rise to power, IOs respond by adopting strategies of appeasement and sidelining—both of populist leaders and their constituents—to counteract the perceived threats these leaders pose to global governance. These strategies reflect a calculated effort by IOs to mitigate populist disruptions while safeguarding their missions and legitimacy.

Having developed our theoretical argument and clarified key concepts and definitions, we now turn to empirical tests that systematically examine these ideas. In the chapters that follow, we present innovative approaches to demonstrate how populists disproportionately undermine IOs, employing the tactics we have outlined. We then delve into the strategies IOs use to push back, shedding light on their capacity to navigate these challenges.

By building on existing scholarship on IO legitimacy and the driving forces behind populism, we also assess the broader implications of these defensive strategies. Ultimately, we argue that these approaches not only counter populist attacks but also enhance IO resilience, enabling these institutions to adapt and endure in an era of rising populist pressures. Through this exploration, we highlight how global governance evolves under strain, offering insights into its capacity to weather existential threats.

3

Populist Attacks on IOs

POPULISM IS a global ideology with broad appeal that has surged dramatically in recent years, creating significant challenges for IOs. As discussed in previous chapters, IOs make convenient targets for populists as elite bureaucracies that constrain domestic sovereignty. Populists thrive by "denouncing the existence of an alliance between domestic and foreign elites seeking to subvert the will of the people" (Rovira Kaltwasser and Taggart 2016, 356). This sentiment is echoed by a former IMF bureaucrat who remarked, "The institution has always been vulnerable to populist, isolationist, and anti-IO leaders."[1]

In this chapter, we delve into the contemporary rise of populism and its implications for IOs. We begin by charting the spread of populism and situating populist opposition to IOs within the context of an evolving multilateral system. Populists, with their disdain for transnational governance and elite-led institutions, have actively worked to undermine IOs in numerous ways. Leveraging novel data on state–IO interactions, we document how populist leaders employ a range of tactics to weaken these institutions.

Our analysis reveals a pattern: Compared with other leaders, populists are far more likely to reduce their participation in IMF programs, withhold or distort critical information from organizations like the World Bank and UNFCCC, and deploy aggressive rhetoric aimed at discrediting the global trade system. These actions highlight the systematic approach populists take to erode the legitimacy and functionality of IOs.

This chapter lays the foundation for the more detailed empirical analyses that follow. By establishing the nature and scope of the populist challenge to

---

1. Former IMF Resident Representative. Interview by authors. November 7, 2024.

IOs, we set the stage in the rest of the book for exploring how IOs adapt to, respond to, and defend themselves against these threats.

3.1.   The Rise of Populist Discontent

Populist ideology has left its mark throughout history, with modern populism often traced back to movements in Russia and the United States in the late nineteenth century. Over the past several decades, populism has flourished across North America, Europe, and Latin America, and its influence has now extended to nearly every corner of the globe. While populist rhetoric varies depending on the particular grievances of each country's population, its core remains the same: a narrative that pits the "common people" against a "corrupt elite." We offer a broad overview of populism's evolution and its regional manifestations; for a deeper dive, see Mudde and Rovira Kaltwasser (2017); Mudde and Rovira Kaltwasser (2018).

Latin America stands out as a hot spot for populist appeals, with leaders achieving significant success in countries such as Argentina, Bolivia, Brazil, Peru, and Venezuela. Here, populism often hinges on economic inequality and has gained momentum alongside democratic expansion in the region. Broadly, Latin American populism can be categorized into three distinct waves: The first (1929–1960s) capitalized on mass urban migration and industrialization. Leaders mobilized workers—though often excluding indigenous populations—against elites perceived as obstacles to the import substitution industrialization model. The second wave (1990s) occurred in the wake of economic crises, with politicians blaming political elites for blocking liberalization and clinging to protectionist policies. The IMF's involvement in implementing economic reforms was a flashpoint, driving resentment that fueled anti-IO populist rhetoric. The third wave (2000s) thus saw the rise of left-wing leaders like Hugo Chávez, Evo Morales, Rafael Correa, and Daniel Ortega. These leaders rejected the neoliberal reforms of the previous wave, instead prioritizing economic equality and national sovereignty. Their campaigns often emphasized the exploitation of natural resources by foreign entities and were highly critical of international institutions' promotion of globalization.

Populism in North America, particularly the United States, has evolved along different lines, often reflecting a divide between "heartland" values and perceived elitism on the coasts. Populism in the United States can be traced to the Jacksonian era. Andrew Jackson's presidency (1829–1837) was marked by opposition to elite-controlled institutions like the Second Bank of the United States and a preference for direct democratic mechanisms over intermediaries like the Electoral College. Populist appeals intensified during the mid-twentieth century, driven by anxieties over communism. Leaders like Richard Nixon leveraged the idea of a "great silent majority," a rhetorical device later revived by Donald Trump. Third-party candidates such as George Wallace and Ross Perot also tapped into populist sentiment during this time. The 2008 financial crisis marked a turning point for modern American populism. Movements like Occupy Wall Street (from the left) and the Tea Party (from the right) emerged in response to government bailouts of major banks. This discontent culminated in the 2016 election of Donald Trump, whose populist rhetoric appealed to many Americans frustrated by globalization and elite governance.

Populism in Europe also has deep roots, with modern populist thought often linked to nineteenth-century Russia. The Narodnik movement, led by intellectuals seeking to mobilize peasants against Tsarist elites, marked an early example of anti-capitalist populism. However, disunity and the lack of grassroots support limited its success. Modern European populism has surged since the 1990s, fueled by two primary grievances: European integration and immigration. These issues have given rise to far-right populist parties like the Freedom Party of Austria, France's National Rally, Italy's League, and Germany's Alternative for Germany. These parties emphasize nationalism, nativism, and anti-immigration policies, often framing welfare as a privilege for a native "in-group." While less prominent than its far-right counterpart, left-wing populism gained traction during the eurocrisis. Parties like Syriza in Greece and Podemos in Spain emerged by criticizing austerity measures imposed by the IFIs.

However, populism's appeal extends well beyond these traditional geographic strongholds. For example, in Australia and New Zealand, right-wing populism mirrors Western European trends, focusing on immigration and welfare concerns. In Asia, populist leaders in the region opposed globalization and the involvement of IFIs following the 1997 Asian financial crisis, echoing Latin American critiques. In Africa, land rights and economic exploitation have become rallying cries for populist leaders across the continent. In the Middle East, populist movements have also gained traction in democracies like Turkey, where Recep Tayyip Erdoğan has combined populism with authoritarianism, and Israel, where populist rhetoric has targeted elite institutions and foreign intervention.

These examples clearly show that populism transcends ideology, geography, and political systems. Whether emerging from the left or right, in wealthy democracies or developing nations, populists successfully mobilize discontent against elites. This enduring and adaptable appeal underscores populism's power to challenge established systems, including IOs, on a global scale.

3.2.   Populism and the Evolution of IOs

The inherent tension between IOs as supranational governing entities and populism as a nationalist, anti-elite ideology has grown sharper as IOs have expanded in both scale and influence. This friction is rooted in a significant historical shift: While IOs have proliferated dramatically since World War II, their scope, authority, and autonomy have also deepened, making them both indispensable and polarizing players on the global stage.

The post–World War II international order was initially built on a foundation of a few major IOs with global reach and focused mandates. The Bretton Woods twins—the IMF and the World Bank—were designed to stabilize the global economy. The GATT provided a platform for trade negotiations, and the United Nations sought to prevent future military conflicts. These institutions were crafted to address the immediate challenges of the postwar world, namely economic reconstruction, monetary stability, and peacekeeping.

Fast forward to today, and these organizations have transformed into sprawling entities with expanded mandates. The GATT evolved into the WTO, which now enforces binding international trade rules. The IMF shifted its focus to emergency loans tied to stringent policy conditions. The World Bank diversified into infrastructure financing, climate change mitigation, and conditional development aid. Meanwhile, the UN has grown into a vast network of specialized agencies addressing issues from health to human rights. The EU has also evolved from a coal- and steel-trading bloc into one of the most integrated political and economic unions in the world.

These expansions were fueled by the increasing complexity of global challenges, from financial crises and pandemics to climate change and technological disruption. IOs responded by hiring elite specialists, investing in cutting-edge technologies like AI and satellite surveillance, and broadening their missions to tackle emerging global issues. This growth has come with enhanced authority, enabling IOs to influence domestic policies and shape international norms more dramatically than ever before.

The end of the Cold War marked an inflection point for IOs, catalyzing a rapid proliferation of institutions and a corresponding expansion of their roles (Johnson 2014; Morse and Keohane 2014; Pratt 2021). With the dissolution

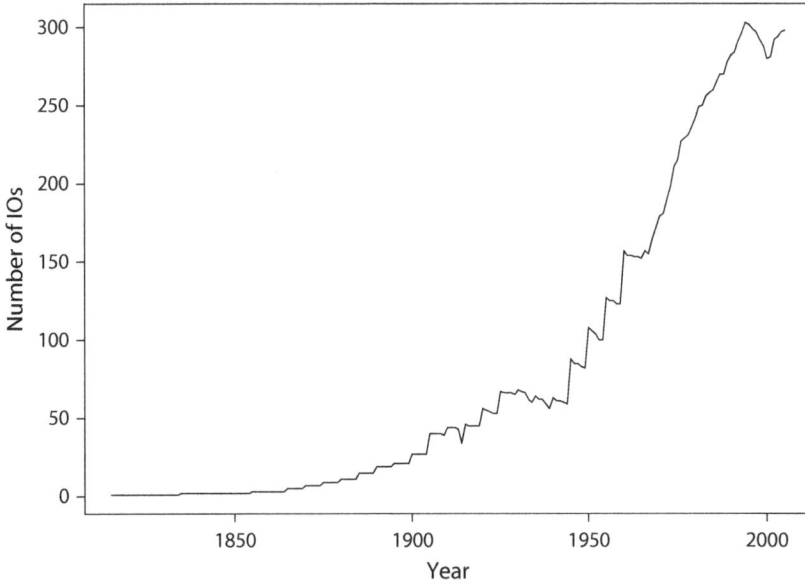

FIGURE 3.1. Number of IOs active over time. Data from (Pevehouse, Nordstrom, and Warnke 2004).

of the USSR, member states and IO bureaucrats seized the opportunity to address gaps in global governance. New organizations emerged, and existing ones reinterpreted their mandates to address previously neglected issues like gender equality, climate change, and cybersecurity (Jupille, Mattli, and Snidal 2013).

This explosion of IOs, while addressing many global challenges, also enabled states to shop among overlapping institutions to secure the most favorable terms (Busch 2007; Clark 2022). While this institutional diversity has enabled flexibility and innovation (Pratt 2018; Henning and Pratt 2020; Eilstrup-Sangiovanni 2021), it has also sparked redundancies and inefficiencies. For example, the development sector is now governed by twenty-eight multilateral organizations alongside a web of bilateral and informal arrangements. Similarly, the emergency lending regime, once dominated by the IMF, now includes eight regional financing arrangements. Figure 3.1 illustrates the dramatic increase in the number of IOs operating on the global stage over time.

The increased complexity and authority of IOs have provoked widespread criticism, particularly from populist leaders who view them as intrusive and elitist. These leaders argue that IOs undermine state sovereignty, operate with democratic deficits, and prioritize elite-driven agendas over national interests. The populist resurgence is deeply tied to globalization—a catch-all term to describe the increased economic interconnectedness of the post– Cold War era—and to the perceived "denationalization" of political rule as global governance has grown more technocratic and detached from everyday citizens.

Indeed, many populists have found IOs to be easy targets for their anti-elite narratives. As bureaucratic entities staffed by highly educated international elites, IOs epitomize the foreign control populists rally against. Their mission to constrain state behavior, whether through trade rules, environmental standards, or financial oversight, further fuels accusations of sovereignty erosion.

Key developments have exacerbated these tensions. First, IOs have expanded their autonomy. IOs have grown more independent from member states, with bureaucrats and leaders leveraging their positions to pursue specialized agendas. For instance, the IMF's increasing focus on climate change reflects not just member-state priorities but also bureaucratic initiatives (Clark and Zucker 2024). Organizations like the WTO and the EU have similarly been criticized for stretching their mandates to encompass broader regulatory roles, further intensifying populist opposition.

Second, elite staffing of IOs has increased as bureaucracies have expanded in size. IOs increasingly hire large numbers of credentialed experts from prestigious institutions, reinforcing perceptions that they are out of touch with ordinary citizens (Chwieroth 2015).

Third, IOs have been affected by technological advancements. Real-time surveillance, AI, and big data analytics have enabled IOs to operate more independently, often without direct state oversight. While these technologies enhance IO effectiveness, they also deepen perceptions of their unaccountability.

The populist backlash against IOs is not simply a rejection of their missions but a broader critique of how they wield power. While nonpopulist critics, such as former US president Barack Obama, have expressed concerns about whether global commitments overstretch state resources, populist leaders frame their opposition ideologically. For them, IOs represent a fundamental incompatibility with national sovereignty and the will of "the people."

In this evolving landscape, IOs face mounting challenges to their legitimacy and functionality. Yet these threats have also spurred innovation and adaptation. By expanding their missions, forming partnerships with NGOs and private actors, and embracing new technologies, IOs are finding ways to remain relevant in an increasingly polarized world. The central question is whether IOs can balance their growing authority with the need for legitimacy among both member states and global publics. Populists argue that they cannot, and have taken it upon themselves to challenge IOs' central role in global governance.

3.3. How Populists Undermine IOs: An Empirical Examination

Previously, we detailed the primary strategies populists employ to undermine IOs: withholding resources such as effort, information, and funding, and engaging in adversarial communication. While these are not the only tactics available to populists, we argue that they form a representative and impactful categorization of the most prevalent methods used to weaken IOs.

In this section, we put these claims to the test with empirical evidence. First, we illustrate that populists contribute less effort to IOs by demonstrating their lower participation rates in IMF programs compared with those of other leaders. Next, we delve into the manipulation of information, revealing how populists withhold or distort crucial data that IOs, like the World Bank, depend upon to function effectively. Finally, we analyze how populist leaders, such as Donald Trump, employ particularly combative rhetoric against the world trade system, amplifying antagonism through oppositional communication.

Our findings point to a clear pattern: Populist leaders exhibit deliberate and persistent resistance to IOs, actively working to diminish their effectiveness and credibility. These actions are not isolated or incidental but represent a concerted effort to weaken the organs of global governance. In the chapters that follow, we shift our focus to examine how IOs counter these populist attacks and seek to maintain their resilience in the face of such challenges.

3.3.1. Effort Withholding

We begin by investigating whether populist leaders systematically withhold effort from IOs, focusing specifically on their engagement with the IMF. This analysis draws on our previous research published in the *Journal of Politics* (Carnegie, Clark, and Kaya 2024), which also contains additional details. We examine whether populist leaders are less likely than their nonpopulist counterparts to participate in IMF programs. Our choice to focus on the IMF stems from its substantive importance, its role as a global lender of last resort, and the transparency of its loan operations, as outlined in the prior chapter.

The IMF occupies a unique space in global governance, providing financial support, policy advice, and technical assistance to member states. It also conducts multilateral surveillance, publishing reports that assess economic trends and risks. Engagement with the IMF, particularly through its conditional lending programs, is both highly public and politically sensitive. These programs impose stringent conditions on borrowing countries in exchange for financial support, often requiring significant policy adjustments that can incur steep domestic costs.

For populist leaders who often reject IOs in their rhetoric and portray them as encroaching on national sovereignty, these costs are particularly problematic. Public engagement with the IMF through loan programs can clash with populists' anti-elite messaging, making such interactions politically risky. Examples abound: Yanis Varoufakis, Greece's finance minister from the left-wing populist party Syriza, famously referred to the IMF–EU bailout of Greece as "nothing short of cruel and unusual punishment" (Varoufakis 2017, 19). Similarly, Donald Trump and his supporters expressed consistent disdain for US financial support of institutions like the IMF and World Bank (Brutger and Clark 2022). Other populists, such as Venezuela's Hugo Chávez, even threatened to exit the IMF altogether.[2]

Despite their rhetoric, populists may find it difficult to entirely avoid the IMF's support because of its critical role in mitigating balance-of-payments crises as global lender of last resort. This makes their participation a particularly stringent test of our theory: Populists' being systematically less likely to engage with the IMF even when their countries face severe economic distress underscores their broader reluctance to cooperate with IOs.

In this analysis, our dependent variable is IMF program initiation, which we code for the first year that a program begins. This approach ensures that we exclude instances where leaders inherit ongoing programs. The data needed to construct this measure come from Kentikelenis, Stubbs, and King (2016), and our primary independent variable is a binary measure of populist leadership derived from Funke, Schularick, and Trebesch (2023). This comprehensive dataset of global populism classifies more than 1,500 leaders between 1900 and 2020 as populist or nonpopulist, based on their alignment with the core tenets

2. *Reuters*, 2007, https://reut.rs/41Nx004.

of populist ideology—whether or not leaders purport to represent the "true, common people" against "corrupt elites." We choose this populism dataset over others given its superior temporal and geographic coverage.

We employ ordinary least squares regressions, clustering standard errors at the country level and incorporating both country and year-fixed effects. To ensure robust results, we test a range of political and economic covariates that could also influence IMF participation. We include political characteristics, such as democracy scores (Polity2) and the political orientation of the executive (right-wing or not).[3] We also include international variables such as UN voting alignment with the United States, US aid receipts, and membership on the UN Security Council.[4] We then add economic indicators including per capita GDP, GDP growth, unemployment rates, and total debt service to GNI ratios.[5] We also control for institutional dynamics, including vote-power asymmetry at the IMF (Pratt 2021), capturing the gap between a country's economic power and formal IMF voting power. To address missing data, particularly for developing countries, we employ multiple imputation, a standard approach in recent IO studies (Schneider and Tobin 2020; Clark 2022).

The results, presented in table 3.1, align with our expectation: Populist leaders are significantly less likely to initiate IMF programs compared with nonpopulist leaders. The estimated effect size—approximately an 8 percentage point reduction in the likelihood of program participation—is both substantively and statistically significant. This aligns with our theory that populists avoid visible cooperation with IOs, even when doing so could address pressing economic needs.

We subjected our findings to several robustness checks, including binomial probit specifications, substituting country-fixed effects with random effects, and conducting sensitivity analysis by iteratively removing countries from the sample. In all cases, the results held firm (see Carnegie, Clark, and Kaya 2024).

These findings support our contention that populist leaders systematically withhold engagement from the IMF, even when economic circumstances

---

3. Polity data come from the Center for Systemic Peace, while political ideology data come from the Database of Political Institutions.

4. UN voting data come from (Bailey, Strezhnev, and Voeten 2017), US aid data come from the World Development Indicators (WDI), and UNSC membership data are updated from Dreher, Sturm, and Vreeland (2009).

5. All economic data come from the WDI.

TABLE 3.1. IMF program participation

	IMF program initiation				
	Model 1	**Model 2**	**Model 3**	**Model 4**	**Model 5**
Populism	−0.071**	−0.080**	−0.080**	−0.082**	−0.080**
	(0.023)	(0.029)	(0.029)	(0.029)	(0.029)
GDPPC		−0.017***	−0.017***	−0.018***	−0.017***
		(0.003)	(0.003)	(0.003)	(0.003)
Polity2		0.002	0.002	0.002	0.002
		(0.002)	(0.002)	(0.002)	(0.002)
UN voting		−0.004	−0.005	−0.003	−0.002
(ideal pt dist)		(0.020)	(0.020)	(0.020)	(0.020)
Right-wing		0.014	0.016	0.013	0.014
government		(0.015)	(0.015)	(0.015)	(0.015)
Debt		−0.001	−0.001	−0.001	−0.001
service/GNI		(0.001)	(0.001)	(0.001)	(0.001)
Vote-power			−0.370***		
asymmetry			(0.072)		
US aid				0.005*	
				(0.002)	
UNSC member				−0.016	
				(0.019)	
GDP growth					−0.003***
					(0.001)
Unemployment					−0.0004
					(0.001)
Country-fixed effects	Yes	Yes	Yes	Yes	Yes
Year-fixed effects	Yes	Yes	Yes	Yes	Yes
N	5122	4190	4190	4190	4190
Adj. R-squared	0.109	0.114	0.115	0.115	0.116

Note: Robust standard errors are clustered at the country-level. Model specification is LPM.
***$p < .001$; **$p < .01$; *$p < .05$

might dictate otherwise. This reluctance underscores the broader antagonism that populists display toward IOs and the political risks they associate with visible cooperation. Having established this, we now turn to another populist strategy: manipulating the flow of information to IOs, with a focus on the World Bank.

3.3.2. *Information Withholding and Manipulation*

We examine another tool populists use to undermine IOs: withholding or manipulating scientific information. This analysis replicates our results published in *World Politics* (Carnegie, Clark, and Zucker 2024). Using data from the World Bank and the United Nations Framework Convention on Climate Change (UNFCCC), we demonstrate that populist governments are more likely to withhold critical scientific data or provide data of lower quality compared with that of nonpopulist governments. This dynamic arises both from a desire to avoid international scrutiny and from the domestic erosion of scientific capacity under populist regimes.

Specifically, we find that environmental and public health data, essential for the World Bank's activities, are disproportionately missing when populists are in power. As a placebo test, we analyze data not supplied by states, showing that this trend does not hold for information collected or estimated by other sources. We further show that data reported to the UNFCCC by populist governments, particularly greenhouse gas emissions figures, are of significantly lower quality compared with that of nonpopulist counterparts.

Why examine scientific data specifically? Scientific information occupies a unique position in global governance, serving as a powerful tool that legitimizes expertise and empowers technocrats (Eichengreen 2018, 7). This has made it a prime target for populists, who frequently frame their rhetoric around distrust of elites. Recent examples illustrate this tension: Populist leaders withheld or misrepresented data to the WHO regarding the origins and spread of the COVID-19 pandemic (Worsnop 2019); countries with populist governments have been hesitant to share accurate climate data with IOs;[6] and populists have failed to supply reliable development-related data to financial IOs like the IMF (Jones and Hilbers 2004).

The reluctance to provide such data stems partly from their technical nature, which requires the input of highly educated experts. For populists, whose base often harbors skepticism toward elite-driven processes, the value of producing and sharing scientific data may seem limited. In contrast, nonpopulist leaders tend to cater to constituencies that trust scientific expertise and expect high-quality data to inform decision making.

6. "Burning the Data: Attacks on Climate and Energy Data and Research," Center for American Progress, 2018, https://www.americanprogress.org/article/burning-the-data/; "Science Under Attack: How Trump Is Sidelining Researchers and Their Work," *New York Times*, 2019, https://www.nytimes.com/2019/12/28/climate/trump-administration-war-on-science.html.

Polling data underscore this divide: While 73 percent of US Democrats and left-leaning independents believe scientists should have an active role in policy decisions, only 43 percent of populist-aligned supporters share this view.[7] This trend is not limited to the United States, as trust in scientific expertise is generally higher among nonpopulist constituencies globally.[8]

Beyond withholding data, populists often degrade domestic institutions that produce them. Budget cuts, staff dismissals, and the replacement of technocrats with loyalists are common practices that diminish the ability of bureaucracies to collect and analyze scientific information. Examples abound. Populist president Andrés Manuel Lopez Obrador slashed funding for Mexico's scientific institutions, framing them as part of the "golden bureaucracy"; Bolivia's Evo Morales reduced investment in research institutions, viewing science primarily as a tool to serve nationalist ends; Donald Trump dismissed scientific advisors, reduced budgets for agencies like the Environmental Protection Agency, and spread misinformation contrary to established scientific findings; and Brazil's Jair Bolsonaro purged environmental agencies of scientists monitoring deforestation in the Amazon. These actions disrupt the production of reliable data, leaving IOs with incomplete or inaccurate information, which undermines their ability to address global challenges effectively.

To assess the relationship between populism and missing data, we analyze the World Bank's World Development Indicators (WDI), focusing on two domains: environment and public health. The Bank relies heavily on data from member states to monitor environmental impacts, evaluate project outcomes, and address public health crises. Missing data in these domains can signal a deliberate lack of cooperation.

We calculate the share of missing scientific indicators in the WDI for each country in each year, standardizing the results for interpretation. Our key independent variable is the populism indicator from Funke, Schularick, and Trebesch (2023), and we again control for variables such as democracy levels, economic capacity (GDP per capita), and IMF program participation. Our

7. "Key Findings About Americans' Confidence in Science and Their Views on Scientists' Role in Society," Pew Research Center, February 2020, https://www.pewresearch.org/short-reads/2020/02/12/key-findings-about-americans-confidence-in-science-and-their-views-on-scientists-role-in-society/.

8. "Global Survey Reveals What People Around the World Think About Science," Editage Insights, June 2019, https://www.editage.com/insights/global-survey-reveals-what-people-around-the-world-think-about-science.

TABLE 3.2. Information withholding (placebo test)

	Missingness of scientific variables			
	Raw state-reported			Estimated or imputed
	(1)	(2)	(3)	(4)
Populism	0.084***	0.065***	0.058***	0.045
	(0.020)	(0.016)	(0.018)	(0.028)
Polity2		−0.008***	−0.005***	−0.010***
		(0.002)	(0.002)	(0.002)
Right-wing			0.0002	0.016
			(0.008)	(0.015)
GDP per			0.001	0.004
capita (ln)			(0.022)	(0.046)
IMF program			−0.0004	0.005
			(0.008)	(0.015)
Observations	7,656	4,614	4,026	4,026

Note: All models include country and year fixed effects and standard errors clustered by country. Independent variables are lagged by one year. Estimated via OLS. DV is standardized.
$^{*}p<0.1$; $^{**}p<0.05$; $^{***}p<0.01$

models include country- and year-fixed effects to account for unobservable factors, with standard errors clustered by country.[9]

The results, summarized in table 3.2, show that populist leadership is associated with a statistically significant increase in missing scientific data. Specifically, populists in power contribute to a 1.75 percent increase in missing scientific indicators annually, translating to missing data for three to four additional indicators on average. The effect is concentrated in raw, state-provided data, as shown in the placebo tests, which reveal no significant relationship for data sourced from nonstate providers like IOs or NGOs.

To further explore the quality of data provided by populist governments, we examine greenhouse gas emissions reporting under the UNFCCC (see table 3.3). Using data from Annex I countries (industrialized and transition economies), we calculate the absolute difference between emissions figures reported to the UNFCCC and those independently estimated by the Emissions Database for Global Atmospheric Research (EDGAR).

Our analysis finds that populist governments report significantly less accurate emissions data, with a 25 percent increase in discrepancies compared with

9. Further details and robustness checks can be found in Carnegie, Clark, and Zucker (2024).

TABLE 3.3. Information quality

	Emissions data gap (ln)		
	(1)	**(2)**	**(3)**
Populism	0.277**	0.268**	0.233*
	(0.118)	(0.121)	(0.116)
Polity2		−0.007	0.011
		(0.025)	(0.023)
Right-wing			0.122
			(0.137)
GDP per capita (ln)			−0.189
			(0.390)
IMF program			−0.054
			(0.131)
Fossil fuel (% energy			0.033*
consumption)			(0.016)
Value added by agriculture,			0.022
forestry, and fishing (% GDP)			(0.032)
Observations	936	871	790

Note: Regressions of the absolute difference (ln) between the total emissions estimate provided by Annex I Parties to the UNFCCC in a given year and the total emissions figure estimated by EDGAR (as reported in the WDI) in that same year on populism. All models include country and year fixed effects and standard errors clustered by country. Independent variables are lagged by one year. Estimated via OLS. $^{*}p<0.1$; $^{**}p<0.05$; $^{***}p<0.01$

nonpopulist governments. This suggests that populist leaders undermine not only the quantity but also the quality of information provided to IOs.

Our findings reveal that populists systematically withhold or distort critical scientific data, creating significant challenges for IOs. This behavior weakens IOs' ability to execute their mandates, from addressing climate change to responding to global health crises. If IOs are unable to determine the scope of these issues, it is extremely difficult to craft solutions to them. Furthermore, the erosion of domestic scientific capacity under populist regimes poses long-term risks, as it diminishes the foundation upon which IOs rely for cooperation and decision making.

3.3.3.   Toxic Communication

Populist leaders can also harm IOs with toxic communication—a strategy characterized by harsh rhetoric aimed at discrediting IOs, often through speeches, party platforms, or social media. This approach sows doubt among domestic and international audiences about the legitimacy and efficacy of these institutions. In this section, we delve into a compelling case study: former US president Donald Trump's aggressive rhetoric on trade during his first term. By comparing his communication strategies with those of nonpopulist US presidents George W. Bush and Barack Obama, we illustrate how Trump leveraged rhetoric to weaken confidence in the global trade regime. The results presented here are reproduced from Carnegie and Carson (2019), which provides further details.

Trade occupies a particularly salient and contentious space in global governance, overseen by the WTO and a web of preferential trade agreements (e.g., USMCA, EU-MERCOSUR). Despite a decline in actual trade violations during Trump's presidency, his rhetoric consistently alleged widespread noncompliance, creating the impression of a fundamentally broken system.

Trump's rhetoric frequently accused other nations of violating trade rules. For example, he declared, "We are going to end the international abuse, the foreign cheating, and the one-sided rules that govern NAFTA and the WTO."[10] Trump amplified his trade rhetoric through Twitter (now X), posting more than 130 tweets accusing countries of unfair trade practices during this time. For example: "We cannot keep a blind eye to the rampant unfair trade practices against our Country!" (March 14, 2018) and "After many decades, fair and reciprocal Trade will happen!" (June 9, 2018). By targeting key trade partners like China, Canada, and the EU, Trump reinforced the perception of widespread noncompliance, even in cases where no violations existed.

To evaluate Trump's rhetoric, presidential documents archived in the American Presidency Project were used, including speeches, press conferences, and official remarks by Bush, Obama, and Trump. The focus of the analysis was on instances where the word "trade" appeared, identifying trends in word frequency, usage patterns, and sentiment. This analysis revealed a stark contrast between Trump and his immediate predecessors. By extracting the top 100 words associated with "trade" in the speeches of all three presidents, 30 words unique to Trump were identified. These words fall into two distinct categories: First, those related to unfairness and cheating like "deficit," "terrible," "unfair," "bad," and "worst" highlight perceived injustices in trade

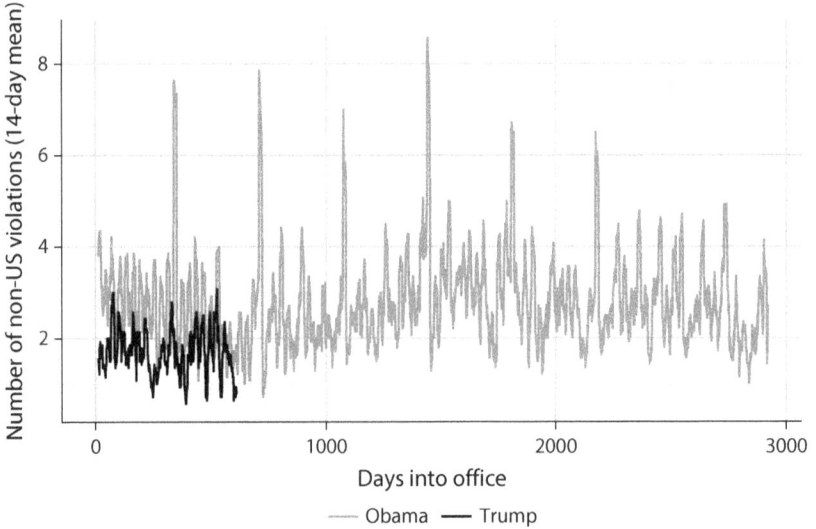

FIGURE 3.2. All trade violations

agreements. Second, those related to demands for change like "renegotiate," "reciprocal," "reform," and "stop" emphasize Trump's calls to overhaul existing trade arrangements.

This analysis raises an important question: Were trade violations increasing, as Trump claimed? To test whether Trump's rhetoric reflected actual increases in trade violations, data from the Global Trade Alert database on trade infractions from 2009 to 2018 were analyzed. Surprisingly, trade violations under Trump were fewer than during Obama's presidency (figure 3.2), suggesting that Trump's rhetoric was largely decoupled from reality.

These results support the idea that Trump's communication strategy was a deliberate attempt to undermine the global trade regime rather than a response to actual changes in trade behavior. Trump's toxic communication had far-reaching consequences. By consistently alleging widespread cheating, he fostered a climate of mistrust, leading other countries to question the fairness of the system and, in some cases, preemptively violate trade rules. Moreover, his rhetoric likely emboldened other populist leaders to adopt similar tactics, further eroding the credibility of global trade institutions.

While this analysis focuses on Trump, the findings have broader implications. Populists across the ideological spectrum use similar strategies to delegitimize IOs, exacerbating challenges to global governance. In subsequent chapters we explore how IOs adapt to counter these rhetorical attacks, seeking to maintain their legitimacy and operational capacity.

3.4.   Conclusion

This chapter explored the multifaceted ways in which populists challenge IOs, grounding these dynamics in their historical context and providing empirical evidence. Our analysis revealed that populist leaders systematically disengage from IOs like the IMF, withhold critical information from institutions such as the World Bank, and deploy toxic rhetoric to undermine the global trade regime.

The findings highlight the pervasive nature of populist resistance to IOs. This hostility does not single out individual organizations, instead often spilling over to weaken support for global governance as a whole. By attacking the very principles of international cooperation, populists sow doubt about the viability of international laws and norms, fostering broader skepticism about globalization. Many populists deride "globalists" and the global order at large, further entrenching resistance to IOs beyond specific grievances. This underscores the significant threat populist intransigence poses, especially when the populist leader hails from a powerful member state with the ability to significantly disrupt an IO's functioning.

Yet, as we will show, IOs are not passive actors in this battle. They adapt, innovate, and push back, employing strategies designed to counter populist resistance and protect the global architecture from being dismantled. These strategies are not only reactive but also pivotal in shaping the resilience of the international system. In the chapters that follow, we delve into the specific methods IOs can use to confront populist hostility. From appeasement and sidelining to direct engagement and public-facing initiatives, these strategies illuminate how IOs strive to uphold their missions and safeguard the principles of global governance in the face of populist challenges.

4

Sidelining Populist Leaders

SWIFT AND coordinated action was crucial to managing the rapidly spreading virus after the COVID-19 outbreak. The WHO was at the center of the global response, tasked with an ambitious mandate: identifying and containing outbreaks, distributing personal protective equipment, and spearheading efforts to develop effective vaccines and treatments.

To fulfill this mission and save lives, the WHO relied heavily on timely, accurate information from member states and other stakeholders, including pharmaceutical companies, medical NGOs, and peer IOs. Granular data on case counts and death rates informed travel advisories, insights on treatment efficacy shaped government policies, and accurate inventories of medical supplies ensured equitable distribution of critical resources.

However, the WHO faced significant resistance from some leaders, many of them populists. Leaders like Donald Trump in the United States and Jair Bolsonaro in Brazil withheld crucial information, failed to standardize reporting at local levels, and even used public platforms to disparage the WHO, blaming it for the pandemic's rapid spread. These actions exacerbated the challenges of responding to the crisis, further complicating the organization's already formidable task (Worsnop 2019).

Despite this noncooperation, the WHO adapted and innovated. Its operational bureaucrats, leaders, and cooperative member states identified creative solutions to fill the information gaps. They leaned on reliable data from countries with robust reporting systems, sought input from third-party sources, and enhanced the WHO's own surveillance capabilities. These efforts demonstrated the organization's resilience and its ability to navigate around uncooperative member states.

The WHO's approach highlights a broader phenomenon: IOs' sidelining of intransigent leaders by circumventing their resistance and sourcing essential resources elsewhere. The proliferation of information-gathering technologies and overlapping institutional mandates has created a network of actors capable of filling these gaps. When one state or leader withholds cooperation, IOs increasingly turn to alternative sources, showcasing their adaptability.

The withholding of information from IOs is not unique to the WHO. Leaders have resisted sharing climate data with the United Nations,[1] suppressed development-related statistics required by the IMF,[2] and obstructed nuclear oversight by the IAEA (Carnegie and Carson 2020). As detailed in the previous chapters, populists have also withheld and distorted scientific data intended for the World Bank and manipulated greenhouse gas emissions data submitted to the UNFCCC. These actions reflect a broader trend of populists' undermining of IOs through their anti-elite and sovereignty-focused ideologies.

Such behavior threatens global cooperative efforts, raising the question of whether IOs can adapt to overcome these challenges. This chapter explores these dynamics, focusing on the strategies IOs employ to navigate the problem of information suppression.

IOs often opt to collect the needed information from alternative sources when populists refuse to provide it. Advances in technology and the proliferation of actors with relevant data make this strategy increasingly feasible. Whether pooling resources with other IOs, collaborating with NGOs, or leveraging private sector expertise, IOs have found innovative ways to bypass uncooperative states.

For instance, security-focused IOs like the African Union, European Union, and United Nations have increasingly pooled resources to compensate for funding cuts by populist-led states. Similarly, development-focused institutions like the World Bank, African Development Bank, and Asian Development Bank have co-financed projects to share financial and informational risks. Election monitors, too, have coordinated their efforts to ensure comprehensive oversight in the face of populist resistance.

Using a multi-method approach, we show how IOs adapt to these challenges by diversifying their information sources and relying more heavily on

---

1. "Burning the Data: Attacks on Climate and Energy Data and Research," Center for American Progress, 2018, https://www.americanprogress.org/article/burning-the-data/; "Science Under Attack: How Trump Is Sidelining Researchers and Their Work," *New York Times*, 2019, https://www.nytimes.com/2019/12/28/climate/trump-administration-war-on-science.html.

2. See Jones and Hilbers (2004).

one another. Our findings carry important implications for global governance. While states often join IOs based on shared security or economic interests, these organizations are increasingly interconnected. Populist threats have driven IOs to cooperate more closely, creating a global web of institutions that transcends their member states' original agreements. This interconnectedness can enhance IOs' power, enabling them to push their agendas more effectively and making it harder for states to exit or undermine the system.

In doing so, IOs not only safeguard their missions but also strengthen the overall resilience of the international order. As populists continue to challenge the global governance framework by manipulating information, IOs' ability to adapt and innovate will be crucial in maintaining a cooperative and effective international system.

4.1.   How IOs Sideline Leaders

As discussed in chapter 2, sidelining is a widely employed strategy by IOs to work around uncooperative members. By reducing reliance on obstructive actors, sidelining allows IOs to mitigate risks posed by populist leaders who might withdraw their support or disrupt institutional processes. Unlike strategies such as appeasement, which require IOs to offer concessions or alter policies in meaningful ways, sidelining enables institutions to plug resource gaps without undertaking major reforms.

By doing so, they can not only secure critical information but also enhance their autonomy, which strengthens their ability to pursue long-term organizational goals without overreliance on individual states. Autonomy, as noted in prior research, can lead to improved institutional performance and resilience (Pollack 1997; Abbott and Snidal 1998; Johnson 2014), though potentially at the cost of agency slack (Barnett and Finnemore 1999). Even so, autonomy remains a critical asset for IOs navigating a politically volatile environment.

This chapter explores sidelining as a tool to address potential information deficits, a particularly attractive application given the wealth of alternative information sources in today's interconnected global landscape. IOs can enhance their own data-collection capabilities, such as deploying satellites or field agents, or tap into external sources like member states, other IOs, NGOs, and private firms.

In extreme cases of sidelining, IOs could consider expelling intransigent members, but this approach carries significant risks. Institutional rules often make expulsion procedurally complex, typically requiring broad agreement among member states. Additionally, expelling a member could backfire by severing ties with a country that may, under different leadership, become more cooperative. For example, President Joseph R. Biden Jr. re-engaged with many institutions that his predecessor, Donald Trump, had distanced the United States from, illustrating the value of maintaining formal ties. Furthermore, rejoining an IO often involves lengthy and challenging accession processes, as evidenced by China's arduous reforms to join the WTO.

Instead of pursuing such drastic measures, IOs typically opt for calculated sidelining efforts, balancing assertiveness with caution. Overzealous attempts to sideline leaders risk provoking stronger backlash, both from the leaders themselves and from their constituencies. Leaders may intensify their rhetorical attacks, accusing IOs of elitism or overreach, potentially amplifying perceptions of a "democratic deficit"—a criticism that IOs act independently of public accountability (Dahl 1999; Moravcsik 2004). This erosion of legitimacy can weaken IOs' capacity to promote and enforce global norms.

This chapter thus focuses on a more subtle and less contentious form of sidelining—enhanced collaboration among IOs. By pooling resources, sharing information, and coordinating efforts, IOs can reduce their dependence on obstructive actors while reinforcing their collective strength. Cooperation among IOs is not only cost-effective but also minimizes the political risks associated with direct confrontation, offering a practical pathway to address populist resistance.

4.2. The Role of Information in Global Governance

Information is a vital component of global governance, enabling IOs to foster cooperation, ensure compliance, and address transnational challenges. Scholars have long recognized that a core function of IOs is to collect, analyze, and disseminate information across the international community (Keohane 1984; Dai 2002). This information spans an array of critical domains, including compliance with international rules, environmental conditions, economic performance, public health metrics, security concerns, trade patterns, demographics, and more. By providing reliable data, IOs empower states to make informed decisions, promote transparency, and facilitate cooperative solutions. In many cases, the collection and provision of such information are embedded within IOs' formal mandates.[3]

---

3. Interviews with senior officials at health, environmental, and energy IOs conducted by the authors, January and February 2021.

To fulfill their information-related mandates, IOs rely on diverse sources. For example, the IMF needs economic data from member states to forecast global trends and identify systemic risks, while the IAEA depends on accurate reports about nuclear programs to verify compliance with international agreements. A lack of accurate or timely information can have dire consequences, including undermining compliance with international laws, weakening accountability for human-rights violations, and jeopardizing initiatives in peacekeeping or public health.

In some cases, IOs supplement state-provided data with independent means of information collection. The IAEA, for example, dispatches inspectors to nuclear facilities (Thorne 1992), the European Commission sends monitors to assess the fairness of elections (Kelley 2009), and the IMF conducts field missions to assess economic conditions on the ground (Clark and Zucker 2024). Satellite imagery, open-source intelligence, and other technologies also play a role in expanding IOs' informational reach. However, IOs are often constrained by limited authority to gather data independently, as member states typically hesitate to empower them with far-reaching surveillance capacities (Abbott and Snidal 1998). States worry that granting IOs extensive autonomy might diminish their own sovereignty, lead to bureaucratic overreach, or even enable IOs to pursue independent agendas at odds with state interests (Barnett and Finnemore 1999).

As a result, IOs frequently rely on member states to provide critical information, whether related to their own activities or to the behavior of other states (e.g., through naming and shaming tactics [Hafner-Burton 2008]). Yet, as emerging scholarship highlights, states' willingness to share accurate information is often governed by self-interest. Leaders may provide information that serves their agendas while withholding or distorting data that could be politically damaging (Terman and Voeten 2018). For example, democratic leaders might suppress information that reflects poorly on their policies or governance (Kono 2006; Schuessler 2010).

While these dynamics apply broadly, an important and underexplored source of variation in information-sharing behavior is whether a state is led by a populist leader. As argued throughout this book, populist leaders have distinct incentives to withhold or distort information. Their skepticism of elites, aversion to technocratic expertise, and emphasis on state sovereignty all contribute to a general hostility toward IOs. Populists often view IOs as "elitist" entities that impose constraints on state behavior and sovereignty. This makes information withholding a particularly appealing tactic for them, as suppressing critical data can obstruct IOs' ability to justify interventions or enforce rules. The prior chapter offered evidence in this vein.

Populists are especially likely to withhold data that are costly or difficult to collect independently. For example, producing accurate economic or environmental data requires specialized expertise, significant funding, and time-consuming analysis (McGarity and Wagner 2010). By cutting funding to domestic expert bureaucracies or politicizing their operations, populist leaders can weaken the capacity for data generation. Examples abound: Populist leaders have suppressed data on pesticide use, pollutant levels, and greenhouse gas emissions to limit IOs' ability to monitor or critique their policies.[4]

In contrast, data that are more accessible to IOs through independent means—such as satellite imagery or other publicly available sources—is harder for populists to manipulate. For instance, GDP data can be approximated using satellite-based measures of nighttime light density (Chan et al. 2019), and large-scale manipulation of metrics like unemployment rates would require coordinated efforts across multiple bureaucracies (Li 2017).

4.2.1. Strategies of Information Withholding

Populist leaders, with their hallmark skepticism of elites and technocrats, often undermine IOs by obstructing their ability to gather information. This obstruction can take several forms, both direct and indirect, and reflects populists' broader disdain for the authority and oversight IOs represent.

Populists may deliberately withhold or manipulate data to impede IOs' work. This can involve selectively reporting data to create a distorted picture of reality, outright lying, or altering information to fit political narratives. Appointing loyalists to key bureaucratic positions ensures that the information supplied serves political rather than technical or scientific ends (Oliver and Wood 2014; Busby, Gubler, and Hawkins 2019). For instance, populists might submit incomplete or misleading reports to evade scrutiny, banking on the assumption that IOs lack the resources to investigate thoroughly. This tactic can shield populist governments from accountability while sowing distrust in the IO's processes. Chapter 3 provided evidence consistent with this form of information suppression.

---

4. Interviews with IO officials, January and February 2021; see also Cory, Lerner, and Osgood (2021).

Populists may also seek to discredit alternative sources of information, casting doubt on their reliability and creating confusion about which data can be trusted. This approach undermines the perceived legitimacy of IOs and weakens their ability to enforce compliance (Oreskes and Conway 2011).[5]

Populists often use indirect strategies as well, such as degrading domestic information-collection systems, thereby curtailing the flow of data to IOs. This may involve cutting funding for scientific or statistical agencies, dismissing or politicizing experts, or changing the mandates of agencies responsible for data collection (Potter 2021). These actions appeal to populists' preference for loyal bureaucracies that uncritically implement their policies, as opposed to expert bureaucrats who might challenge their decisions (Bellodi, Morelli, and Vannoni 2024, 5).

The result is a decline in the overall quality of bureaucracy and governance, which inevitably affects the quantity and quality of information available to IOs (Bellodi, Morelli, and Vannoni 2024, 25). This pattern is evident across the ideological spectrum. These strategies leave IOs without reliable data or force them to rely on information so distorted that it can become unusable. In some cases, populists' broader anti-IO policies exacerbate the problem. Cutting funding to IOs or withdrawing entirely from membership (though rare) can further reduce the organization's ability to obtain necessary information (von Borzyskowski and Vabulas 2019b).

Populists weigh several factors when deciding how to obstruct information flows. First, they consider the feasibility of manipulation. The extent to which data can be falsified without raising suspicion varies; for example, emissions data regulated by international treaties must align with stringent reporting standards, limiting the opportunity for manipulation.[6] Populists also think about their control over the domestic bureaucracy: Some leaders lack direct control over agencies that generate critical data, constraining their ability to manipulate or withhold information. In addition, leaders' time horizons matter. Strategies like ceasing data collection entirely may have longer-term consequences, as rebuilding capacity under a new government could take years. Withholding already collected data, by contrast, allows for quicker recovery when leadership changes.

---

5. Suspicious or incomplete data flagged by IOs may simply be omitted, appearing as missing data in official reports. Interview conducted by authors. Senior official at an environmental and energy IO, January 25, 2021.

6. Senior official at an environmental IO. Interview by authors. January 25, 2021.

The mix of tactics employed depends on a government's incentives, constraints, and strategic calculations. Compared with other anti-IO tactics, such as exiting institutions or creating competitor organizations, withholding information is generally faster and less costly. Regardless of the method chosen, the result is the same: IOs lose access to critical information, undermining their ability to fulfill their mandates.

4.2.2.   IOs Fight Back: Information Sharing

When faced with gaps in critical information, IOs must quickly adapt to maintain their effectiveness. To replace the information lost when states under populist leadership withhold or distort data, IOs employ several strategies.

One approach involves leveraging open-source data or partnering with third parties, such as NGOs. However, while these sources can be useful, they often lack the granularity required for comprehensive analysis, and IOs may struggle to verify their accuracy independently. Another option is to turn to cooperative member states, particularly those with robust intelligence capabilities, advanced technologies, and sophisticated data systems. This solution, however, is limited by geopolitical considerations, the willingness, if any, of states to share sensitive information, and the availability of relevant data outside the IO's membership. States may possess detailed information on only a subset of members, such as allies, and may be hesitant to share other states' data.

A particularly effective method involves collaboration between IOs themselves. Each organization brings distinct expertise, infrastructure, and access to specialized data streams, making inter-IO cooperation a powerful tool for filling information gaps (Abbott et al. 2015). For instance, the World Bank augments its US-provided emissions data with insights from the EU's EDGAR database, constructing a more comprehensive picture of global environmental trends. These partnerships allow IOs to pool resources and knowledge, enhancing their ability to address complex issues.

Information sharing among IOs offers several advantages. Agreements to share data typically bypass the need for member-state approval, enabling IO bureaucrats to act independently (Clark 2021). By tapping into one another's unique strengths, IOs can access specialized expertise, build more reliable datasets, and reduce redundancy. This interconnectedness also enhances their resilience; for example, during the eurozone crisis, the IMF and the World Bank collaborated to gather insights on European banking systems, helping to compensate for data withheld by uncooperative member states.

Interviews with IO officials underscore the importance of these strategies. One senior environmental IO official noted that when states fail to provide accurate data, the organization turns to alternative sources, including other IOs. This official explained, "We compare notes, involve [other IOs] in eventual papers, and ensure everyone is satisfied with the results."[7] Similarly, a UNAIDS official highlighted how collaboration with WHO and UNICEF helps validate questionable data, emphasizing that political motivations often influence member states' reporting.[8]

This collaborative approach has been applied across sectors. When the Trump administration restricted energy and environmental data shared with the World Bank, the organization signed agreements with Arab multilateral development banks to fill the gaps.[9] Similarly, in the security realm, the UN addressed the reluctance of the US government to share intelligence by partnering with the EU, NATO, the OPCW, and the African Union, bolstering its peacekeeping operations through shared resources.[10]

Despite its benefits, information sharing poses challenges. Member states may hesitate to share sensitive data because of fears of leaks or mistrust of partner IOs. Establishing the necessary infrastructure and protocols for collaboration can impose significant economic and political costs, while staff accustomed to existing systems may resist change. Moreover, IOs often compete for funding and influence, which can deter partnerships. Differences in ideologies and organizational cultures may further complicate cooperation (Clark 2022).[11]

Given these obstacles, IOs typically engage in information sharing when faced with significant threats, such as the rise of populist leaders in powerful member states. These leaders often curtail information flows, forcing IOs to seek alternative sources to maintain operational effectiveness. For instance, the United States, a dominant stakeholder in many development IOs, exerts substantial influence over their policies. Under a populist leader like

7. Senior official at a leading environmental IO. Interview by authors. January 26, 2020.

8. Senior official at a leading health IO. Interview by authors. January 22, 2021.

9. Data collected by authors.

10. See "US 'Hid Iraq Chemical Weapons Incidents.'" *BBC News.* October 15, 2014. https://www.bbc.com/news/world-us-canada-29631829.

11. Former IMF official. Interview by authors. June 8, 2021.

Donald Trump, IOs may lose critical data streams, prompting them to seek new partnerships to mitigate the impact.

Ultimately, information sharing is a vital tool for IOs to navigate populist challenges and maintain their functionality. By pooling resources and expertise, IOs can mitigate the effects of data withholding, safeguard their missions, and reinforce the broader architecture of global governance. This interconnectedness strengthens their ability to address complex global issues, ensuring that international cooperation continues to thrive even in the face of adversity.

4.3.   Testing Alternative IO Information Acquisition

We examine the strategies that IOs employ to navigate information shortfalls in the development space, a domain particularly suited to studying information-sharing dynamics. Development IOs often engage in formalized agreements to exchange data, which are publicly documented and therefore conducive to empirical analysis.

We define information sharing as the structured exchange of knowledge between organizations, as formalized through agreements such as memorandums of understanding. These arrangements typically outline specific areas for collaboration, as seen in the 2018 agreement between the Asian Infrastructure Investment Bank (AIIB) and the Eurasian Development Bank (EDB), which aimed to enhance the "exchange of information and promotion of knowledge-sharing to benefit from each other's experience, resources, and expertise. Potential areas for information sharing may include: (i) economic, financial and business information on common areas of interest; (ii) information with respect to processing of potential projects for co-financing; and (iii) information in relation to mitigation and management of risks, arising from the co-financing of projects."[12]

Notably, these agreements are initiated and signed by IO staff without the direct oversight of member states, granting IOs autonomy in broadening their informational networks. This autonomy allows IOs to circumvent potential interference by powerful stakeholders, who may be unaware of the extent to which data shared with one IO are subsequently disseminated to others. By

12. See "Memorandum of Cooperation Between the Eurasian Development Bank and the Asian Infrastructure Investment Bank." https://www.aiib.org/en/about-aiib/who-we-are /partnership/_download/MOU-Eurasian-Development-Bank.pdf.

formalizing these arrangements, IOs can address critical informational gaps while maintaining their operational independence.

To empirically investigate these dynamics, we utilize a unique dataset from Clark (2021) on information-sharing agreements in the development sector, covering the period from 1956 (when multiple IOs first began operating in the space) to 2018.[13] These data capture agreements that were signed between twenty-eight development IOs, including prominent regional banks such as the African Development Bank and the Asian Development Bank. Our primary analysis focuses on the years 1990 to 2018 because information-sharing agreements are most prevalent during this period.

The development sector provides fertile ground for studying information sharing. First, despite being characterized as ripe for competition among IOs in the literature (Lipscy 2015, 2017), it exhibits high levels of interorganizational cooperation.[14] This cooperation persists across decades, as information-sharing agreements are rarely revoked once established. Second, information collection and dissemination are central to the mandates of most development IOs. For instance, the World Bank collects raw data for constructing influential datasets like the World Development Indicators, which inform global decision making across economic, health, and environmental domains. A senior official from a regional development bank affirmed this mandate, noting that member states are expected to provide statistics when requested.[15]

Development is representative of many economic issue areas in terms of the sensitivity of the information collected and shared by IOs. Therefore, development does not constitute an easy case for information sharing, and we anticipate that our argument generalizes to other economic IOs as well.

Development IOs vary widely in their propensity to sign information-sharing agreements. Figure 4.1 visualizes the evolution of information-sharing networks among development IOs, revealing that while collaboration is widespread, it is pursued unevenly. Some newer organizations, like the AIIB, have quickly become prolific participants in these networks, while smaller

---

13. Information-sharing agreements could not have been signed when the World Bank was the only IO active in the development area (1945–1956).

14. Development is distinct from areas like emergency lending, in which few IOs operate (Lipscy 2015), or environmental governance, where IOs are fragmented and hierarchically ordered (Keohane and Victor 2011; Green 2020).

15. Interview with an official from a development IO (January 25, 2021).

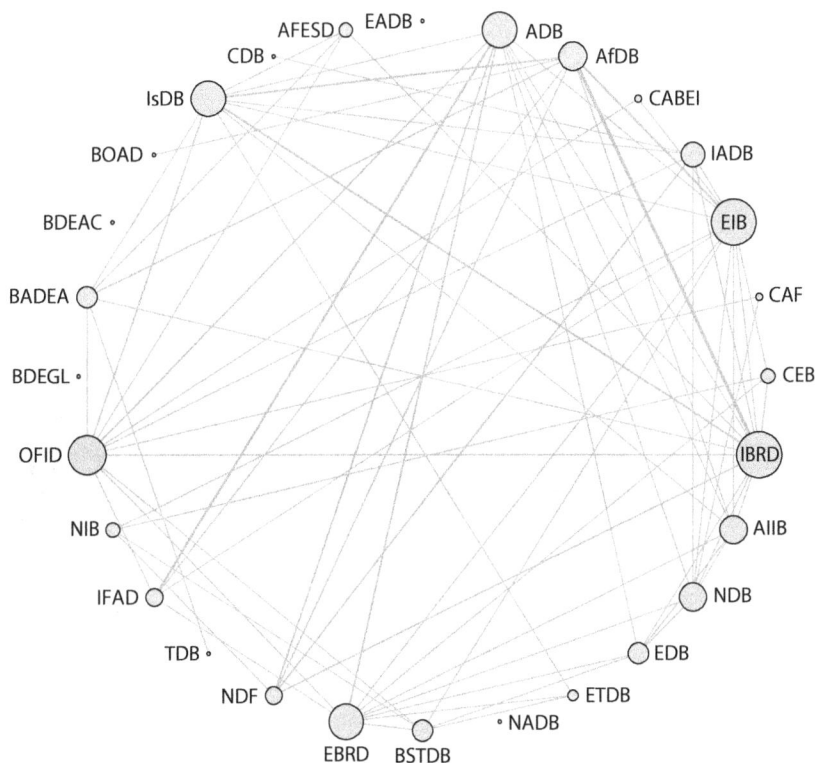

FIGURE 4.1. Average levels of information sharing among development IOs. The size of the circles is increasing in the information sharing of the IO in question. Thicker lines connecting IOs indicates more information sharing on average. Averages are calculated by taking the total number of agreements signed by a given dyad and dividing it by the total number of years the IOs have both operated and thus could have shared information.

banks, such as the Development Bank of the Great Lakes, have yet to sign any agreements. On average, established IOs sign new agreements every two to three years, indicating that information sharing is a common and sustained practice.

The nature of information shared through these agreements varies considerably, ranging from economic statistics to technical expertise. For example, some agreements focus on co-financing projects and mitigating associated risks, while others emphasize exchanging managerial best practices or strategies for delivering development assistance. Figure 4.2 categorizes these agreements using hand-coded data, highlighting the breadth of informational exchange in the development sector.

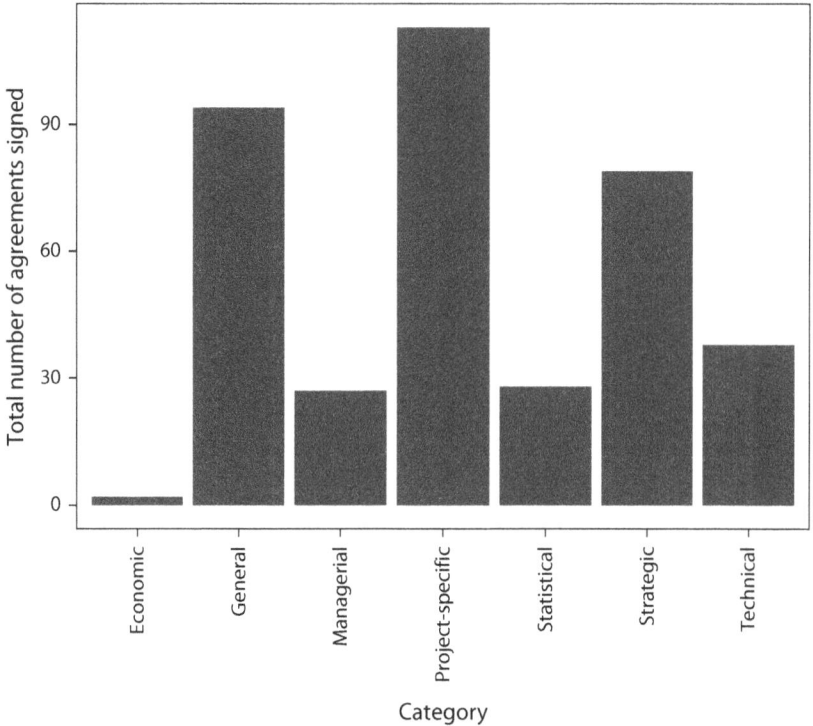

FIGURE 4.2. Total number of information-sharing agreements signed by information category. These data reflect all information-sharing agreements signed by dyads of development banks between 1956 and 2018.

"Economic" agreements involve the sharing of economic statistics; "General" agreements speak broadly (and often vaguely) about improving cooperation and information sharing; "Managerial" agreements mention sharing information about best practices and administration; "Project specific" agreements discuss the transmission of information related to co-financing operations; "Statistical" agreements specifically mention the sharing of country statistics; "Strategies" correspond to information about assistance strategies and development plans; and "Technical" agreements discuss the sharing of knowledge about policies, research, and expertise. Note that while each agreement corresponds to at least one category, some correspond to several.

The IOs in the issue space vary in terms of their propensity for signing information-sharing agreements. Figure 4.3 shows the average number of information-sharing agreements signed by each IO in the development space in a given year. Newer IOs, such as AIIB and NDB, sign such agreements most

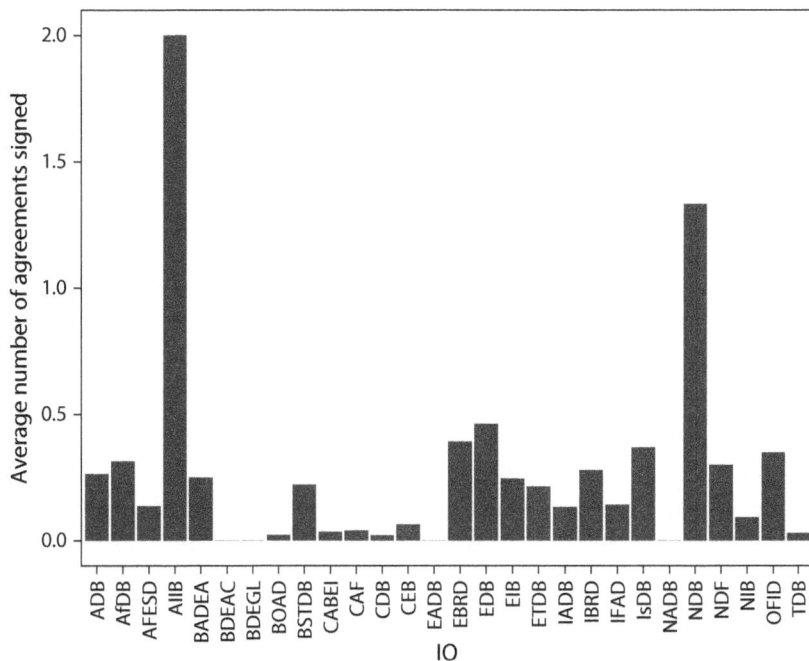

FIGURE 4.3. Average number of information-sharing agreements signed by IOs.

frequently, while some smaller IOs, such as BDEAC, BDEGL, and the EADB, have never shared information. However, most IOs—including prominent regional banks like the ADB, AfDB, and IADB—sign a new information-sharing agreement about once every two to three years, which suggests that information sharing is a fairly widespread form of interorganizational cooperation. Moreover, because AIIB and NDB are in the data for only 2016–2018 and 2015–2018 respectively, they sign few agreements in absolute terms even if their relative propensity to sign agreements is high.

To test our theoretical claims, we analyze dyadic data between pairs of development IOs. To test our claims, we conduct an analysis using dyadic IO-level data. We specifically examine dyads with substantive and geographic overlap (i.e., those that perform similar functions and have overlapping memberships). Only such IO pairs should cooperate (Clark 2021). There are just over 5,700 dyads of overlapping development IOs in our data.

Our primary variable of interest is whether the leading stakeholder in each IO is governed by a populist leader. Leading stakeholders are identified based on voting power within the organization, supplemented by the influence of positions like IO president or managing director in cases of ties.[16] This measure varies between 0–2 (zero if neither most powerful state is led by a populist, one if one of the two states is led by a populist, and two if both are led by populists). As in other chapters, we utilize populism data from Funke, Schularick, and Trebesch (2023). Our dependent variable measures the number of information-sharing agreements signed between two IOs in a given year.

In some of our models, we include additional control variables, following Clark (2021). First, we control for the difference in the number of member states belonging to each IO—existing work suggests that IOs with relatively few resources prefer to cooperate with richer IOs. We also account for geopolitical ties between leading stakeholders across IOs by including a binary equal to one if such states are allies. Last, we control for geographic proximity between IOs.

We use negative binomial models with dyad and year-fixed effects. Standard errors are robust and clustered at the dyad level. Our parsimonious baseline model includes no additional control variables, and we subsequently add the control variables described previously.

Our analysis, the results for which are found in table 4.1, reveals a strong and statistically significant relationship between populist leadership in an IO's leading stakeholder and the frequency of information-sharing agreements. When one of the two IOs in a dyad is led by a populist stakeholder, the likelihood of signing such agreements increases by approximately 20 percent.[17] This suggests that IOs actively compensate for the informational gaps created by populist resistance by seeking alternative sources of data through collaboration with other IOs.

These findings hold across various robustness checks, including alternative model specifications, additional control variables, and different fixed-effects structures. For instance, we account for the geographic proximity of IO headquarters, differences in organizational size, and geopolitical alliances between leading stakeholders, all of which might influence the propensity for cooperation. In all cases, the results confirm our central contention: IOs respond to the challenges posed by populist leadership by forging stronger interorganizational connections.

---

16. This is a common measure of institutional power in the literature (see, e.g., Kaya 2015; Lipscy 2015). Countries with large vote shares in a given IO may also possess veto power; for example, this is the case for the United States at the World Bank.

17. The mean number of agreements signed by a given pair of IOs in a given year is 0.19.

TABLE 4.1. Information-sharing results

	Information sharing	
	Model 1	Model 2
Populism	0.200**	0.214***
	(0.085)	(0.079)
Alliance		−0.083
		(0.099)
Difference in IO size		0.009**
		(0.004)
HQ distance		−0.349***
		(0.077)
N	5747	5747

Note: Model type is negative binomial. Dyad and year-fixed effects are included. Robust standard errors are clustered at the dyad-level.
***p < .01; **p < .05; *p < .1

By expanding their informational networks through formal agreements, IOs not only mitigate the impact of populist-driven information withholding but also enhance their resilience. These partnerships enable organizations to pool resources, share expertise, and maintain their operational effectiveness, even in the face of significant political and institutional challenges. As such, information sharing emerges as a critical strategy for safeguarding the functionality and credibility of global governance institutions.

4.4. Illustrative Example: IO Information Dynamics Under Trump

This section traces the impact of populist leadership on the dynamics of information sharing among IOs, using the election of Donald Trump during his first term as a case study. Trump's presidency provides a valuable lens for examining how populist leadership influences IO behavior, particularly within US-led institutions. This case is especially significant because of the geopolitical weight of the United States and the availability of detailed data on information sharing and suppression.

Our theory predicts that US-led IOs would respond to increased information suppression and distortion under Trump by intensifying their efforts to establish information-sharing agreements with other IOs. To test this, we

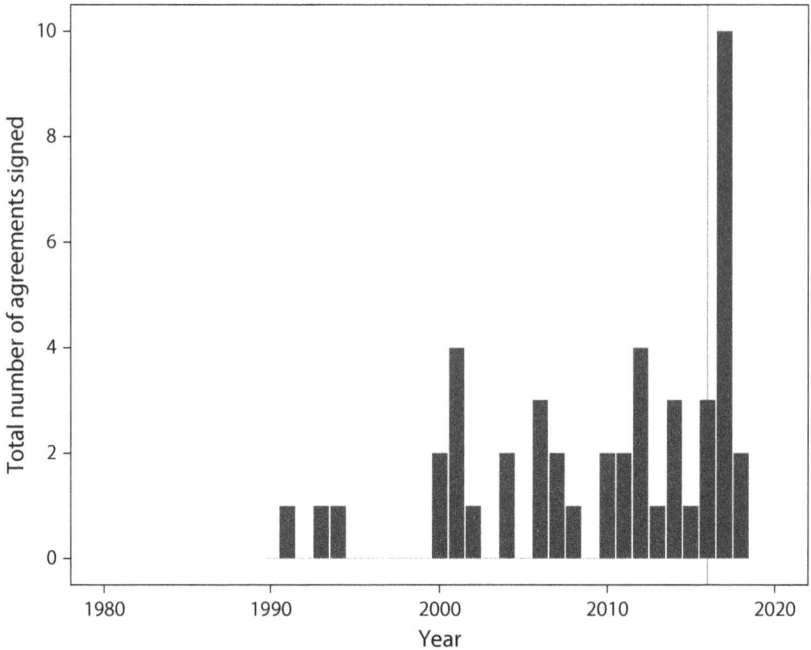

FIGURE 4.4. Number of information sharing agreements signed by US-led development IOs, 1980–2018. The vertical line demarcates 2016 (the year of Trump's election).

first analyzed trends in the number of such agreements over time. We then examined evidence of information suppression during Trump's tenure, finding a simultaneous rise in formal information-sharing agreements and a decline in the provision of accurate data by the United States. While causality cannot be firmly established, the evidence aligns with our theoretical expectations.

The number of information-sharing agreements signed by US-led development IOs, such as the World Bank, Inter-American Development Bank, and others, surged dramatically after Trump's election in 2016. As shown in figure 4.4, 2017 marked a significant increase in these agreements compared with those of prior years. This uptick is not merely a byproduct of new opportunities presented by recently established IOs, such as the New Development Bank and the Asian Infrastructure Investment Bank. Instead, US-led IOs also actively sought cooperation with long-standing institutions like the Arab Coordination Group, which includes IOs specializing in energy and infrastructure.

Before Trump's election, US-led IOs had limited interaction with the Coordination Group (CG) institutions, despite decades of potential

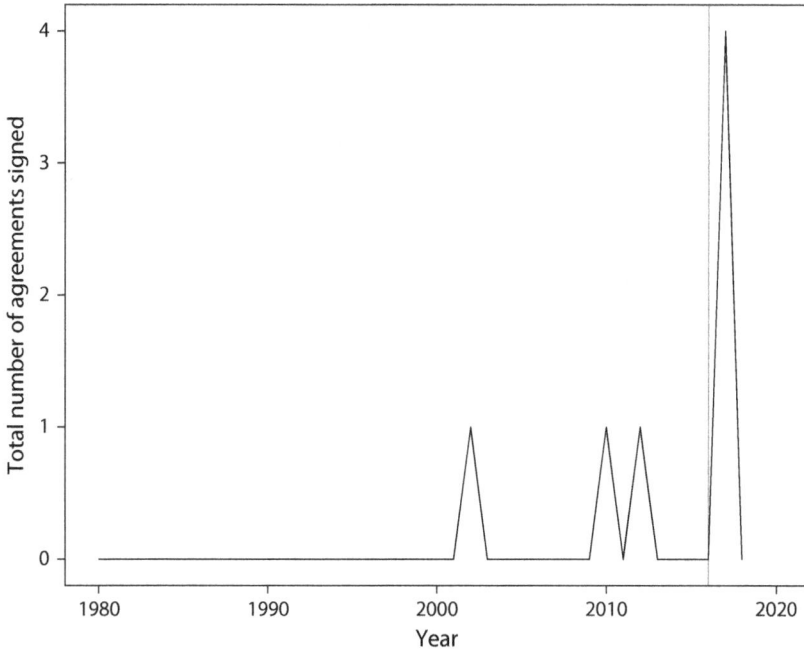

FIGURE 4.5. Number of information-sharing agreements signed by US-led development IOs with Arab IOs, 1980–2018. The vertical line demarcates 2016 (the year of Trump's election).

collaboration. However, following Trump's inauguration, these IOs signed multiple agreements with CG institutions, likely aiming to diversify their informational inputs, as shown in figure 4.5. This pivot highlights a strategic effort to compensate for the anticipated reduction in US-sourced data. While we are unable to observe specific flows of information between US- and Arab-led IOs, it is likely that at least some of the information sharing pertained to elite-driven areas like energy and the environment that are prone to populist withholding, as the prior chapter illustrated. Given that American and Arab IOs had more than three decades of opportunities to cooperate before Trump's election, it seems plausible that US-led IOs more aggressively sought cooperation with the CG to diversify their information base as Trump took office.

To investigate the underlying mechanism, we turned to data on information suppression by the Trump administration, particularly in the domains of public health and climate change—critical areas for development IOs. The Silencing Science Tracker documents numerous instances of restricted

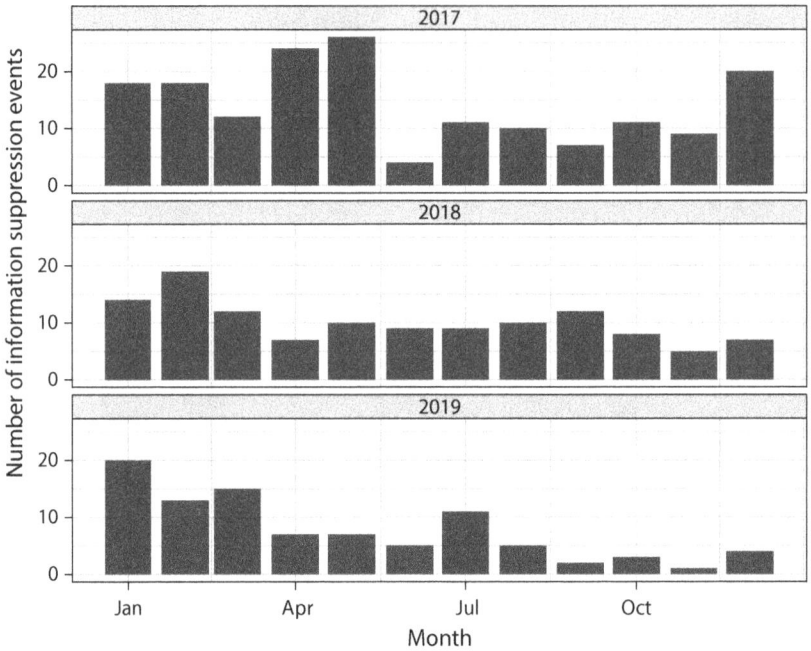

FIGURE 4.6. US information suppression, 2017–2019. Data come from Silencing Science Tracker.

scientific research, altered publications, and budget cuts to research agencies.[18] As shown in figure 4.6, suppression events escalated sharply after Trump assumed office in 2017, with categories like "Bias," "Budget Cuts," and "Research Hindrance" dominating the landscape (figure 4.7).

These suppression tactics included blocking US scientists from contributing to international reports, cutting funding for NASA's Carbon Monitoring System (essential for UN deforestation programs), and injecting political bias into environmental assessments.[19] For example, the US Bureau of Land Management published a report downplaying climate risks in Arctic drilling proposals. Similarly, the Trump administration's budget proposals targeted research agencies central to IO information flows, such as the EPA, NIH, and NSF, with substantial funding reductions.[20]

18. See https://climate.law.columbia.edu/Silencing-Science-Tracker.

19. Brad Plumer and Coral Davenport, "Science Under Attack: How Trump Is Sidelining Researchers and Their Work." *The New York Times.* December 28, 2019.

20. Luke Bassett, Kristina Costa, and Lia Cattaneo, "Burning the Data: Attacks on Climate and Energy Data and Research." *Center for American Progress.* June 13, 2018. Indeed, two US

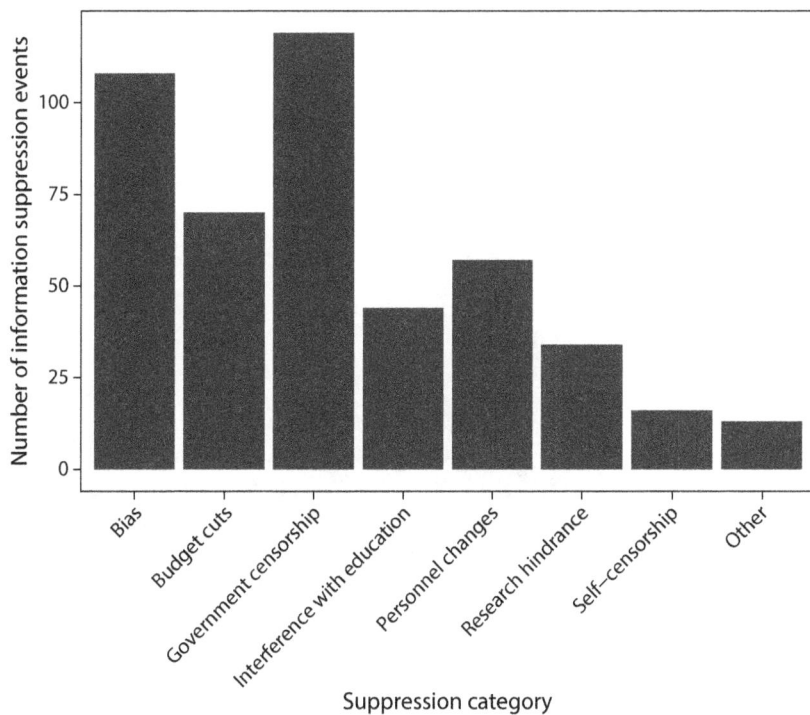

FIGURE 4.7. US information suppression events by category, 2017–2019. Data come from Silencing Science Tracker.

Our analysis of data from the World Development Indicators further corroborates these findings. The share of missing US data in the WDI dataset—a proxy for transparency and information sharing (Hollyer, Rosendorff, and Vreeland 2014)—rose steeply from under 20 percent in 2015 to nearly 60 percent by 2019 (figure 4.8). This dramatic increase suggests a systemic effort to curtail data sharing, consistent with Trump's populist orientation and skepticism toward IOs.

These trends are not unique to the United States. A similar pattern emerged in Turkey following the election of populist leader Recep Tayyip Erdoğan in 2014. As shown in figure 4.9, Turkey also exhibited a significant increase in WDI data missingness under Erdoğan. Concurrently, the Turkish-led Economic Cooperation Organization Trade and Development Bank signed

federal datasets proved pivotal to its 2014 conclusions, and the Department of Energy's carbon emissions data is a key source for its determinations regarding precipitation patterns (ibid).

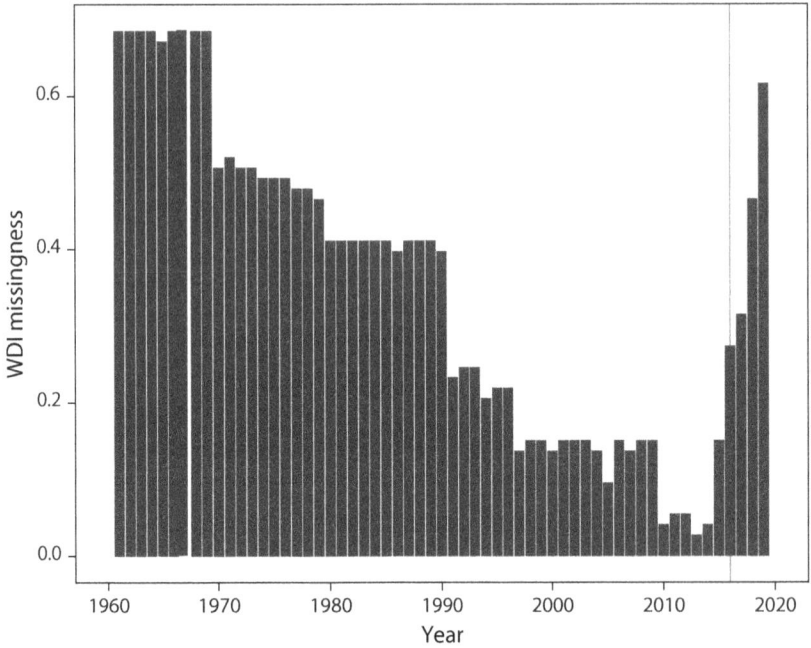

FIGURE 4.8. Share of US missing WDI data, 1960–2019. Data come from the World Development Indicators. Variables are matched with those from Hollyer, Rosendorff, and Vreeland (2014). The vertical line again demarcates 2016 (the year of Trump's election).

multiple information-sharing agreements post-2014, having signed only one in the preceding decade.

The evidence presented in this illustrative case aligns closely with our theoretical framework. Under Trump, the United States curtailed information flows to development IOs through suppression, distortion, and funding cuts, prompting US-led IOs to actively forge new information-sharing agreements. This response was not limited to new partnerships but extended to long-standing institutions, indicating a deliberate strategy to diversify information sources.

These dynamics generalize to other populist-led states, reinforcing the broader relevance of our findings. By highlighting the interplay between populist governance and IO behavior, this analysis underscores the importance of adaptive strategies like information sharing in preserving the functionality of global governance structures amid political disruption.

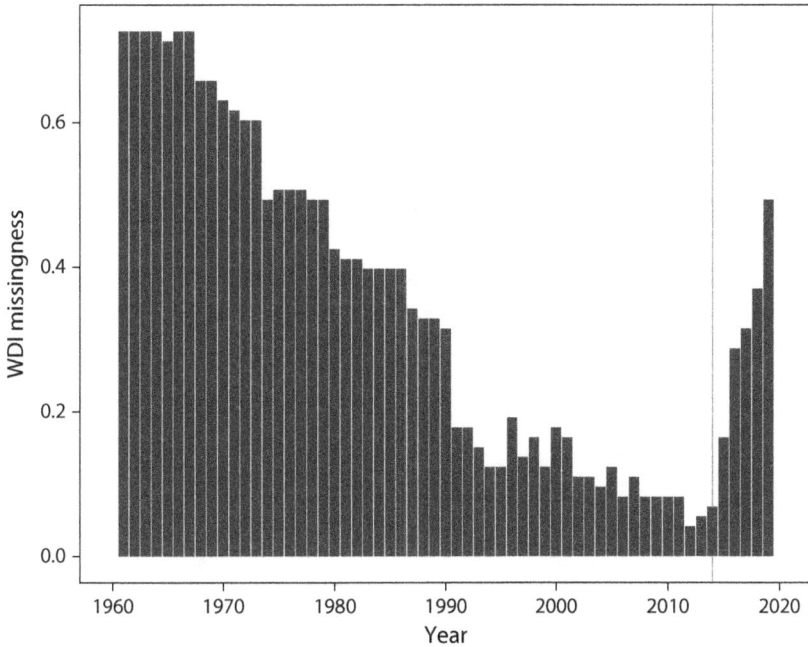

FIGURE 4.9. Share of Turkish missing WDI data, 1960–2019. Data come from the World Development Indicators. Variables are matched with those from Hollyer, Rosendorff, and Vreeland (2014). The vertical line demarcates 2014 (the year of Erdoğan's election).

4.5. Concluding Thoughts: The Role of Sidelining in Combating Populist Resistance

This chapter explored and tested our theory of sidelining populists via information sharing among IOs, demonstrating how IOs adapt when faced with the challenge of a populist-led major stakeholder. We found that populists' resistance often leads to a loss of crucial member-provided information, prompting IOs to collaborate more closely by sharing knowledge among themselves. This pattern was supported through quantitative analysis in the development sector and a case study focusing on Trump's presidency and its impact on US-led IOs.

Our analysis makes clear that sidelining strategies are a key element of IOs' adaptive toolkit. Sidelining can enable IOs to navigate hostile environments while safeguarding their missions and values. By leveraging their networks and cooperating with other organizations, IOs can maintain operational effectiveness and relevance on the global stage. Crucially, this approach allows IOs to circumvent the need to compromise their goals or norms to appease populists.

However, sidelining also has downsides. This strategy may further alienate populist states, potentially exacerbating tensions and depriving IOs of the contributions these members might otherwise offer. Moreover, its success depends on the availability and quality of alternative information and resources. In such cases, combining sidelining with appeasement may be necessary to strike a balance between maintaining core principles and ensuring broader organizational stability—a topic we turn to in the next chapter.

5

Appeasing Populist Leaders

DONALD TRUMP took a particularly hostile stance toward the WTO during his first term. Throughout, he openly criticized the organization, threatened to withdraw the United States from it entirely, and disregarded its rules and norms. This hostility was not simply rhetorical: Trump blocked the appointment of judges to the WTO's dispute-settlement body and imposed tariffs on trading partners that directly violated WTO rules.[1] These actions sparked concerns about cascading noncompliance, with fears that other states might follow suit, potentially destabilizing the global trade regime and jeopardizing the WTO's very survival.

In response, the WTO made several attempts to appease the United States, focusing on reforms to its Appellate Body—the primary target of Trump's criticism. Proposed changes included limiting the length of appeals, introducing term limits for Secretariat staff, establishing an audit committee, removing advisory opinions, and ensuring that precedents would not bind future cases. While these concessions failed to satisfy Trump, they demonstrate the lengths to which the WTO was willing to go to mollify his administration.[2]

This pattern of IOs making concessions to defuse populist pressure is not unique to the WTO. The European Union faced similar challenges when Hungary, under populist leader Viktor Orbán, blocked the ratification of the post-Cotonou Agreement with seventy-nine African, Caribbean, and Pacific states in 2021. Orbán objected to the agreement's migration policies and its promotion of LGBTQ+ rights, framing them as violations of Hungarian sovereignty. In response, the EU attempted to placate Hungary by

---

1. Ben Horton and Kristen Hopewell. "Lessons from Trump's Assault on the World Trade Organization." *Chatham House*. August 3, 2021.

2. "New Proposal Seeks to Save World Trade Organization." *Forbes*. December 9, 2019.

emphasizing that national governments would retain control over education and migration policies.[3]

These examples illustrate a broader dynamic: IOs often respond to populist-led states by granting concessions to secure their participation and support. Unlike other leaders who might face domestic backlash for defying international norms, populists often find that their hostility toward IOs resonates with their constituents. This political calculus makes their threats to disengage from IOs more credible. Populists' behavior creates significant challenges for IOs, which rely on member participation to remain effective and legitimate (Gray 2018). To maintain these relationships, IOs may cede ground, granting populists concessions that they can showcase as victories at home, while continuing to benefit from IO resources.

These concessions take various forms, including material incentives, fewer constraints, and increased institutional influence. For instance, in the financial sphere, institutions like the World Bank and IMF often attach stringent conditions to their loans, such as privatization mandates, budget cuts, or compliance with transparency requirements. These conditions are politically and economically costly, particularly for populists, who campaign on sovereignty and resistance to elite interference. Accepting such terms risks alienating their domestic base and contradicting their anti-elite rhetoric.

We hypothesize that populist leaders receive less onerous loan conditions from the World Bank and IMF compared with their nonpopulist counterparts, ensuring their continued engagement with these institutions. We present the results of statistical analyses of loan conditionality, which show that populists consistently secure more favorable terms.

While this dynamic helps IOs retain populist participation, it raises serious normative concerns about equity and legitimacy in global governance. By granting populists preferential treatment, IOs may appear to reward defiance while punishing compliance. This could erode the perception that IOs operate based on fairness and need, undermining their broader mandate to promote global welfare. In financial institutions, for example, conditions are designed to prevent moral hazard and ensure sustainable economic reforms (Reinsberg, Stubbs, and Kentikelenis 2022). Deviating from these principles to appease populists risks undermining these objectives.

---

3. Benjamin Fox, "Post-Cotonou Deal in Danger as Concerns Grow Over Ratification Delay." *Euractiv.* November 4, 2022.

Furthermore, empowering populists within IOs can allow them to reshape the organizations to align with their agendas. For example, the EU faced pressure to reinstate funds it had withheld from Hungary because of democratic backsliding, a move that could have compromised its commitment to upholding core EU values.[4] World Bank president Ajay Banga similarly looked to shift institutional activities to "focus on mutual benefits" like job creation in a pitch to preserve US cooperation ahead of Trump's second term.[5] Concessions such as increased control within IOs might enable populists to erode institutional missions, clawing back sovereignty or pursuing policies counter to the IO's founding principles.

Finally, such concessions may bolster populists' domestic standing, reinforcing their image as effective negotiators who can stand up to international elites. By securing tangible victories over IOs, populists can strengthen their political support at home, potentially emboldening further defiance on the international stage. Thus, while concessions may preserve short-term institutional stability, they risk enabling populists and undermining IOs' long-term goals and legitimacy. In the concluding chapter, we discuss how using sidelining strategies in conjunction with strategies of appeasement may help ameliorate some of these undesirable outcomes.

5.1.   How IOs Appease Populists

When populist leaders grow disenchanted with IOs, they often engage in a range of oppositional tactics, as explored in earlier chapters. In response, IOs strive to counter this resistance, motivated by a need to keep these states engaged. One of their key strategies is to lower the political and economic costs of participation, effectively enticing populists to remain within the fold. While populists may bristle at IOs' elite character and perceived encroachments on sovereignty, they also recognize the tangible benefits of membership. These include access to economic assistance, expert policy advice, valuable information, dispute-resolution mechanisms, and reduced barriers to trade and investment (Keohane 1984; Dai 2002).

Participation in an IO operates like a renewable contract: For states to remain engaged, the benefits must outweigh the costs (Keohane 1984). To tip

4. Anna Meyerrose, "The Hungary Games." *Devex Newswire.* April 21, 2023.

5. Helen Murphy, "Can the World Bank get Trump on board?" *Devex Newswire.* January 15, 2024.

this balance in favor of continued membership even as populist leaders perceive relatively high costs, IOs can offer populist leaders enhanced benefits or reduced burdens. These adjustments might take the form of temporary concessions, such as increased aid during a populist leader's tenure, or longer-term structural reforms, like granting a populist-led state more control or influence within the organization. Similarly, IOs can mitigate the perceived costs of participation by softening policies that populists find objectionable, such as stringent rules or what they see as onerous loan conditions.

While existing scholarship highlights various reasons why IOs show favoritism to their members—including political competition between organizations (Lipscy 2015) and concerns over institutional legitimacy (Imerman 2018; Lenz, Burilkov, and Viola 2019)—we emphasize the importance of populism. Politically significant states, such as those with temporary seats on the UN Security Council or the World Bank board, have long been shown to secure preferential treatment, such as receiving more projects or fewer loan conditions (Dreher, Sturm, and Vreeland 2009; Kaja and Werker 2010; Kilby 2011; Lim and Vreeland 2013; Clark and Dolan 2021). However, we argue that populist leaders, with their heightened and more credible threats to disengage, are especially likely to reap such rewards.[6] Populists' vocal opposition and ideological divergence compel IOs to attempt to mollify them.

By incorporating populism into an analysis of IO favoritism, this chapter contributes to a broader understanding of global governance reform. Much of the literature on institutional change focuses on systemic shocks—political or economic disruptions that create opportunities for transformation (Krasner 1976; Wallander 2000). These moments of upheaval, or punctuated equilibria, are often seen as prerequisites for overcoming institutional inertia (Bennett and Elman 2006; Page 2006).

However, we challenge this perspective and demonstrate that IOs frequently implement reforms to appease skeptical leaders even in the absence of dramatic external shocks. Populists, with their intense and credible opposition, create localized pressures that can drive change. This recalibration may result in concessions but can also have long-term policy implications, potentially shifting power dynamics and organizational priorities over time (Blyth 2002; Mahoney and Thelen 2010; Campbell 2021).

Understanding these processes offers critical insights into the inner workings of IOs. By examining how populists shape institutional behavior, we

---

6. Also see Clark (2024).

reveal the extent to which IOs are willing to adapt to maintain their membership and relevance. These adjustments, while often pragmatic, highlight the delicate balancing act IOs must perform to navigate political resistance without compromising their foundational principles.

5.2. IOs, Loans, and Conditionality: Appeasing Populist Leaders in International Finance

IFIs play a pivotal role in global governance by providing financial assistance to member states through grants, loans, and technical expertise. This assistance often comes with strings attached—mandatory policy reforms known as conditionality. While conditions aim to foster macroeconomic stability and ensure the responsible use of funds, they also ignite controversy. Populist leaders, in particular, often push back against these requirements, creating a complex dynamic between IOs and their members (Clark 2024).

Conditionality is a cornerstone of lending for institutions like the IMF and, to a lesser extent, the World Bank. IMF loans frequently mandate sweeping reforms, including trade liberalization, privatization of state-owned enterprises, fiscal austerity, anti-corruption measures, and tax increases (Li, Sy, and McMurray 2015; Kentikelenis, Stubbs, and King 2016; Clark and Meyerrose 2025). These conditions are controversial, often sparking domestic unrest and political resistance, especially from organized labor and other affected groups (Caraway, Rickard, and Anner 2012). The World Bank, while less stringent, imposes conditions related to governance, environmental policies, and long-term economic restructuring that can also prove contentious (Clark, Dolan, and Zeitz 2025).

IFIs justify conditionality as a safeguard against moral hazard and recidivism, ensuring that loans are used effectively and that borrowing countries adopt reforms to address the root causes of their financial distress (Reinsberg, Stubbs, and Kentikelenis 2022). Conditions are often linked to disbursement: Funds are released in tranches only after borrowers meet specific benchmarks. At the IMF, subsequent tranches are contingent on compliance unless a waiver is granted, while the World Bank's conditional lending arm operates on an all-or-nothing basis, requiring that all conditions be met before funds are disbursed (Clark and Dolan 2021).

Loan recipients frequently resist conditionality, citing both practical and ideological concerns. Critics argue that the IMF's "one-size-fits-all" approach often fails to deliver economic growth or stability over the medium term (Bulir and Moon 2004; Li, Sy, and McMurray 2015). Conditions can exacerbate inequality, unemployment, and economic contraction, eroding public trust and fueling political instability (Vreeland 2005; Handlin, Kaya, and Günaydin 2023).

The eurozone crisis provides a vivid illustration of conditionality's contentious nature. Strict austerity measures imposed by the IMF and EU, including tax hikes, pension cuts, and labor market reforms, provoked widespread backlash in Greece and Portugal. Populist parties, such as Syriza in Greece, capitalized on public discontent, achieving electoral success by opposing these reforms. Syriza even threatened to exit the eurozone, compelling the IMF to soften its stance and reduce the number of conditions attached to Greek loans, from forty-six in 2014 to just eight in 2015 when Syriza came to power.[7] These concessions underscore the challenges IFIs face when dealing with populist leaders who can credibly threaten disengagement.

IOs relent to populists because populist leaders present a unique challenge to IFIs. Their ideological opposition to IOs and their emphasis on sovereignty allow them to credibly threaten withdrawal or disengagement, raising the stakes for IFIs. To maintain member participation and avoid irrelevance, IFIs have strong incentives to appease populists by reducing the stringency of loan conditions.

Several factors drive this leniency. First, IFIs rely on loan-interest income to fund concessional programs, such as the World Bank's IDA loans. Maintaining a robust loan portfolio minimizes dependence on direct member contributions, which can themselves become threatened under populist regimes. Second, active lending preserves IFIs' relevance and legitimacy, demonstrating their ability to address members' needs. Powerful member states also benefit from IFI lending, as it allows them to exert influence over recipient countries (Andersen, Hansen, and Markussen 2006; Kilby 2013). Third, IO bureaucrats, motivated by what has been termed the "disbursement imperative," prioritize getting funds out the door to justify their work and advance their careers (Weaver 2008).

Given these dynamics, we hypothesize that countries led by populist leaders receive fewer and less stringent conditions on loans from IFIs. By easing the burdens of conditionality, IFIs can retain populist participation, balancing the need for engagement against the risks of populist exit. This hypothesis

---

7. Information comes from IMF program documents.

aligns with broader patterns of IO behavior, where institutional flexibility is employed to navigate political resistance and sustain participation in a fragmented global order.

5.3.   Testing IO Concessions to Populists through Conditional Lending

To investigate whether IOs appease populist leaders by granting concessions, we analyze data on conditional lending from the IMF and World Bank. Conditionality, which is politically sensitive and economically significant, serves as an ideal lens to examine these dynamics. Countries with leverage, like those that are close to the United States, hold temporary membership on the UNSC, or belong to competitor institutions, often obtain relatively lenient conditionality packages (Stone 2011; Vreeland and Dreher 2014; Clark 2022). We argue that populists, by credibly threatening disengagement from IOs, can achieve similar outcomes.

In both cases, we use a count of binding conditions imposed in a given project as a proxy for the intrusiveness of conditionality.[8] This count serves as our primary dependent variable. As a robustness check, we also measure the number of policy areas covered by these conditions, which offers an additional metric of the burden of conditionality (Stone 2008). Programs encompassing more policy areas are presumed to be more onerous.

We sourced data on IMF conditionality from Kentikelenis, Stubbs, and King (2016) covering 1978–2014 and on World Bank conditional loans from Clark and Dolan (2021) covering 2000–2018. Our unit of analysis is the country-year. The IMF models include country- and year-fixed effects to account for temporal shocks and country-specific factors, while the World Bank models incorporate only country-fixed effects; Clark and Dolan (2021) formally reject the use of year-fixed effects in this setting. Robust standard errors are clustered at the country level, and our specifications employ negative binomial models because of the overdispersion of our count variables.

The primary independent variable is again a binary indicator of whether a country's executive leadership was populist, derived from Funke, Schularick, and Trebesch (2023). We include as controls economic and political

---

8. Structural benchmarks and indicative targets at the IMF were excluded because of their weaker enforceability, as were nonbinding conditions at the World Bank (Clark and Dolan 2021).

variables relevant to each IO's context, following the literature on each (Vreeland 2003, 2005; Stone 2011). For the IMF, controls include GDP per capita, trade openness, debt-to-export ratios, FDI flows, democracy scores (Polity2), institutional checks on executives, US aid receipts, UNSC membership, and ideological alignment with the United States on votes in the UN General Assembly. For the World Bank, additional controls include Chinese aid receipts, colonial relationships with the EU president's home country, and inflation rates. IMF-specific controls include program type (e.g., PRGF loans), program duration, and a country's IMF quota.[9]

In subsequent tests, continuous variables are standardized for ease of interpretation and to assist the convergence of the negative binomial models.[10] All independent variables are lagged by one year except program characteristics in the IMF case. We opt for a one-year lag because there is a temporal gap between when a country applies for assistance and when loan terms are agreed upon, which is when projects first appear in the data. To address missing data, economic covariates were imputed using multiple imputation, following best practices in the field (Lall 2016).[11]

The results, summarized in tables 5.1 and 5.2, indicate that populist leaders receive significant breaks in conditional lending: Regarding IMF lending, populist-led states experienced a 35 percent reduction in the number of conditions and a 20 percent reduction in policy areas covered by these conditions in our data. These results are statistically significant at the 0.01 level, underscoring the bargaining power of populist leaders in negotiations with the Fund.

9. Economic statistics come from WDI; Polity data comes from Jaggers and Gurr (1995); checks and election data come from DPI; US aid data come from the aid greenbook; UN voting data come from Bailey, Strezhnev, and Voeten (2017); conflict data come from UCDP; data on UNSC membership are hand-coded; data on domestic officials' ideology come from Nelson (2017). Data on quotas come from MONA, while data on program features come from Kentikelenis, Stubbs, and King (2016). Data on Chinese aid comes from AidData, see Dreher et al. (2022); data on colonial relationships with the country in control of the EU presidency are hand-coded; World Bank Board membership data are hand-coded; inflation data come from WDI; IMF program data come from Kentikelenis, Stubbs, and King (2016).

10. Standardization is done with the `scale` function in R, which subtracts the column mean from a given value and then divides by the column standard deviation.

11. A similar approach to missing data in the development space is taken by Schneider and Tobin (2020); as they note, "crisis countries with missing data tend to be poorer and have weaker democratic institutions ... coefficient estimates would likely be inefficient and biased if listwise deletion [was utilized] for missing data."

TABLE 5.1. IMF conditionality results

	Conditions Model 1	Categories Model 2	Conditions Model 3	Categories Model 4
Populism	−0.489***	−0.276***	−0.437***	−0.234***
	(0.124)	(0.082)	(0.134)	(0.088)
Duration			0.021	0.016
			(0.022)	(0.014)
Quota			−0.010	0.004
			(0.031)	(0.019)
PRGF			0.253***	0.201***
			(0.060)	(0.037)
Time from last IMF program			0.007	0.004
			(0.006)	(0.003)
Outside option member			−0.263**	−0.146**
			(0.117)	(0.068)
Polity2			−0.049*	−0.013
			(0.026)	(0.016)
UN voting (ideal pt dist from US)			−0.030	−0.008
			(0.025)	(0.016)
UNSC member			−0.124**	−0.086**
			(0.059)	(0.040)
Checks			0.021*	0.012
			(0.012)	(0.008)
US aid			−0.045**	−0.006
			(0.021)	(0.013)
FDI/GDP			−0.026**	−0.013*
			(0.011)	(0.007)
GDPPC			0.014	0.005
			(0.020)	(0.013)
Openness			0.026	−0.004
			(0.021)	(0.015)
Debt service/ exports			−0.002	−0.001
			(0.013)	(0.009)
Short-term debt/exports			−0.022	−0.016
			(0.014)	(0.010)
War			−0.071*	−0.014
			(0.043)	(0.026)
Election year			0.023	0.007
			(0.047)	(0.026)

(*Continued on next page*)

TABLE 5.1. (*continued*)

	Conditions Model 1	Categories Model 2	Conditions Model 3	Categories Model 4
Country-fixed effects	Yes	Yes	Yes	Yes
Year-fixed effects	Yes	Yes	Yes	Yes
Model type	Negative binomial	Negative binomial	Negative binomial	Negative binomial
N	2121	2121	2121	2121

Note: All independent variables except for duration and PRGF are lagged by one year. Robust standard errors are clustered at the country-level. Missing data is imputed with multiple imputation in columns 3 and 4.

***p < .01; **p < .05; *p < .1

For the World Bank, populists receive a 55 percent reduction in the number of policy areas covered by conditions, though the results for the number of conditions imposed are weaker and fail to achieve statistical significance. This discrepancy likely reflects the softer nature of World Bank conditionality (Clark and Dolan 2021), which focuses on governance and environmental reforms rather than the harsher economic measures often imposed by the IMF.

We performed extensive robustness checks to validate these findings. In these models, we accounted for selection into loan programs by utilizing an instrumental variable for IMF participation and using inverse probability weighting for World Bank loans. We also tested models with and without imputed data. For the IMF, we next excluded waived conditions to ensure that they did not skew results. We further employed alternative specifications using Poisson models and different combinations of covariates. In each case, our results were corroborated.[12]

Our analysis reveals that populist leaders successfully leverage their opposition to IOs to secure favorable loan terms. By threatening to withdraw from or disengage with IOs, populists compel organizations like the IMF and World Bank to reduce the burden of conditionality, preserving their participation. This dynamic underscores the strategic calculus of IOs, which often prioritize retaining members—even contentious ones—to maintain their relevance and legitimacy.

---

12. Robustness checks for this chapter are available from the authors upon request.

TABLE 5.2. World Bank conditionality results

	Conditions Model 1	Categories Model 2	Conditions Model 3	Categories Model 4
Populism	−0.221	−0.759***	0.116	−0.698***
	(0.153)	(0.194)	(0.203)	(0.189)
Duration			0.309***	0.075***
			(0.041)	(0.021)
Quota			−0.072	0.027
			(0.101)	(0.068)
PRGF			−0.197	−0.089
			(0.135)	(0.124)
Time from last IMF program			−0.125	−0.003
			(0.078)	(0.053)
Outside option member			−0.042	−0.004
			(0.030)	(0.020)
Polity2			0.001	0.001
			(0.031)	(0.016)
UN voting (ideal pt dist from US)			0.025	−0.031
			(0.067)	(0.048)
UNSC member			−0.014	−0.014
			(0.027)	(0.016)
Checks			0.024	−0.019
			(0.026)	(0.020)
US aid			−0.068***	−0.007
			(0.023)	(0.018)
FDI/GDP			0.072	−0.001
			(0.044)	(0.018)
GDPPC			0.0005	−0.025
			(0.029)	(0.015)
Openness			0.035	0.010
			(0.051)	(0.033)
Debt service/ exports			0.018	−0.067
			(0.070)	(0.044)
Short-term debt/ exports			−0.002	0.061
			(0.095)	(0.053)
War			0.077	−0.048
			(0.106)	(0.064)
Election year			0.033	0.001
			(0.055)	(0.034)

(*Continued on next page*)

TABLE 5.2. (*continued*)

	Conditions Model 1	Categories Model 2	Conditions Model 3	Categories Model 4
Country-fixed effects	Yes	Yes	Yes	Yes
Year-fixed effects	Yes	Yes	Yes	Yes
Model type	Negative binomial	Negative binomial	Negative binomial	Negative binomial
N	766	766	766	766

Note: All independent variables are lagged by one year. Robust standard errors are clustered at the country-level. Missing data is imputed with multiple imputation in columns 3 and 4.
***p < .01; **p < .05; *p < .1

While the IMF exhibits stronger evidence of concessions, likely because of the harsher nature of its conditions, the World Bank also shows a tendency to appease populists, albeit to a lesser degree. These findings highlight the adaptability of IOs in the face of political resistance and their willingness to compromise to ensure institutional survival.

5.4.   Concluding Thoughts: The Role of Appeasement in Combating Populist Resistance

This chapter has highlighted appeasement as one of the key strategies IOs can use to navigate populist opposition. By offering concessions, IOs can incentivize populist leaders to remain engaged, ensuring their participation despite ideological resistance. Focusing on the realm of loan conditionality at the IMF and World Bank, our analysis revealed that populist-led governments tend to receive fewer and less stringent conditions on their loans. These findings were robust across a variety of analytical models and approaches.

Appeasement, however, is rarely a stand-alone solution. As discussed in the previous chapter, it often operates in tandem with sidelining populists and their constituents. While appeasement provides rewards to encourage cooperation, IOs can simultaneously prepare for diminished populist engagement. For instance, IOs may forge new information-sharing partnerships or reduce their reliance on populist-led states for critical inputs. This dual approach allows IOs to manage populist threats more holistically, balancing short-term incentives with long-term contingency planning.

The need for a multipronged approach stems from the costs of appeasement. Offering concessions—whether in the form of fewer loan conditions or the provision of other benefits—raises important questions about fairness and equity. IOs are fundamentally tasked with distributing resources and imposing requirements based on objective needs, ensuring that assistance generates welfare-enhancing outcomes. Concessions to populist states may undermine these principles, creating perceptions of favoritism and unfairness among other members. This could erode trust in IOs and strain relationships with more cooperative member states. Additionally, by granting populists domestic victories, such as reduced economic conditions or new tangible benefits, IOs may inadvertently bolster their political standing, prolonging their influence both domestically and within the organization.

The next chapter delves into the use of secrecy by IOs to sideline populists' constituents. By limiting the flow of sensitive information to domestic audiences, IOs can reduce populists' ability to rally support against global governance. This form of sidelining complements appeasement and leader-focused sidelining, yielding a multifaceted approach to counter populist threats while maintaining the efficacy and legitimacy of international institutions.

6

Sidelining Populists' Constituents

IN 2011, as Italy faced its most severe economic downturn in decades, the IMF offered the country a critical bailout opportunity. Yet populist leader Silvio Berlusconi rebuffed the package, dismissing it as "not needed."[1] This move was emblematic of Berlusconi's broader hostility toward the IMF, a stance he underscored with sharp public criticisms of the organization.

Berlusconi's refusal was fueled by concerns about political survival. Amid dwindling approval ratings and growing economic turmoil, he sought to distance himself from the IMF, an institution deeply unpopular with his populist-leaning coalition. Many Italians viewed the IMF as a symbol of foreign intrusion and a threat to national sovereignty, often conflating it with the similarly criticized European Union. Accepting IMF aid, Berlusconi feared, would signal the failure of his leadership and economic policies, undermining his precarious hold on power.[2]

For the IMF, Berlusconi's resistance presented a formidable challenge. Italy's economic instability posed significant risks not only to the eurozone but also to major economies holding Italian debt, including the United States, the UK, and northern European countries. The IMF's ability to stabilize Italy's economy was crucial for preventing the crisis from spreading. Yet engaging Berlusconi openly was politically unfeasible.

Rather than retreating, the IMF pivoted to a subtler strategy: engaging Italy behind closed doors. Using private forums like executive board meetings, the IMF worked closely with Italian representatives to monitor the country's economic reforms and maintain a dialogue with Berlusconi. These covert

---

1. "Defiant Silvio Berlusconi Refuses IMF Bailout." *Daily Mail*. November 4, 2011.

2. Tom Kington, "Silvio Berlusconi Shrugs Off IMF's Financial Checks on Italy." *Guardian*. November 4, 2011.

FIGURE 6.1. Word cloud from Italian board statements, 2010–2012. Data come from IMF archival documents. Common stop words are removed.

communications proved effective. Despite his public defiance, Berlusconi privately engaged with the IMF on issues such as fiscal policy, tax reforms, and structural adjustments. Between 2010 and 2012, Italy's executive director (ED) at the IMF submitted 202 pre-meeting statements, the highest number of any country during that period, underscoring the depth of behind-the-scenes engagement.[3] A word cloud of these statements (figure 6.1) reveals the breadth of topics discussed, ranging from fiscal consolidation to economic stability.

Berlusconi's case exemplifies a broader phenomenon—populist leaders often publicly reject IO engagement to avoid domestic backlash, creating challenges for IOs that rely on member cooperation to function effectively. Yet, as Berlusconi's private dealings with the IMF show, overt resistance doesn't

3. Data assembled by authors from IMF archives.

always equate to complete disengagement. IOs can sidestep public defiance by engaging populists discreetly, leveraging forums for private dialogue and collaboration.

Indeed, doing so allows populist leaders to escape public scrutiny for cooperating with elite-driven IOs. Italian prime minister Giorgia Meloni, for instance, has been described as less than a "true" populist despite her outsider status and far-right platform as a result of her willingness to work publicly with the EU; the *Economist* has referred to her as "Mainstream Meloni."[4] This could erode her appeal with populist constituents moving forward. More subtle engagement with the EU and other multilateral bodies may have limited such backlash.

Alternatively, IOs can sideline populist constituents by shifting support toward domestic nonpopulist actors. For example, the EU has withheld funds from populist-led governments like Poland's Law and Justice party, promising to release them once EU-aligned leaders assume power. This strategy bore fruit in Poland, where the center-left coalition led by Donald Tusk, a staunch EU advocate, took office in 2023.

Sidelining constituents thus offers IOs a pathway to maintain cooperation in politically fraught situations. Secrecy—the focus of this chapter's empirical analysis—allows IOs to navigate populist opposition while still delivering critical public goods. Scholars have long argued that private communication facilitates effective diplomacy, allowing leaders to bypass public posturing and reach mutually beneficial agreements (Morgenthau 1948; Krasner 1978; Stasavage 2004).

However, secrecy can also have unintended consequences. It can undermine transparency and accountability, exposing IOs to accusations of elitism and corruption. Public trust in IOs depends on visible adherence to norms and rules, and secrecy can erode this trust, creating fertile ground for populist narratives about IO overreach. Moreover, secrecy does not address populist grievances; instead, it obscures IO engagement, potentially deepening public perceptions of IOs as distant and unaccountable if word of such backroom engagement leaks out.

Indeed, when IOs actively intervene in domestic politics, such as by withholding funds from populist governments to favor opposition parties, they risk further exacerbating political tensions. These actions can reinforce populist claims of IO interference and sovereignty violations, further entrenching

---

4. "Giorgia Meloni's Not-So-Scary Right-Wing Government." *Economist.* January 24, 2024.

anti-IO sentiment. While secrecy can help IOs maintain functionality, it is not a panacea. Balancing covert engagement with visible efforts to address populist concerns is essential to fostering long-term cooperation.

6.1. How IOs Sideline Populists' Constituents

Sidelining populists' constituents involves working around the voter base that populist leaders rely on, either by obscuring interactions between populists and IOs or by empowering nonpopulist groups. This approach helps IOs maintain functionality while reducing the domestic political costs stemming from populists' engaging with them. By shielding their cooperation with IOs from public scrutiny, populist leaders can avoid alienating their base, while IOs can focus on their objectives without the friction of overt populist opposition. Alternatively, IOs can shift the domestic political balance by bolstering nonpopulist constituencies, reducing the influence of anti-IO voices. We begin with this latter approach before delving into secrecy, which is the focus of our empirical tests in this chapter.

6.1.1. *Shifting the Domestic Calculus*

IOs can shape domestic politics either deliberately or incidentally. For example, they may provide material benefits to nonpopulist groups, endorse reformist leaders, or promote governance structures that strengthen democratic institutions and weaken populist rhetoric. The EU's support for nonpopulist candidates in Poland, through its strategic withholding of funds from the populist-led government, exemplifies how IOs can leverage their influence to affect domestic politics. By signaling that compliance with IO norms brings tangible rewards, IOs can tilt domestic power dynamics in favor of actors more aligned with their values.

Though such strategies might appear unconventional for organizations with limited authority delegated by member states, they align with broader patterns in international cooperation. IOs frequently engage in democracy promotion, election monitoring, and judicial reforms as part of their mandates to foster global stability (Hyde 2011; Kelley 2012). Economic IOs like the IMF and World Bank have long encouraged governance reforms and transparency initiatives, a reflection of their broader role in spreading liberal norms championed by dominant powers like the United States and the European Union. However, these efforts can backfire, unintentionally consolidating executive power in ways that undermine democratic norms, as seen in cases of democratic backsliding enabled by external interventions (Meyerrose 2020).

IOs can also shape voter perceptions through endorsements and elite cues. For instance, research demonstrates that IOs' legitimacy often enables them to influence public opinion and policy. UN authorizations for the use of force, for example, tend to increase public support for military interventions (Voeten 2005), while EU conditionality has shaped party platforms and policy outcomes in various member states. In some cases, IOs have explicitly acknowledged their intent to undermine populist support, as the EU did when it passed strict migration measures to weaken populist momentum ahead of elections.[5]

6.1.2.   Secrecy

While altering domestic political dynamics offers one route to sidelining populists' constituents, secrecy often provides a more straightforward approach. Populist leaders who genuinely distrust IOs or take anti-IO stances for political gain frequently face a tension between their stated anti-IO positions and the practical benefits IOs provide. Cooperation with IOs offers access to critical resources like economic assistance, dispute-resolution mechanisms, and security guarantees. However, engaging with IOs openly risks backlash from populist constituents who view such organizations as elite institutions infringing on national sovereignty. This is consistent with canonical research on audience costs in international relations (Fearon 1994; Trachtenberg 2012).

Secrecy mitigates these risks by allowing leaders to engage with IOs discreetly, shielding their participation from public scrutiny. This enables populists to reap the benefits of IO cooperation while maintaining their public image as critics of international institutions. For leaders who perform populism strategically, secrecy reduces the risk of their being penalized by voters for perceived hypocrisy, particularly when cooperation involves politically sensitive issues like economic austerity or structural reforms.

Even genuine populists, who harbor deep ideological distrust of IOs, may find secrecy appealing. While they face ideological costs from engaging with IOs, hidden cooperation minimizes the domestic fallout, increasing

5. Martin A. Schain, "Shifting Tides: Radical-Right Populism and Immigration Policy in Europe and the United States." *Transatlantic Council on Migration.* 2018.

the likelihood that the benefits of engagement will outweigh the costs. Moreover, many IOs have robust confidentiality measures—such as classification schemes and professional penalties for leaks—that reassure leaders of the low risk of exposure. For instance, the IMF employs stringent archival practices to protect sensitive communications, making covert interactions viable even for leaders wary of leaks.

Interviews with IMF officials illustrate how secrecy facilitates engagement with skeptical leaders. A former IMF resident representative recounted the case of Namibia in the 2000s, where the left-leaning government publicly resisted the Fund's advice while privately acknowledging its merit. The official described a dual reality in which Namibian leaders were cooperative behind closed doors but performed opposition publicly to align with their domestic political narrative. This dynamic underscores the role of secrecy in enabling IOs to work constructively with populist governments while allowing leaders to maintain their political personas.[6]

From the perspective of IOs, secrecy is a pragmatic but imperfect solution. While it fosters cooperation and preserves organizational relevance, it also allows populists to scapegoat IOs publicly while reaping the rewards of private engagement. This duality erodes public confidence in IOs, as citizens often rely on elite cues to form opinions about IOs (Brutger and Clark 2022; Dellmuth and Tallberg 2023). By enabling populists to denounce IOs while benefiting from their support, secrecy can reinforce narratives of IO elitism and unaccountability.

Furthermore, secrecy does little to address the underlying grievances that drive populist resistance to IOs. Instead, it perpetuates the perception of IOs as opaque and out-of-touch institutions, fueling populist criticism. Efforts to sideline constituents through covert engagement may also exacerbate concerns about IO interference in domestic politics, further entrenching populist narratives about sovereignty violations.

In this chapter, we demonstrate that IOs use secrecy to combat populist resistance. This idea fits with a large literature that finds states often use secrecy to enact policies that domestic audiences find troublesome (Schuessler 2010). IOs help states funnel controversial foreign aid (Dreher et al. 2018) and make secret deals (Dreher and Jensen 2007; Dreher 2009; Vreeland and Dreher 2014). Secrecy also allows IOs to link disparate issues without mobilizing domestic resistance (Davis 2004) and can allow leaders to compromise

---

6. Former IMF Resident Representative. Interview by authors. November 7, 2024.

more easily (Stasavage 2004; Hafner-Burton, Steinert-Threlkeld, and Victor 2016).

Secrecy can, however, also raise concerns about a lack of transparency in IOs, especially given that they often demand transparency from member states. Balancing covert engagement with efforts to address populist grievances transparently is essential to maintaining the legitimacy and effectiveness of IOs. By pairing secrecy with other strategies like appeasement, IOs can better navigate the challenges posed by populism while reinforcing their foundational principles, as we discuss further in the concluding chapter.

6.2.   Forms of Covert Engagement

To maintain relationships with populist leaders while mitigating public backlash, IOs often employ covert engagement strategies. These strategies range from partial to full secrecy and can leverage both existing and novel channels for discreet interaction.

Partial secrecy involves obscuring certain aspects of state–IO interactions while maintaining an outward semblance of transparency. For example, many IOs redact sensitive portions of public-facing documents to conceal populist participation without withholding the broader findings entirely (Carnegie and Carson 2020). This allows them to share information without revealing the identity of contributing countries. The IAEA, for instance, produces reports on nuclear developments but refrains from disclosing the sources of its data.

Another common practice is restricting access to specific proceedings and documents. This can be achieved through classification systems, encryption, or limited distribution methods. The WTO, for example, uses stand-alone computers accessible only in person to minimize data breaches. Similarly, the IMF classifies many documents in its archives, keeping them inaccessible to the public for extended periods. Liability mechanisms also deter unauthorized leaks, further reinforcing the confidentiality of such processes.

At the other end of the spectrum lies complete secrecy, where IOs refuse to produce or disclose certain documents altogether. This approach is frequently used in high-stakes areas like security or arbitration. For instance, many cases at the International Centre for Settlement of Investment Disputes remain fully opaque, depending on the transparency preferences of panelists (Hafner-Burton, Steinert-Threlkeld, and Victor 2016). In the security domain, sensitive information is often shared only under strict confidentiality guarantees, enabling states to cooperate without fear of exposure.

Some IOs also adopt hybrid approaches, combining transparent and opaque elements. WTO dispute-settlement procedures, for instance, allow for private bargaining sessions before or instead of formal adjudication. Similarly, the IMF might publicly share broad economic data about a country while withholding more sensitive details, such as those related to banking stability.

It may seem implausible that IOs shield interactions with populist-led states from public scrutiny or other member states. Some IOs, such as the United Nations, have been criticized for leaks (Taylor 1991), and their staffing by member-state nationals might appear to complicate confidentiality. However, certain IOs have demonstrated strong track records in maintaining secrecy. The IAEA, for example, has consistently upheld nuclear confidentiality, earning trust through decades of reliable secret-keeping. IOs also safeguard information to protect international norms, preserve state security (Busch and Pelc 2010; Coe and Vaynman 2020), and ensure that proprietary data remain confidential (Hafner-Burton, Steinert-Threlkeld, and Victor 2016).

The likelihood of leaks significantly influences populists' willingness to engage covertly. When the risk is low, populists are more inclined to participate in secretive forums, which mitigate the domestic costs of IO cooperation. In contrast, nonpopulist leaders, whose constituencies are less critical of IO engagement, often find secrecy unnecessary.

Covert and overt engagement with IOs can function as either complementary or substitutive strategies. Nonpopulist leaders, for example, may combine public and private channels to maximize the benefits of IO membership. Populist leaders, however, face higher domestic costs for overt engagement because of their anti-elite rhetoric. As a result, we hypothesize that populists are more likely to substitute overt cooperation with private participation.

This hypothesis aligns with evidence from previous chapters. In chapter 3, we demonstrated that populist leaders initiate fewer IMF programs publicly than nonpopulist leaders. This chapter shows that such leaders are more likely to leverage behind-the-scenes methods of engagement. Together, these findings suggest that populist governments rely more heavily on covert multilateral cooperation, opting for private channels to balance the benefits of IO engagement against their need to appear anti-IO.

6.3.   Empirical Analysis: Testing Populist Reliance on Private IMF Participation

Tracking secrecy in IOs is inherently challenging, as covert interactions are, by definition, designed to escape detection. However, novel data from the IMF offer a unique lens into these behind-the-scenes engagements. This section leverages that data, introduced in Carnegie, Clark, and Kaya (2024), to analyze covert participation.

Focusing on the IMF allows for a systematic exploration of covert engagement within a normatively and substantively significant institution. As discussed in chapter 2, the IMF is a cornerstone of global economic governance, shaping states' economic policies through loans, surveillance, and technical assistance. Its visibility and influence make it particularly salient for both populist and nonpopulist leaders. For many countries, the IMF serves as a lender of last resort, providing essential financial and technical support during crises (Vreeland 2005; Kentikelenis, Stubbs, and King 2016).

Yet public engagement with the IMF often comes at a steep political cost. Given these dynamics, populist leaders are expected to favor more discreet methods of interaction with the IMF, avoiding public scrutiny while still reaping some of the institution's benefits. One key avenue for covert IMF engagement is through executive board meetings, where member states influence the organization's policies and programs. A crucial mechanism for shaping discussions at these meetings is the submission of pre-meeting written statements, known as "Grays." These documents, filed by executive directors, outline countries' stances on issues ranging from conditionality and lending to institutional reforms. Grays are housed in the IMF's archives and declassified after three to five years, making them an ideal proxy for private participation.

Grays are meaningful: They reflect careful deliberation and encapsulate the official positions of member states. Executive directors, who represent their home governments, craft these statements in consultation with national authorities. Deviations from a government's stance can lead to tensions or even recalls, ensuring that Grays align closely with state preferences. Additional details and analysis can be found in Carnegie, Clark, and Kaya (2024).

The content of Grays underscores their significance. Table 6.1 provides examples of these documents, including submissions from populist-led countries. These statements demonstrate a focus on substantive economic deliberations rather than public grandstanding. Our interviews with IMF staff corroborate this, highlighting that Grays are rarely used as a platform for

TABLE 6.1. Illustrative Grays

Country	Date	Topic	Representative detail from Gray
Argentina	2/10/10	The Fund's mandate in post–2008 crisis period	"The Fund must therefore play a bolder role in fostering a fundamental change in the form and degree of international cooperation."
China	7/27/95	Exchange-rate restrictions	"We do understand that it is necessary to consider an enlargement of the GAB [General Agreements to Borrow] in order for the Fund to play an effective role in assisting its member countries in financial emergencies."
Greece	5/9/17	Fiscal capacity in fragile states	"We commend staff and local stakeholders for the efforts deployed in ensuring continuity in surveillance and assistance often under very challenging circumstances."
India	3/24/98	Fund surveillance post–East Asian crisis	"I agree that there should be a periodic review of the policies of countries which may have a regional impact, particularly when there is a formal grouping of countries such as ASEA, SAARC, etc. . . ."
Turkey	5/29/15	Fiscal policy and long-term growth	"In addition to its analysis on energy subsidies, we wonder whether the Fund plans to revisit its work on other common subsidies with the view of taking stock of recent experience in member countries and providing reform options."

IMF-bashing.[7] To validate this claim, we conduct sentiment analysis in subsequent sections.

Our analysis draws on approximately 55,000 Grays from the IMF Archives Online, covering the period 1987–2017. These documents encompass the IMF's global membership and represent the complete set of declassified Grays available under the IMF Open Archives Policy.

The primary dependent variable is the annual count of Grays submitted by a country or constituency leader. While constituencies often comprise multiple countries, we attribute Grays to the leading country, as its ED drafts these documents in alignment with national priorities. Constituency members may influence the content, but the leading state's preferences typically dominate.

Given their covert nature, we hypothesize that populist-led countries submit more Grays than their nonpopulist-led counterparts. Populists, who face greater domestic costs from overt IMF engagement, are expected to rely heavily on private communication channels. Both qualitative and quantitative evidence supports this hypothesis. Interviews with IMF staff reveal that populist leaders often adopt a dual approach, publicly criticizing the Fund while privately cooperating through their EDs. One official noted that even when leaders publicly distance themselves from the IMF, their EDs "gloss over differences" and "try not to make enemies with staff or management."[8]

Historical examples illustrate this dynamic. Venezuelan populist Hugo Chávez publicly denounced the IMF and threatened to exit the institution but remained an active participant in private.[9] Under Donald Trump, the United States maintained regular behind-the-scenes engagement with the IMF despite Trump's dismissive rhetoric.[10] Similarly, Poland submitted significantly more Grays under populist governments (2005–2007, 2015–2017) than under nonpopulist leadership, suggesting a strategic reliance on covert channels.[11]

To delve deeper into the content of Grays, we employed Latent Dirichlet Allocation topic modeling. After pre-processing the documents to remove extraneous elements (e.g., punctuation and stop words), we identified

7. IMF official. Interview by authors. August 24, 2021.

8. IMF official. Interview by authors. August 24, 2021.

9. "Venezuela Says to Quit IMF, World Bank," Reuters, August 9, 2007, https://www.reuters.com/article/us-imf-venezuela/venezuela-to-quit-imf-world-bank-idUSN3047381820070501/.

10. IMF official. Interview by authors. August 24, 2021.

11. Authors' calculation.

nine coherent topics, ranging from global financial markets to labor and employment issues. Figure 6.2 illustrates the temporal salience of these topics, revealing shifts in focus that align with global economic shocks and helping to validate their use. For instance, concerns about labor and employment spiked during the early 1990s recession and the 2007–2009 Great Recession.

6.3.1. Statistical Analysis

To evaluate whether populist leaders rely more heavily on private engagement with the IMF than their nonpopulist counterparts, we employ our measure of private participation: the submission of pre-meeting statements, or "Grays," by IMF executive directors. Our dependent variable is the logged count of Grays submitted by a country or a constituency leader in a given year. Because the data are overdispersed, we take the natural logarithm to normalize the distribution. This analysis replicates results from Carnegie, Clark, and Kaya (2024) appearing in the *Journal of Politics*.

The key independent variable, as in other chapters, is a binary populism measure drawn from Funke, Schularick, and Trebesch (2023). To account for the IMF's constituency system, where seven powerful members have their own executive directors while others belong to multicountry groupings, we weight this populism measure by a country's GDP share within its constituency. This reflects the expectation that larger, more influential countries have a greater impact on ED behavior. For robustness, we confirm that unweighted results align with these findings.[12]

A preliminary analysis reveals strong support for our hypothesis. On average, executive directors representing populist-led governments submit 24.4 Grays annually, compared with just 9.9 from nonpopulist counterparts. This difference is statistically significant ($p = 0.000$) and suggests that populist governments engage behind the scenes at the IMF to a much greater extent than nonpopulist governments.

To systematically assess the relationship between populism and private IMF participation, we begin with a parsimonious baseline model and progressively add controls for political, economic, and institutional factors—many of which were present in analyses in the previous chapters. These include Polity2 democracy scores, right-wing leadership, UN voting alignment with the United States, US aid receipts, UNSC membership, an array of economic

---

12. See Carnegie, Clark, and Kaya (2024) for further details and robustness checks.

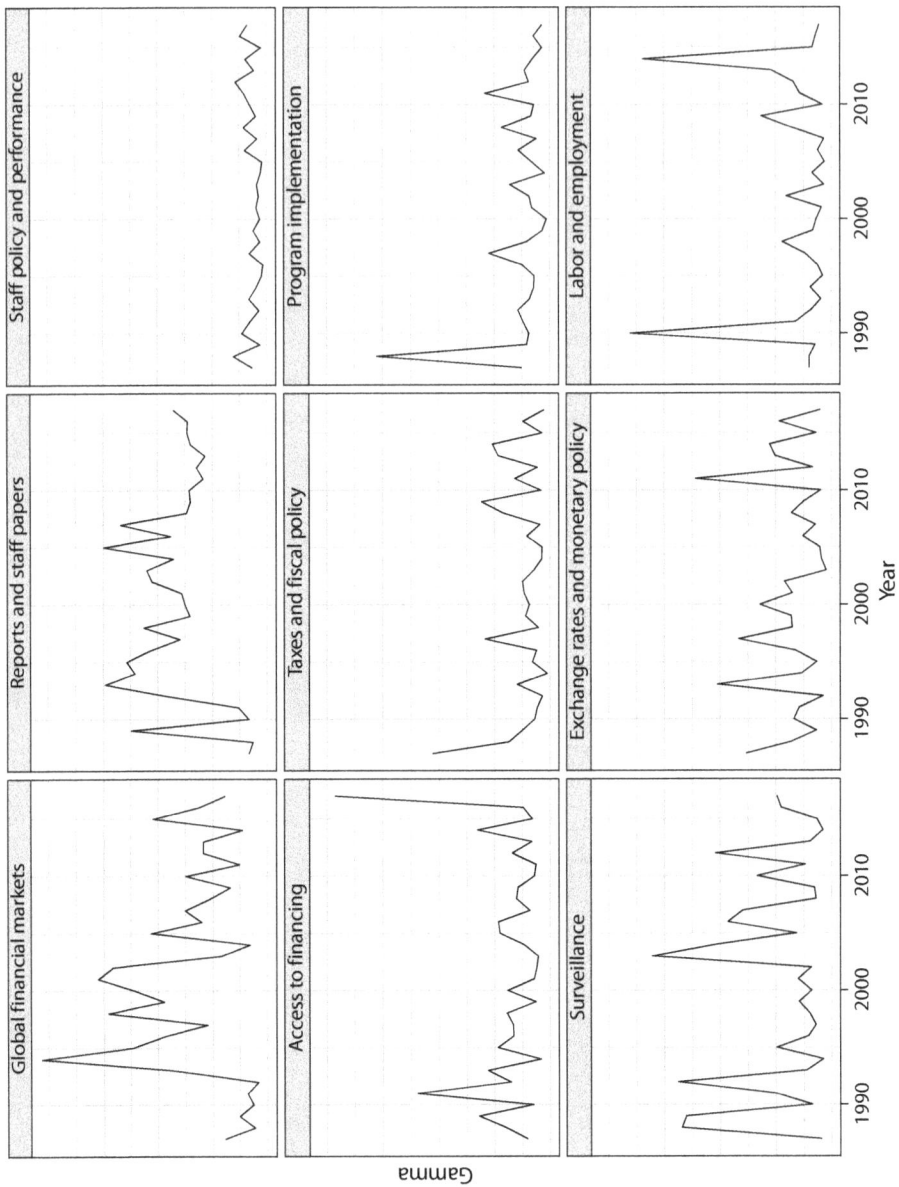

FIGURE 6.2. Topics in Grays.

indicators, IMF program participation, and vote-power asymmetry, which measures the gap between a country's economic power and its voting influence at the IMF (Pratt 2021). We again address missing covariate data through multiple imputation.

The results, presented in table 6.2, strongly support our theoretical expectations. Across all models, countries with populist leaders exhibit significantly higher levels of private participation at the IMF. The effect is both statistically significant and substantively meaningful: Moving from a nonpopulist- to a populist-led government corresponds to an approximately 80 percent increase in Grays filed annually.

To validate these findings, we conduct several robustness checks. We include region-fixed effects to account for potential regional clustering, perform sensitivity analysis in which we iteratively drop each country from the sample to ensure that no single observation drives the results, employ random effects models to test whether results hold under alternative assumptions about data structure, use the `PanelMatch` method from Imai, Kim, and Wang (2023), and show robustness to an alternate dependent variable using the average word count of Grays as a proxy for engagement intensity. Results remain consistent across all tests.

A potential alternative explanation is that populists use Grays to echo their public criticisms of the IMF in private. If this is true, Grays might serve as a platform for venting grievances rather than constructive engagement. To test this, we compare the sentiment of Grays filed by populist and nonpopulist governments. Word clouds (figure 6.3) reveal no major tonal differences, with both groups focusing on technical economic issues like debt, markets, and fiscal policy. For a more systematic approach, we perform sentiment analysis using the Loughran and McDonald financial sentiment dictionary (Loughran and McDonald 2011), tailored to economic and financial topics.

The results confirm that Grays from populist and nonpopulist governments have similar sentiment scores. A simple difference-in-means test yields no statistically significant difference ($p = 0.874$), and regression analysis (table 6.3) corroborates this finding. These results indicate that populists' private IMF engagement is substantive rather than merely critical.

Our analysis demonstrates that populist-led governments participate in the IMF more heavily through private channels than their nonpopulist counterparts. This aligns with our theory that populists avoid overt engagement because of possible domestic political costs but still recognize the benefits of IMF cooperation. These findings underscore the dual strategy of public antagonism paired with private collaboration that populists often employ.

TABLE 6.2. Covert participation in the IMF

	Covert participation				
	Model 1	**Model 2**	**Model 3**	**Model 4**	**Model 5**
Populism	0.811**	0.805*	0.735*	0.776*	0.804*
	(0.303)	(0.334)	(0.290)	(0.331)	(0.333)
GDPPC		0.087***	0.087***	0.088***	0.088***
		(0.010)	(0.010)	(0.010)	(0.010)
Polity2		−0.011*	−0.011*	−0.010*	−0.011*
		(0.005)	(0.005)	(0.005)	(0.005)
UN voting (ideal		−0.006	−0.012	−0.013	−0.005
pt dist)		(0.057)	(0.058)	(0.057)	(0.057)
Right-wing		0.077	0.087	0.081	0.077
government		(0.053)	(0.053)	(0.053)	(0.053)
Debt service/		0.010***	0.010***	0.010***	0.010***
GNI		(0.003)	(0.003)	(0.003)	(0.003)
IMF program			0.017		
			(0.047)		
Vote-power			−3.240***		
asymmetry			(0.749)		
US aid				−0.013	
				(0.009)	
UNSC member				−0.086	
				(0.080)	
GDP growth					−0.001
					(0.002)
Unemployment					0.0004
					(0.003)
Year-fixed effects	Yes	Yes	Yes	Yes	Yes
Country-fixed effects	Yes	Yes	Yes	Yes	Yes
N	5122	4190	4190	4190	4190
Adj. R-squared	0.634	0.645	0.647	0.645	0.645

Note: Robust standard errors are clustered at the country level. Model specification is OLS.
***p < .001; **p < .01; *p < .05

6.4.   Concluding Thoughts: The Role of Sidelining Constituents in Combating Populist Resistance

In this chapter, we uncovered how IOs counter populist resistance by sidelining their constituents, particularly by engaging with populist leaders through covert channels. This strategy encompasses a variety of methods aimed

(a) Populists

(b) Nonpopulists

FIGURE 6.3. Most common words appearing in Grays. Common stop words, punctuation, words systematically used in headers and document-naming conventions, and numbers are removed. We constructed the clouds using the program Wordle.

at reducing the domestic political costs that populist leaders face when cooperating with IOs. Using novel data, we demonstrated that populists rely on private interactions with IOs significantly more than their nonpopulist counterparts do. While secrecy mechanisms are not exclusively designed to address populist challenges, our findings reveal that IOs frequently leverage these channels in the face of populism.

Earlier chapters illustrated how IOs adapt to bolster resilience against populist threats by appeasing or sidelining leaders. This chapter switched the focus to the "two-level games" IOs must play in order to secure cooperation, balancing relationships with member-state leaders while managing the perceptions and reactions of domestic audiences (Putnam 1988). In doing so, we showed that IOs often work not just to counter populist leaders but also to neutralize the influence of their domestic supporters.

TABLE 6.3. Sentiment and participation at the IMF

	Sentiment				
	Model 1	**Model 2**	**Model 3**	**Model 4**	**Model 5**
Populism	−0.036	−0.041	−0.039	−0.041	−0.040
	(0.021)	(0.026)	(0.025)	(0.027)	(0.027)
GDPPC		0.001	0.005	0.001	0.004
		(0.018)	(0.019)	(0.019)	(0.019)
Polity2		0.002	0.003	0.002	0.002
		(0.001)	(0.001)	(0.001)	(0.001)
UN voting (ideal		0.008	0.013	0.008	0.009
pt dist)		(0.012)	(0.012)	(0.012)	(0.012)
Right-wing		0.013	0.011	0.013	0.010
government		(0.008)	(0.008)	(0.008)	(0.008)
Debt service/		−0.00001	−0.0002	−0.00001	−0.0001
GNI		(0.0004)	(0.0005)	(0.0004)	(0.0004)
IMF program			0.034**		
			(0.012)		
Vote-power			−0.023		
asymmetry			(0.061)		
US aid				−0.0001	
				(0.001)	
UNSC member				0.002	
				(0.008)	
GDP growth					−0.002*
					(0.001)
Unemployment					0.002
					(0.001)
Country-fixed effects	Yes	Yes	Yes	Yes	Yes
Year-fixed effects	Yes	Yes	Yes	Yes	Yes
N	1158	1004	1004	1004	1004
Adj. R-squared	0.515	0.500	0.506	0.499	0.504

Note: Model type is OLS. Robust standard errors are clustered at the country-level.
***$p < .001$; **$p < .01$; *$p < .05$

However, the use of secrecy as a tool for resilience also presents IOs with trade-offs. Increased reliance on confidential engagement risks undermining the transparency and accountability that often underpin IO legitimacy, and specifically process legitimacy (Buchanan and Keohane 2006). Greater secrecy could exacerbate populists' accusations that IOs are elitist and disconnected from ordinary citizens, potentially deepening public distrust. This dynamic reinforces perceptions that IOs operate in the shadows, inaccessible and unresponsive to the populations they ostensibly serve. These concerns warrant careful consideration, and we delve deeper into the implications of such trade-offs in the concluding chapter.

To mitigate the potential drawbacks of secrecy, IOs could integrate this strategy alongside the other tools we have explored. Combining secrecy with concessions, strategic workarounds, and direct engagement could enhance IO resilience while managing the risks of alienating domestic publics. Moreover, to counteract the potential backlash secrecy might generate among populist-leaning constituencies, IOs can simultaneously deploy strategies aimed at appeasing domestic populations—an approach we examine in the next chapter.

7

Appeasing Populists' Constituents

IN CHAPTER 5, we demonstrated how IOs and their member states respond to populist attacks by offering to appease populist leaders. These strategies, including awarding states favorable loan terms, overlooking rules violations, or reforming institutional structures, aim to increase the benefits of IO participation for populist leaders. However, while effective in some respects, such measures often fail to address the significant ideological and domestic costs populists face when engaging with IOs.

As discussed in chapter 2, these costs arise on two fronts. Ideologically, populists often reject IOs as elite institutions that impose unwanted constraints. Domestically, positive engagement with IOs can clash with populists' anti-elite rhetoric, leading to perceptions of hypocrisy. Constituents may penalize leaders for these contradictions through protests or reduced political support, or at the ballot box. To mitigate these costs, IOs can go beyond appeasing leaders and address public opposition to IO engagement. The previous chapter explored one method of achieving this—operating out of public view. This chapter examines another strategy: improving public perceptions of IOs.

Public support is critical for IOs to maintain legitimacy and effectiveness (Milner and Tingley 2012; Bearce and Scott 2018; Zvogbo 2019; Brutger and Clark 2022), especially when faced with populist hostility. By increasing public approval, IOs can reduce the domestic pressure on populist leaders to oppose their operations, smoothing the way for such leaders to pursue open cooperation with IOs.

Public backlash against IOs has grown as their influence has expanded into daily life. Populist leaders have capitalized on this discontent, portraying IOs as overreaching and out of touch. Examples are plentiful. The European

Court of Human Rights faced protests after rulings on crucifixes in Italian schools[1] and prisoners' voting rights in the UK (Voeten 2020). In Costa Rica, a controversial ruling by the Inter-American Commission on Human Rights helped propel an anti-IO candidate to prominence.[2] Similarly, IMF bailouts in Argentina, Syria, and Greece; WTO rulings on controversial trade disputes; and WHO policies during the COVID-19 pandemic have sparked widespread disapproval.

In response, IOs have sought to counteract public hostility by engaging directly with domestic audiences in several ways. First, they provide tangible benefits to citizens, such as branded aid or direct support for local firms, ensuring public recognition of their contributions (Oliveros, Weltz-Shapiro, and Winters 2023). Second, IOs may present themselves as less elitist by reducing bureaucratic constraints, diversifying their leadership, or exercising judicial discretion to avoid inflammatory rulings (Voeten 2020). Third, and central to this chapter, IOs use rhetorical strategies to reshape their public image, emphasizing their alignment with ordinary citizens rather than elite interests.

We focus on rhetorical framing specifically through the lens of social media. Social media platforms provide IOs with a direct channel to engage domestic publics, counter populist narratives, and humanize their institutions. Anecdotal evidence suggests that IOs are already leveraging this approach to reshape their public images. Interviews with IMF officials, for instance, revealed deliberate efforts during the European financial crisis to frame the Fund as working for "the people." Similarly, WTO staff sought to rebrand the organization as an advocate for common citizens to sustain its relevance.[3] These efforts extend to public speeches, such as IMF managing director Kristalina Georgieva's emphasis on her humble origins to connect with everyday people: "As someone who grew up behind the Iron Curtain, I could never have expected to lead the IMF."[4] The EU, too, has launched a public relations campaign to bolster its image through the erection of "Europa Experience" exhibitions in all twenty-seven member countries that showcase how European countries

1. "Vatican Protests Ruling on Crucifixes in Italy." *NBC News*. November 3, 2009.

2. Elisabeth Malkin, "In Costa Rica Election, Gay-Marriage Foe Takes First Round." *New York Times*. February 5, 2018.

3. Interviews with former senior IMF officials, February 2021, and WTO officials, October 2022.

4. Kristalina Georgieva, speech at the IMF, 2019.

are working together to better ordinary people's lives and combat global challenges.[5]

To probe the use of such rhetorical strategies, we conducted two analyses. First, we analyzed Twitter data to show how IO officials frame their messaging to emphasize connections with ordinary citizens,[6] resulting in increased public engagement. Second, we used survey experiments to manipulate how IOs are characterized in political rhetoric. Messaging that highlighted IOs' alignment with ordinary people outperformed messages emphasizing technocratic credentials, boosting public support. Finally, we examined how IOs respond to populist threats by centralizing their communications to enhance their social media outreach and the consistency of their public messaging.

These findings illustrate how IOs work to appease domestic audiences in member states and demonstrate that this approach can achieve meaningful success. By engaging directly with publics, IOs not only counter populist resistance but also bolster their legitimacy and relevance in a period of increasing scrutiny.

7.1. Methods of Appeasement

IOs have several means at their disposal to win over domestic audiences and mitigate public hostility. In this section, we explore three approaches: providing tangible goods and services, easing constraints, and issuing direct appeals. We examine each method's potential and pitfalls, ultimately focusing this chapter on the power of rhetorical outreach through social media.

7.1.1. Providing Goods and Services

A widely employed strategy for improving public perceptions is delivering tangible benefits to citizens. Aid organizations, for instance, frequently tailor programs to specific populations. Such targeted assistance often enhances public support for the donor organization (Blair, Marty, and Roessler 2022), particularly as IOs are often seen as more effective and impartial than domestic agencies (Milner, Nielson, and Findley 2016; Dietrich, Mahmud, and Winters 2018).

---

5. "Europa Experiences." *Visiting European Parliament.* https://visiting.europarl.europa.eu /en/visitor-offer/other-locations/europa-experience. Accessed January 15, 2024.

6. Our data precede the rebrand of Twitter to X, and so we use the term Twitter here.

Branding plays a critical role in this process. Roads, schools, or hospitals built with IO funds often display signage crediting the donor(s). Similarly, food aid packages or social media campaigns may highlight the IO's contributions, ensuring that the organization's role is visible and recognized (Dietrich, Hyde, and Winters 2019; Oliveros, Weltz-Shapiro, and Winters 2023). These efforts help raise awareness of IO activities and foster goodwill among local communities.

Critics, however, argue that foreign aid can undermine confidence in domestic governments, as citizens may view them as unable to provide essential services (Knack 2001; Dietrich and Winters 2015). Furthermore, targeting aid toward populations aligned with populist leaders may provoke resentment from other groups, reducing the net benefit of such initiatives. The effects of branding and aid provision can also be limited, with some studies finding only marginal improvements in public perceptions (Dietrich, Mahmud, and Winters 2018; Blair, Marty, and Roessler 2022).

Another limitation is that not all IOs are equipped to provide direct benefits. Judicial bodies or institutions with constrained budgets may lack the capacity to engage in large-scale aid distribution. Others may face resistance from influential member states, limiting their ability to target resources effectively. Thus, while providing goods and services is a valuable tool, it is not universally doable and can be costly.

7.1.2. Rolling Back Constraints

Another method for reducing populist resistance is scaling back the constraints that IOs impose on member states and their populations. Populists often frame IOs as overreaching institutions that infringe on sovereignty, making it politically costly for leaders to comply with their mandates. By easing these constraints, IOs can reduce public hostility and maintain engagement.

This approach can take several forms. IOs might refrain from calling out rule violations when doing so could anger domestic audiences, delay sanctions to avoid backlash, or strategically time public criticism to minimize its impact. For instance, international courts sometimes practice judicial economy, declining to rule on contentious cases that could fuel populist narratives (Voeten 2020).

While selective leniency can help mitigate populist opposition, it comes with its own risks. Favoring some states over others can create perceptions of bias, undermining the fairness and legitimacy of IOs (Stone 2011). Moreover, temporary rollbacks of authority may evolve into long-term compromises that weaken the institution's effectiveness and relevance. IOs must therefore navigate these trade-offs carefully. While temporary leniency may help maintain states' engagement, overuse of this strategy risks alienating other members and eroding the organization's credibility.

7.1.3.   *Direct Rhetorical Appeals*

A third approach to combating populist hostility is directly appealing to domestic audiences. Historically, IOs have focused on disseminating information to elite audiences through press releases, research papers, and technical reports (Clemens and Kremer 2016; Goes and Chapman 2024). However, the rise of social media has transformed how IOs communicate, allowing them to bypass traditional channels and engage directly with the public.

Unlike press releases or policy briefs, social media enables IOs to tailor messages to specific audiences, particularly those skeptical of IOs. By emphasizing their alignment with ordinary people and highlighting the tangible benefits they provide, IOs can counter populist narratives that paint them as out-of-touch elites. For instance, IMF officials have rebranded the organization as a defender of "the people" during financial crises, and WTO staff have emphasized their advocacy for everyday citizens.[7]

This strategy is particularly appealing because it is low-cost and scalable. Unlike targeted aid or relaxed constraints, rhetorical appeals do not require significant financial resources or institutional compromises. Moreover, they avoid the equity and legitimacy concerns that can arise from selective leniency or aid distribution. Instead, they foster transparency and inclusivity.

While all three methods of appeasement are important, this chapter concentrates on IOs' rhetorical strategies, particularly their use of social media. This focus allows us to explore a cost-effective and widely available approach that has become increasingly central to IOs' public engagement efforts. Through social media, IOs can reach mass audiences, counter populist narratives, and enhance their legitimacy in an era of growing skepticism toward international cooperation.

---

7. Interviews with former senior IMF officials, February 2021, and WTO officials, October 2022.

7.2. IOs, Public Opinion, and Social Media

Historically, IOs have relied on government intermediaries, traditional media outlets, and elite networks to disseminate data, policy advice, and messaging to audiences like academics, policymakers, and subject-matter experts. In the past decade, however, IOs have embraced social media platforms like Twitter and Facebook, bolstering their ability to reach broad, transnational audiences quickly and cost-effectively. These platforms also enable citizens to engage directly with IO messaging, fostering discussions and debates online (Gil de Zúñiga, Koc Michalska, and Römmele 2020).

Among social media platforms, Twitter/X has emerged as the most prominent for IOs (Twiplomacy 2017). Its microblogging format provides a powerful avenue for IOs to communicate directly with domestic audiences, bypassing national governments and traditional media filters. Importantly, citizens don't need to follow IO accounts explicitly to see their content—retweets, promoted posts, and trending topics often extend the reach of IO messages to a broader audience. While Twitter is far from the only place IOs seek public engagement—the World Bank now has a TikTok account—its broad use by IOs makes it attractive for empirical study.

Although citizens may pay little attention to IO social media feeds during routine periods (Guisinger and Saunders 2017; Brutger and Clark 2022), their engagement spikes during times of crisis or heightened salience. For instance, IOs like the WHO became globally prominent during the COVID-19 pandemic, while the IMF gains visibility when countries undertake controversial loan programs. Similarly, populist critiques often amplify IO salience by linking them to politically charged issues, such as when the WTO faced heightened attention after the United States levied heavy tariffs on China under the Trump administration. These moments are particularly significant, as public opinion tends to exert the greatest influence on policymaking during times of crisis (Bailey 2003; Verdier 1994).

Public opinion during these critical junctures, as well as during more business-as-usual periods, is critical to IO legitimacy and effectiveness (Dellmuth and Tallberg 2023). Recognizing this, IOs actively seek to enhance their visibility and favorability among domestic audiences. They do so in several ways, including claiming relevance on salient issues—for instance, the IMF's recent foray into climate change, which has increased its prominence in vulnerable states like Barbados (Clark and Zucker 2024). IOs also invest in online communication strategies and centralize their public messaging to ensure

TABLE 7.1. Growth in Twitter followers of most-followed IOs

International Organization (IO)	Follower count (2017)	Follower count (2022)	Growth (% Increase)
United Nations	9.3 million	15.9 million	70.9%
UNICEF	6.3 million	9.3 million	47.6%
World Health Organization	3.9 million	11.8 million	202.6%
World Wildlife Fund	3.7 million	3.9 million	5.4%
Human Rights Watch	3.5 million	5 million	42.9%
World Economic Forum	3.1 million	4.2 million	35.5%
UNESCO	2.7 million	3.6 million	33.3%
World Bank	2.5 million	3.7 million	48%
Total	35 million	57.4 million	64%

Sources: Authors collected 2022 data from Twitter; historical data from Twiplomacy (2017).

consistency and effectiveness (Ecker-Ehrhardt 2018b; Bjola and Zaiotti 2020; Özdemir and Rauh 2022).

The widespread presence of IOs on social media underscores their commitment to engaging with global audiences. For example, a 2016 study identified ninety-seven institutional accounts and seventy-four personal accounts of IO leaders, collectively boasting more than 64 million followers. These accounts include major organizations like the UN, UNICEF, WHO, and the World Bank, alongside high-profile leaders such as NATO's Jens Stoltenberg and former IMF managing director Christine Lagarde (Twiplomacy 2017). Table 7.1 highlights the continued growth of IO social media followings, demonstrating their enduring popularity.

Interestingly, IOs' social media audiences are not primarily composed of elites. A cursory analysis of IMF and World Bank followers reveals that fewer than 1 percent of these users are verified accounts, indicating that most followers are everyday citizens rather than prominent public figures or policy-makers.[8]

Social media is thus more than just a broadcasting tool for IOs—it constitutes a strategic platform. IOs develop long-term communication plans,

8. Using Twitter's API, we retrieved user data for followers of the IMF ($\sim$ 2.2 Mil.) and the World Bank ($\sim$ 3.7 Mil.). Verified Twitter accounts (prior to November 9, 2022) must confirm the account owner's identity with Twitter, represent or be associated with a "prominently recognized individual or brand," and be active (Twitter 2022). Employing an alternative measure that classifies a user as elite if the account is verified or has at least 500 followers, 9.3 percent of World Bank followers and 11.1 percent of IMF followers are elites.

assess their impact, and refine their messaging to improve public perceptions (Ecker-Ehrhardt 2018a). Doing so can have a meaningful effect on perceptions of IO legitimacy (Dellmuth 2018; Tallberg and Zürn 2019; Dellmuth et al. 2021; Dellmuth and Tallberg 2023), bolstering IOs' ability to achieve their mandates. Indeed, legitimacy is crucial if IOs are to maintain member-state participation and secure funding in areas like trade and development (Keohane 1984; Milner and Tingley 2012; Morse and Keohane 2014).

Many IOs have actively sought domestic buy-in to bolster their legitimacy. The EU, for example, has long attempted to "reconnect with the European public," reshaping its messaging to address democratic deficits and public concerns about accountability (Michailidou 2008; Barisione and Michailidou 2017b). Similarly, international courts and other IOs have employed democratic narratives to emphasize fairness and inclusivity, hoping to resonate with diverse audiences (Dingwerth, Schmidtke, and Weise 2020; Lenz and Söderbaum 2023).

Scholarship suggests that these initiatives have achieved mixed success (Blair, Marty, and Roessler 2022; Dellmuth and Tallberg 2023). This is, in part, because IOs may seem disingenuous when tooting their own horns on social media (see Dellmuth and Tallberg 2023). Endorsements of IOs from domestic politicians or NGOs, who often appear less biased, can be more helpful. The EU's social media strategies exemplify the mixed outcomes of such efforts. While social media has empowered critics, it has also affirmed a sense of European unity and mitigated perceptions of democratic deficits (Barisione and Michailidou 2017a).

We posit that IOs use social media not just to disseminate information but also to strategically counter populist critiques. By portraying themselves as relatable and highlighting their positive impacts on ordinary people, IOs aim to enhance public trust and legitimacy. In the following sections, we explore the effectiveness of these strategies, examining how IOs leverage social media against the backdrop of populist resistance.

7.3. Populists and Social Media: IOs Fight Back

Social media has become a battleground where populists skillfully mobilize public opinion against their opposition, including IOs. Leaders often leverage platforms like Twitter to portray IOs as scapegoats for unpopular policies or as symbols of overreaching global elitism, which helps them consolidate domestic support (Vreeland 1999; Handlin, Kaya, and Günaydin

2023). For instance, European populist actors frequently broadcast anti-EU messages, emphasizing fears about sovereignty loss (Alonso-Muñoz and Casero-Ripollés 2020). Similarly, US president Donald Trump used Twitter to rail against "globalists," criticizing multilateral institutions like the WTO and the UN.[9]

However, little extant research has explored whether IOs counter populist messaging, or if their efforts can effectively sway public opinion (though see Dellmuth and Tallberg [2023]). We examine whether IOs can adopt populist-style communication on social media to influence public sentiment. Populist leaders have demonstrated how anti-elite, people-centered messaging resonates with the public (Bakker, Schumacher, and Rooduijn 2021). We argue that IOs may be able to co-opt this strategy to win back trust and legitimacy.

Reversing public opposition is no easy feat for IOs. Citizens often hold deeply entrenched partisan beliefs, using these affiliations to form opinions on complex issues like international cooperation (Schlipphak, Meiners, and Kiratli 2022). Such partisan attachments make people more likely to accept information that aligns with their preconceptions and reject opposing views (Zaller 1992; Brewer 2001). These dynamics may pose a barrier to IOs' efforts to reshape public attitudes.

Furthermore, adopting populist-style rhetoric could clash with IOs' technocratic and elite identities. Bureaucrats within these institutions may hesitate to use simplified or emotionally charged messaging, fearing that it could undermine their credibility, which is crucial for advancing institutional mandates and sustaining career success. Indeed, some officials may prefer to ignore populist threats and maintain the status quo operationally, hoping such threats are blips that fade over time.[10] Additionally, IOs may be perceived as biased or self-interested actors when touting their people-centrism online (Dellmuth and Tallberg 2023).

Despite these challenges, there are compelling reasons for IOs to counter populist narratives using direct appeals to ordinary citizens. IOs are staffed by mission-driven leaders and bureaucrats committed to upholding the international order and ensuring the organizations' survival (Chwieroth 2015; Honig 2018). Public support is essential for maintaining legitimacy, and IOs often rely on it to fulfill their mandates successfully (Dellmuth 2018; Tallberg and

9. See White House Archives (2020).
10. Interviews with former senior IMF official, February 2021.

Zürn 2019; Dellmuth and Tallberg 2023). Moreover, softening public hostility could reduce the costs for populist leaders to cooperate with IOs, potentially encouraging more constructive engagement.

Importantly, social media provide a cost-effective means for IOs to engage directly with citizens, especially in low-salience issue areas where public familiarity with IOs' roles and operations is limited. This baseline knowledge gap offers IOs an opportunity to influence perceptions by portraying themselves as less elitist and more aligned with ordinary citizens' interests. Countering populist rhetoric on platforms like Twitter is thus a pragmatic strategy for IOs, consistent with their adaptive responses to other political shocks (Ecker-Ehrhardt 2018b). In short, rhetorical engagement has limited downsides given how cheap it is to reach out to public audiences on social media.

We specifically propose that IOs combat populist narratives by adopting "populist-style" messaging, which focuses on themes of anti-elitism, people-centrism, and the preservation of national sovereignty. We highlight here three strands of such messaging that mirror our empirical tests. First, IOs can stress their connections with ordinary people—for instance, the non-elite backgrounds of their staff or leadership, which showcases their relatability. The Georgieva quote from the chapter's onset is illustrative. Similarly, IOs can spotlight initiatives that directly benefit ordinary citizens, such as job creation or public health projects, using simple and engaging language to make their messaging accessible.

Second, IOs can signal alignment with populist leaders who claim to represent "the common man." For example, tweets featuring photos of IO officials meeting with populist leaders and highlighting shared goals can create an impression of collaboration. By showing they are willing to work with populists, IOs can subtly counter the narrative that they are antagonistic to popular interests. For instance, NATO Secretary General Jens Stoltenberg tweeted about a productive meeting with Turkey's populist leader Recep Tayyip Erdoğan, pairing his message with a handshake photo to convey cooperation and respect.[11] Similarly, after Donald Trump repeatedly criticized the UN, Secretary-General António Guterres tweeted a personal message wishing Trump a speedy recovery from COVID-19, signaling goodwill despite political tensions.[12]

---

11. Twitter. July 10, 2023.
12. Twitter. October 2, 2020.

Third, IOs can reframe potential constraints placed on members as benefits. In doing so, IOs can reposition their policies to appeal to citizens by framing them as tools to hold elites accountable. For example, conditions attached to IMF loans could be presented as measures targeting corruption or ensuring elite contributions to social welfare (e.g., the IMF's efforts to emphasize the need for the wealthy to pay their taxes during the eurocrisis). By shifting the focus away from restrictions on sovereignty and toward benefits for citizens, IOs can mitigate perceptions of overreach.

We thus derive two main expectations from this framework. First, we expect that IOs' populist-style messages on social media generate more public engagement (measured with likes and retweets) than traditional, technocratic messaging. Second, we expect that ordinary citizens exposed to populist-style IO messaging will express greater support for IOs compared with those receiving technocratic or neutral messaging. To test these hypotheses, we analyze a large dataset of IOs' social media communications and conduct an original survey experiment to evaluate the effectiveness of various rhetorical strategies. The results shed light on how IOs adapt to counter populist resistance and shape public sentiment in an increasingly polarized global landscape.

7.4.   Empirical Analysis: Testing IOs' Populist-Style Communications

We investigate whether IOs adopt populist-style communication strategies on social media and evaluate the public's response to such messaging. Our analysis comprises two key empirical tests. First, we assess whether populist-style tweets from IOs and their leaders generate higher public engagement, measured by likes and retweets, compared with other types of tweets. We then turn to an original survey experiment that examines whether publics approve more highly of IOs that issue populist-style rhetoric than those utilizing more neutral or technocratic language. These tests draw on evidence and data from Carnegie, Clark, and Fan (2024).

7.4.1.   Twitter-Based Tests of Populist-Style Rhetoric and Engagement

Social media platforms like Twitter have become central to how IOs engage with the public, bypassing government intermediaries and traditional media gatekeepers. We focus on whether IOs use populist-style themes in their tweets and if such messaging resonates more with audiences than other types of tweets.

Our analysis centers on the IMF and World Bank—two prominent IFIs with active social media accounts and significant global influence. As discussed in earlier chapters, these institutions face frequent populist criticism as a result of their elite staffing and imposition of state sovereignty constraints, making them ideal cases for testing our theory. Their large digital footprints also provide a robust dataset for analysis.

We collected tweets from the IMF, World Bank, and their senior officials from 2012 to 2022 using the Twitter API for Academic Research. This dataset spans 89,426 tweets, excluding retweets, comprising 47,225 from the World Bank and 20,675 from the IMF. It also includes 17 senior IO officials' accounts, such as IMF managing directors and World Bank presidents. We selected 2012 as the starting point because this marks a period when IOs began to actively expand their Twitter presence. Both the IMF and World Bank have more than 2 million followers, and their tweets generate significant public interaction. For example, IMF tweets average 58 likes and 27 retweets, while World Bank tweets receive 75 likes and 35 retweets on average. The IMF issues approximately 1,880 tweets annually (157 per month), while the World Bank sends roughly 4,293 tweets per year (357 per month). Senior officials, such as Kristalina Georgieva and Ajay Banga, also actively tweet, with notable engagement levels.

We used supervised machine learning to identify tweets that employ populist-style rhetoric. A training dataset of 7,000 hand-coded tweets served as the foundation for this analysis, with a coding scheme adapted from Ernst et al. (2017). Tweets were classified as "populist-style" if they reflected any of three key characteristics: anti-elitism, where IOs are positioned as opposing elites who act against the interests of ordinary people; people-centrism, where IOs prioritize ordinary citizens' needs; or sovereignty restoration, where IOs highlight how their policies respect or restore national sovereignty.

Examples of populist-style tweets include:

During today's #G20 debt forum I highlighted the progress on debt + transparency. As large creditors + debtors work together, the new debt process can help achieve better development outcomes in which all incomes rise, not just the incomes of the elite, David Malpass, July 8, 2020

RT @IMFLive: Christine @Lagarde: Solid fiscal frameworks together with good governance and transparency give citizens confidence that fiscal policy serves the good of all, not just the wealthy or the well-connected. https://t.co/vZpeQ8gwjN#ArabFiscalForum https://t.co/avAcHInICA, IMF, February 10, 2019

By contrast, nonpopulist tweets emphasized technical expertise and elite credentials:

IMF publishes agenda of global finance ministers and central bank governors' meeting in Washington, 4/20, 1:30p ET http://t.co/QnvllDwExn, IMF, April 17, 2013

Top economists to exchange views on lessons from & the future of unconventional monetary policies. Blog #ARCPOLAK https://t.co/vfQkkv7zvX, IMF, November 2, 2015

Our pre-processing pipeline involved stemming, lowercasing, and removing non-English tweets (translated via Google Translate API). We implemented a Random Forest classifier, which is robust against overfitting and effective for text classification. Out of the total dataset, approximately 10.6 percent (9,465 tweets) were classified as employing populist-style rhetoric. This rate aligns with previous research on populist rhetoric in political texts, such as campaign speeches and party manifestos.

Institutional variation exists, as the majority of populist-style tweets come from the World Bank (5,181) or World Bank officials (1,851). The IMF issued a total of 1,758 populist-style tweets over our period of analysis, while IMF officials sent 675 populist-style tweets. Our classification algorithm also detected higher populist-style tweet activity on average from senior officials such as IMF managing director Kristalina Georgieva and World Bank senior managing director Axel van Trotsenburg.

Figure 7.1 illustrates the proportion of tweets classified as populist-style by year. Our findings reveal that IOs' adoption of people-centric rhetoric corresponds with global trends in populism. IOs have increasingly adopted populist-style messaging alongside an increase in the number of populist leaders and parties (Kyle and Meyer 2020). The proportion of IO tweets that use populist-style language peaks in 2018, which corresponds to the height of populist leadership in the world. Our descriptive findings suggest that IOs employ populist-style rhetoric in their tweets in practice and that this communication strategy corresponds with the rise and decline of populist leadership around the world.

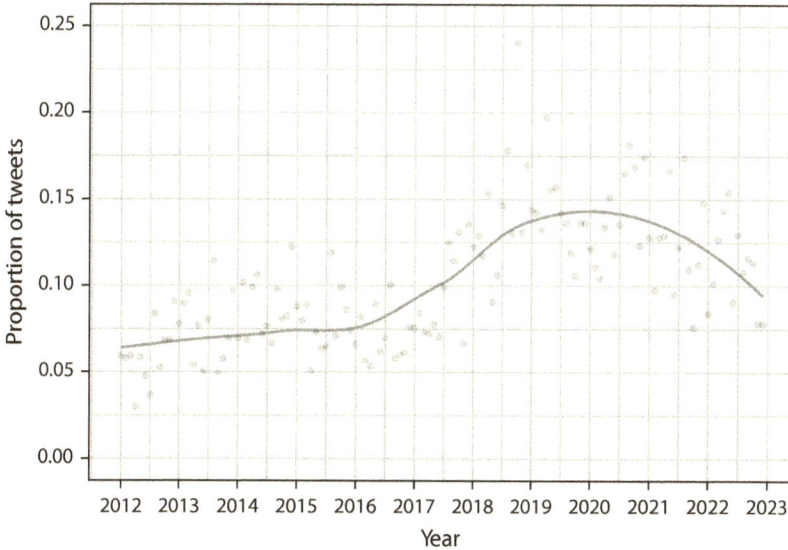

FIGURE 7.1. Proportion of populist-style tweets. Trends in the proportion of tweets classified as "populist-style" given the total number of tweets per year. Points represent month–year averages.

7.4.2. Twitter Engagement Regression Results

We investigate whether tweets classified as populist-style garner greater public engagement compared with other IO tweets. Engagement is measured through likes and retweets, which serve as proxies for public approval and resonance with messaging strategies on social media.

Our primary analysis employs ordinary least squares with robust standard errors. To account for institutional differences, we include IO-fixed effects in all specifications. We further control for additional tweet characteristics that might influence engagement by including a dummy variable to denote whether a given tweet includes a photograph or video attachment as well as sentiment scores assessing whether the tone of the language is relatively positive or negative for each tweet, calculated using the NRC Word-Emotion Association Lexicon. Such covariates allow us to account for stylistic features of the tweet that might drive engagement, as opposed to populist-style rhetoric.

The results, displayed in table 7.2, strongly support our hypothesis: Tweets classified as populist-style by the supervised machine learning model elicit significantly greater engagement. Specifically, populist-style tweets receive

TABLE 7.2. Twitter engagement

	Dependent variable					
	Likes (1)	RTs (2)	Likes (3)	RTs (4)	Likes (5)	RTs (6)
Populist-style	0.096*** (0.012)	0.111*** (0.011)	0.087*** (0.011)	0.110*** (0.011)	0.051*** (0.011)	0.079*** (0.011)
Media			0.593*** (0.009)	0.539*** (0.009)	0.556*** (0.009)	0.469*** (0.009)
Sentiment			−0.00000 (0.004)	−0.028*** (0.004)	0.0004 (0.004)	−0.016*** (0.004)
Constant	1.134*** (0.040)	2.581*** (0.047)	1.124*** (0.040)	2.584*** (0.047)	1.281*** (0.040)	2.744*** (0.044)
IO FE	✓	✓	✓	✓	✓	✓
Month–year FE	✓	✓	✓	✓	✓	✓
Topics			✓	✓	✓	✓
N	89426	89426	89124	89124	88791	88791

Note: Model type is OLS with IO and month–year fixed effects. Standard errors are robust. We add one to zeros and log likes and RTs before proceeding with the analysis.
*** p < .01; ** p < .05; * p < .1

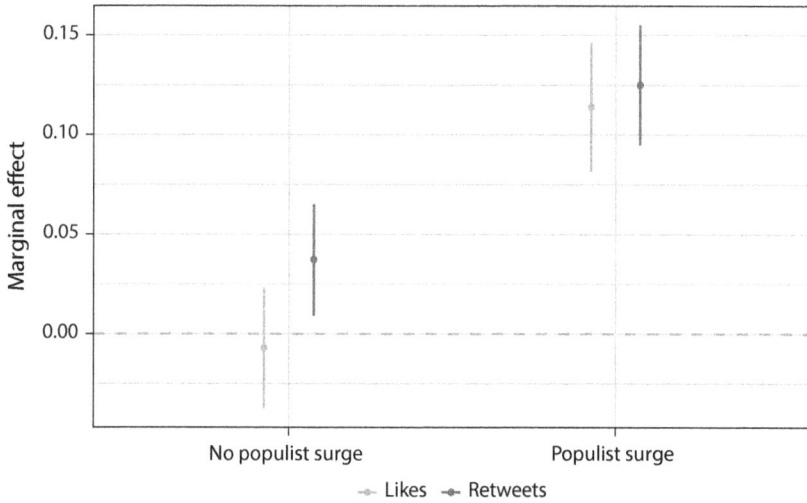

FIGURE 7.2. Marginal effect of populist-style tweets on engagement during populist surge. Specifications include covariates and month–year fixed effects, along with 95 percent confidence intervals. Temporal range of populist surge defined as 2015–2019 (Kyle and Meyer 2020).

approximately 10 percent more likes than other IO tweets, and these tweets are retweeted around 12 percent more frequently.

This increased engagement underscores the effectiveness of populist-style rhetoric in connecting with audiences. Likes and retweets are widely regarded as key indicators of public approval and responsiveness on social media (Schöll, Gallego, and Le Mens 2024). Our findings suggest that the public reacts more positively to communication strategies emphasizing relatable, people-centered messaging.

We further examine whether the impact of populist-style rhetoric on engagement is amplified during periods of heightened global populism. Incorporating a dummy variable to denote the populist surge that manifested during 2015–2019 (Kyle and Meyer 2020), we assess its moderating effect. Figure 7.2 illustrates the estimated marginal effects of populist-style tweets during this period. During the populist surge, people-centric tweets experienced a 12 percent increase in likes and a 13 percent rise in retweets compared with other tweets. These findings align with our expectations, highlighting the heightened receptivity of audiences to populist-style rhetoric during periods of global populist leadership and discourse.

To ensure the robustness of our results, we performed several additional tests. First, to address concerns that differences in public engagement might arise from the tweet's topic rather than from its populist style, we used a Structural Topic Model (Roberts et al. 2013) to assign topics to tweets (we tuned the model to 15 topics). Even after controlling for the tweet's topic, populist-style tweets retained significantly higher engagement levels (columns 5–6, table 7.2). Next, to investigate whether engagement was driven by elite users, we analyzed a random sample of 10,000 tweets and classified retweeters as "elite" if they had a verified account or at least 1,000 followers. Results in table 7.3 show no significant difference in elite engagement with populist-style tweets, indicating that such tweets resonate broadly with general audiences, not elites.

These findings reveal that IOs can significantly increase public engagement by employing populist-style rhetoric, particularly during periods of heightened populist sentiment. This suggests that IOs' strategic use of relatable, people-focused messaging is received warmly by diverse audiences, extending beyond the traditional elite populations often associated with IOs.

7.4.3.   Experimental Test of Populist-Style Rhetoric on IO Support

To further evaluate whether IOs can boost public support by employing populist-style rhetoric, we conducted a survey experiment in the United States in fall 2021. The United States was chosen because of its significant funding role and influence in many IOs, as well as the surge in populist sentiment within the country over the last fifteen years. Notably, President Donald Trump and his supporters have been vocal critics of IFIs like the World Bank, advocating for funding cuts and appointing prominent IO critics like David Malpass to leadership positions.[13] While our findings focus on the United States, we expect similar dynamics to apply in other advanced democracies— Dellmuth and Tallberg (2023) offer evidence in this vein, showing that elite cues about IOs have similar effects across an array of democratic countries spanning all regions of the world.

We recruited 2,000 respondents via Amazon Mechanical Turk (mTurk) and administered the survey through Qualtrics. Recognizing the limitations of mTurk's representativeness, we oversampled conservative respondents to balance political ideology (approximately 40 percent Democrats and 40 percent

---

13. Sophie Edwards, "Trump's 'America First' Budget Slashes Foreign Aid, Multilateral Funding." Devex. March 16, 2017.

TABLE 7.3. Retweets engagement for elites

	Dependent variable	
	(1)	**(2)**
Populist-style	0.0001	0.0001
	(0.001)	(0.001)
Sentiment		0.032***
		(0.001)
Media		0.023***
		(0.002)
Constant	0.063***	0.047***
	(0.018)	(0.018)
Author-fixed effects	✓	✓
Month-year fixed effects	✓	✓
N	236909	236909

Note: Standard errors are clustered at the tweet-level. Model type is OLS.
Author-fixed effects refers to author of the initial tweet. We subset here to retweets
from elite actors, coded as those that are verified or that have at least 1,000
followers.
***$p < .01$; **$p < .05$; *$p < .1$

Republicans). After applying quality control measures such as attention
checks and removing low-quality responses, the final sample comprised 1,600
respondents.

To limit the influence of preexisting knowledge and biases about IOs, we
introduced a hypothetical development organization, the International Development
Fund. Our approach also builds on recent work highlighting the
potential benefits of abstraction in survey design (Brutger et al. 2022).

The control group received the following neutral description of the IDF's
mission: "The International Development Fund (IDF) is an organization
of 190 countries, working with developing countries to reduce poverty and
achieve sustainable growth by financing investment, mobilizing capital in
international financial markets, and providing advisory services to businesses
and governments." This description was modeled closely on the missions of
influential development IOs like the World Bank and the African Development
Bank.

Respondents in the treatment conditions received one of two additional
statements attributed to the fictional IDF president. In addition to the
neutral description, those receiving the populist-style treatment were given

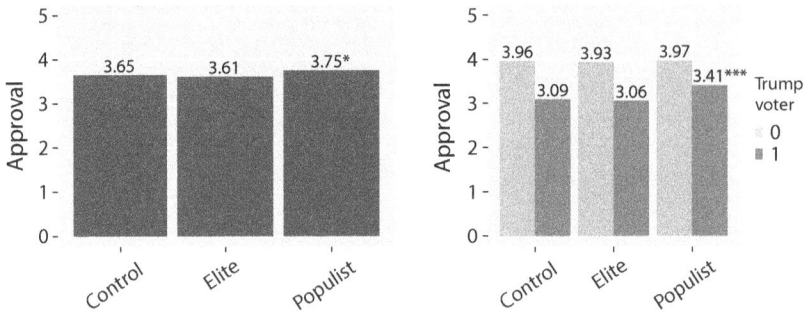

FIGURE 7.3. Approval of IDF by treatment condition. *Left*: Pooled sample. *Right*: Sample broken out by Trump voter. The plots denote average approval by treatment condition and 2020 presidential vote choice. Statistical significance is denoted with respect to the control condition within a given group as determined by a one-tailed t-test. ***p < .01; **p < .05; *p < .1

the following text: "As someone who grew up with few resources or connections, I understand the struggles of the common people. I will make sure they prosper by working with them directly, providing them with crucial public services, and ensuring that wealthy elites do not take advantage of them." Those receiving the elite-style treatment saw this text: "The IDF is staffed by the world's best and most highly educated economists. These experts will ensure that the organization advances development and reduces poverty by efficiently allocating resources to spark economic growth."

Support for the IDF was gauged through two questions, in line with existing work (Bearce and Scott 2018; Zvogbo 2019; Brutger and Clark 2022). We asked: "How much do you approve or disapprove of US participation in the International Development Fund?" (measured on a five-point scale from strongly disapprove to strongly approve) and "To what extent do you perceive the mission and objectives of the International Development Fund to be fair?" (measured on a five-point scale from not Fair at All to Very Fair).

We start by examining the simple difference-in-means across our conditions. Figures 7.3 and 7.4 present the results for approval and fairness, respectively. The populist-style treatment significantly increased support for the IO, particularly among respondents who support populist candidates (operationalized with a binary measure of whether a respondent reported voting for President Trump in the 2020 election). The elite-style treatment did not boost support and, in some cases, slightly reduced perceived fairness and approval, likely because of its focus on technocratic expertise.

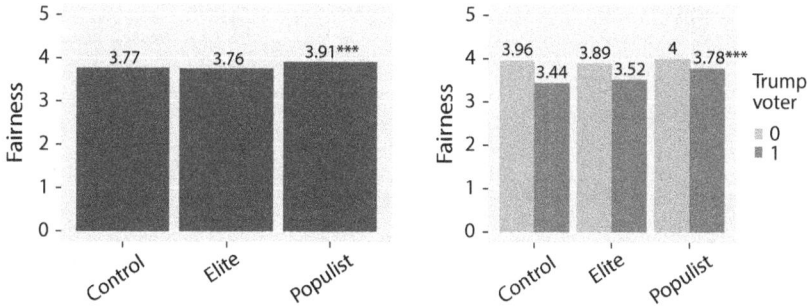

FIGURE 7.4. Perceived fairness of IDF by treatment condition. *Left*: Pooled sample. *Right*: Sample broken out by Trump voter. The plots denote average perceived fairness by treatment condition and 2020 presidential vote choice. Statistical significance is denoted with respect to the control condition within a given group as determined by a one-tailed t-test. ***$p < .01$; **$p < .05$; *$p < .1$

To account for demographic variables, we modeled the data using a regression framework (table 7.4). In the pooled sample, populist-style rhetoric positively affected approval and fairness, though only the fairness outcome reached statistical significance. The interaction between Trump voters and the populist treatment was highly significant for both dependent variables, indicating that these respondents drove the observed effects.

Our findings demonstrate that IOs can enhance public support by adopting populist-style rhetoric, particularly among audiences sympathetic to populist leaders. By framing their mission as aligned with the interests of "ordinary people" and opposing elites, IOs can effectively counter populist narratives and improve their perceived legitimacy.

While the elite-style treatment underscores IOs' technocratic strengths, it appears less effective in resonating with public audiences. This suggests that IOs seeking broader public approval should consider employing messaging strategies that prioritize relatability and accessibility over expertise.

7.5.   Testing an Additional Implication: Centralization

Our theory suggests that IOs respond to populist challenges by centralizing their public communication efforts. Public communication involves the "organizational structures that enable IOs to regularly engage with nongovernmental audiences, including media outlets, experts, lobby groups, movements, and the general public," while centralization entails the creation of dedicated

TABLE 7.4. Experimental regression results

	Dependent variable			
	Approval		Fairness	
	(1)	(2)	(3)	(4)
Populism treatment	0.105	0.010	0.139**	0.058
	(0.066)	(0.076)	(0.060)	(0.071)
Trump voter		−0.860***		−0.480***
		(0.067)		(0.063)
Populism X Trump		0.299***		0.238**
		(0.112)		(0.105)
Elite treatment	−0.035	−0.033	−0.013	−0.012
	(0.068)	(0.064)	(0.061)	(0.060)
Male	−0.065	−0.095*	−0.080	−0.097**
	(0.055)	(0.052)	(0.050)	(0.049)
Income	−0.011	0.004	0.0003	0.009
	(0.017)	(0.016)	(0.015)	(0.015)
Education	0.070***	0.048**	−0.005	−0.017
	(0.022)	(0.021)	(0.020)	(0.019)
Age	−0.004**	−0.001	0.003*	0.005***
	(0.002)	(0.002)	(0.002)	(0.002)
Constant	3.572***	3.792***	3.682***	3.810***
	(0.153)	(0.146)	(0.137)	(0.136)
Observations	1,642	1,642	1,642	1,642

Note: *p<0.1; **p<0.05; ***p<0.01

administrative capacities to manage and deliver consistent messaging to these audiences (Ecker-Ehrhardt 2018b, 522). This centralization might involve hiring additional staff for public outreach, expanding social media operations, or coordinating a unified communication strategy.

For instance, the WTO recently hired personnel solely dedicated to outreach efforts, illustrating a broader trend among IOs.[14] Centralized communications help IOs project coherent and effective messages, particularly when countering negative populist narratives. We thus hypothesize that as the number of populist-led member states increases, IOs will intensify their communication centralization to ensure consistent and effective messaging across their membership and enable them to more effectively leverage public-facing communication outlets like social media.

14. Interview with WTO official. October 2022.

To assess whether this is the case, we use data from Ecker-Ehrhardt (2018b) on the centralization of IOs' communication apparatuses. This measure evaluates the extent to which an IO's communication functions are codified (formally outlined in organizational rules) and departmentalized (supported by dedicated organizational capacities). The centralization index, which ranges from 0 to 12, aggregates information from IO documents across 48 prominent IOs spanning sectors such as security, development, and regional integration.

Our key independent variable quantifies the degree of populism influencing each IO annually. Using IO membership data from Pevehouse, Nordstrom, and Warnke (2004), we calculate the number of member states led by populist executives, as identified by Funke, Schularick, and Trebesch (2023). In addition, we incorporate several controls based on Ecker-Ehrhardt's prior analyses. These include transnational access, or the extent to which civil society and activists direct demands at an IO; protests, measured as a binary indicator of whether an organization faced an anti-IO protest in a given year; and scandals, measured as a binary indicator capturing whether an IO experienced a significant scandal. We also control for member-state democraticness using average Polity2 democracy scores of member states, local intervention using the extent to which IOs engage in operations on the ground in target states, budget size using an IO's minimum budget allocation, and issue areas using dummies capturing sectoral contexts like security or development. The unit of analysis is the IO-year, and we follow Ecker-Ehrhardt (2018b) by employing a negative binomial model with year-fixed effects as our main specification.

Table 7.5 presents our regression results, which strongly support the notion that populism drives IOs to centralize their communication strategies. In the bivariate analysis (column 1), we observe a statistically significant and positive relationship between the number of populist-led member states and the centralization index. Substantively, the rise of populism in one additional member state correlates with approximately a 10 percent increase in the centralization of an IO's communication procedures. These results remain robust when including Ecker-Ehrhardt's key independent variables (column 2) and additional controls (column 3). Even when testing alternative specifications—such as including all covariates simultaneously or excluding specific variables—our findings remain consistent.

The results suggest that populism triggers a structural shift in how IOs approach public outreach. By centralizing their communication operations,

TABLE 7.5. Populism and centralization of communication

	Centralization		
	Model 1	**Model 2**	**Model 3**
Populism	0.130***	0.067***	0.113***
	(0.009)	(0.010)	(0.013)
Transnational access		1.055***	
		(0.071)	
Protest		0.470***	
		(0.053)	
Scandal		0.406***	
		(0.091)	
Democratic membership			−0.020***
			(0.005)
Local implementation			−1.078***
			(0.121)
Development			0.682***
			(0.076)
Environment			−0.666***
			(0.091)
Human rights			0.878***
			(0.185)
Finance			0.268***
			(0.078)
Technology			−2.767***
			(0.202)
Trade			−0.013
			(0.085)
Security			−0.339***
			(0.096)
Commodities			0.409***
			(0.085)
Minimal budget			1.736***
			(0.170)
Year-fixed effects	Yes	Yes	Yes
Model type	Negative binomial	Negative binomial	Negative binomial
N	1853	1809	1644

Note: Robust standard errors are clustered at the country-level. Data for the DV and control variables come from Ecker-Ehrhardt (2018).
***p < .01; **p < .05; *p < .1

IOs aim to craft and disseminate strong, coherent, consistent messages to diverse audiences, including the general public, civil society organizations, and nonstate actors. This strategic adaptation enhances IOs' ability to counter populist criticisms and shore up public support.

Appeasing constituents—including by centralizing communications and employing populist-style rhetoric—is a useful tool for IOs navigating an era of growing populist resistance. It allows them to maintain their legitimacy and effectiveness by ensuring that their communications resonate with and reassure a skeptical public while countering populist leaders' anti-IO narratives. In doing so, IOs bolster their capacity to sustain meaningful international cooperation in challenging political climates.

7.6. Concluding Thoughts: Leveraging Social Media to Counter Populist Challenges

Our analysis demonstrates that IOs use social media strategically to solidify public attitudes about their role and relevance, especially when faced with populist threats. Through a survey experiment, we showed that such efforts can meaningfully improve favorability among populist citizens. Additionally, we provided evidence that IOs actively implement this approach, centralizing their communications and using social media to highlight their value to ordinary people during moments of populist backlash.

In today's fragmented media landscape, reaching broad swaths of the general population can be difficult. Nevertheless, our findings suggest that when IOs do successfully connect with their audiences, their messages can resonate effectively. Social media engagement is also relatively low-cost compared with other outreach methods, making it an attractive option for IOs seeking to shore up their legitimacy. Posting strategically or hiring a dedicated communications director is often a feasible investment. Given these attributes, social media campaigns should serve as one component of a multipronged strategy rather than as the sole approach to countering populist resistance.

While communicating directly with the public enhances IOs' transparency and accountability, adopting populist-style rhetoric carries its own risks. Such messaging may inadvertently raise expectations that IOs will align themselves with a populist agenda. Citizens might begin to expect that IOs reduce demands that impinge on sovereignty, integrate more non-elite voices into their operations, or even mimic populist domestic policies in other ways. For instance, Hungary's populist trajectory under Viktor Orbán has arguably pressured the EU to adopt more populist-leaning policies in response to public sentiment.

If these heightened expectations are fostered but remain unmet, IOs could face backlash, undermining their legitimacy and reinforcing populist narratives that they are undemocratic or out-of-touch with ordinary citizens' needs (Tallberg and Zürn 2019). Striking a balance between engaging public support and maintaining organizational autonomy is thus crucial.

In the next chapter, we illustrate how IOs have deployed the four strategies we have identified—appeasement, secrecy, sidelining, and public outreach—to combat populist challenges in a diverse series of real-world cases. We show that populists have sought to weaken organizations spanning several issue areas and that IOs have responded by utilizing a mix of sidelining and appeasing populists and their constituents. Doing so has helped IOs remain resilient.

8

Institutional Resilience: Illustrative Examples

THIS BOOK makes ambitious arguments about the relationship between IOs and populism, positing that IOs adopt strategies of appeasement and sidelining to withstand populist resistance and maintain their resilience. This chapter examines these claims by tracing how IOs have navigated populist challenges and assessing whether these strategies have been effective.

While we cannot definitively determine what actions IOs would have taken in the absence of populist threats, our focus is to evaluate whether populists have meaningfully weakened these organizations, and if so, to what extent. To do this, we analyze prominent instances of populist resistance, as these represent cases with strong potential for populists to harm IOs. The evidence shows that IOs have largely demonstrated creativity and resilience in maneuvering around these challenges, often mitigating potential damage effectively. This helps explain how and why IOs have persisted in the face of mounting resistance.

Importantly, this chapter provides evidence extending beyond IOs that operate in international finance. Much of the empirical evidence presented so far has centered on IFIs, which ensures coherence and comparability with existing research. In this chapter, we broaden the scope by exploring examples beyond the financial domain to demonstrate the broader applicability of our argument. Across different sectors and regions, the strategies used by populist leaders and the countermeasures adopted by IOs align remarkably well with the framework outlined in this book.

The cases we include reflect a diverse range of countries and organizations, spanning both economically and militarily powerful states as well as weaker nations. The IOs analyzed vary in their design, membership, resources, and functions, encompassing economic and security institutions alike. While many examples stem from North America and Europe—regions with highly constraining and consequential IOs that make them particularly vulnerable to populist challenges—we also consider how IOs responded to populists from smaller or less influential states.

In several cases, we focus on US president Donald Trump's first term, as his second term was in progress as this book went to press. We do so because Trump represents a uniquely consequential populist figure as a result of his vocal and persistent attacks on IOs, coupled with the United States' hegemonic influence in global governance. By examining how IOs responded to the Trump administrations' rhetorical and substantive challenges, we can explore how different organizations addressed a similar populist threat. Moreover, Trump's opposition brought unprecedented salience to many IOs among both domestic and international audiences. If IOs had failed to counter Trump's sustained barrage of criticism, that failure would have undermined our framework.

Beyond Trump, we analyze how IOs confronted other prominent populist leaders, including Jair Bolsonaro in Brazil, Viktor Orbán in Hungary, and Recep Tayyip Erdoğan in Turkey. These comparative cases highlight the adaptability of IO strategies when dealing with varying political contexts and levels of influence. For example, we examine how both Trump's and Bolsonaro's threats to exit the Paris Agreement reshaped the organization, as well as how NATO managed hostilities from both Trump and Erdoğan.

In instances involving smaller states, we also explore how regional populist coalitions have posed collective challenges to IOs. For example, we discuss how the International Criminal Court addressed coordinated resistance from several African countries.

Our analysis relies on a mix of elite interviews, official documents, media reports, and secondary literature. Each case study begins by detailing the nature of the populist threat before examining how the IO deployed appeasement and sidelining strategies. We analyze how these tactics targeted both populist leaders and their constituencies, illustrating the interplay between the two.

Our analysis includes the following examples:

- EU and Hungary: Addressing challenges posed by Viktor Orbán's illiberal governance
- EU and the UK: Managing the populist-led Brexit campaign
- NATO and Turkey: Responding to Erdoğan's geopolitical maneuvering
- NATO and the US: Countering Trump's threats to withdraw support

- UN Peacekeeping and the US: Navigating funding cuts under Trump
- WHO and the US: Addressing populist criticisms during the COVID-19 pandemic
- WTO and the US: Confronting Trump's protectionist rhetoric and actions
- UNFPA and the US: Mitigating attacks on reproductive health initiatives
- Paris Agreement and the US/Brazil: Handling Trump's and Bolsonaro's withdrawal threats
- IMF and Greece: Managing populist backlash during the eurozone crisis
- ICC and African populist states: Countering collective resistance to the International Criminal Court's authority

Across these cases, we find that IOs consistently employed the strategies outlined in our framework to push back against populist resistance. They adapted their responses to the specific challenges posed, using a mix of appeasement and sidelining. These efforts have often succeeded in preserving the IOs' legitimacy and functionality, even in the face of severe populist pressures.

The chapter concludes by reflecting on the implications of these findings for the long-term resilience of IOs and the broader resurgence of populism. By illustrating how IOs navigate these challenges, we shed light on their capacity to adapt in an era of rising populist sentiment.

8.1.   EU and Orbán

The European Union, a governance structure dominated by political and economic elites, exerts significant influence over its member states, often imposing deep constraints in areas such as trade, environmental policy, agriculture, migration, human rights, and data privacy. While this level of integration fosters unity and cooperation, it also creates vulnerabilities: As a primarily consensus-driven organization, the EU can be disrupted by a single defiant member state. Hungary, under the leadership of its populist prime minister Viktor Orbán, exemplifies this challenge. Since his second term began in 2010, Orbán has consistently voiced euroskepticism and has actively worked to obstruct key elements of the EU's agenda.[1]

---

1. Sarah Wheaton and Eddy Wax, "Viktor Orbán Brings Culture War to Brussels." *Politico*. November 15, 2023.

Orbán epitomizes the archetype of populist leadership outlined in this book, combining a staunch hostility to elites with an unrelenting defense of sovereignty. He accuses "liberal elites" of distorting the true purpose of European integration and condemns the EU's "detached and empty elite discourse" (Spandler and Söderbaum 2023). His rhetoric often invokes a vision of a "true Europe," one rooted in white Christian identity, and he positions himself as the defender of "average" Europeans against the "elitist" forces in Brussels. By framing his actions as reclaiming sovereignty from the EU, Orbán amplifies his populist appeal.[2]

The EU, for its part, has been sharply critical of Orbán's domestic policies. Since 2011, his government has enacted sweeping constitutional and legislative changes targeting the media, judiciary, central bank, and electoral system, as well as NGOs. These reforms have insulated Orbán from political competition and weakened institutional checks and balances. The EU has also condemned Hungary's treatment of migrants, the LGBTQ+ community, and academics, viewing these actions as emblematic of a broader erosion of democratic norms. Orbán's actions, characterized by the dismantling of civil society and the reshaping of government institutions to his favor, have led the EU to describe Hungary's elections as "free but not fair" (Spandler and Söderbaum 2023).

In defiance of EU norms, Orbán insists that Hungary alone should dictate its domestic policies, particularly on contentious issues like migration, democratic governance, and the rule of law.[3] He has repeatedly obstructed EU initiatives that challenge his nationalist agenda, portraying the EU's pro-migrant policies as threats to European identity and defending Christianity as the continent's cultural foundation.[4] Beyond migration, Orbán has opposed globalist measures, including aid packages to Ukraine, while forging alliances with populist and authoritarian leaders such as Donald Trump, Jair Bolsonaro, and Giorgia Meloni.

To amplify his influence, Orbán has weaponized Hungary's voting power within EU institutions, such as the European Council and Parliament. He

2. Andrew Higgins, "Orbán's Dream of an Illiberal Pan-European Alliance Is Fading." *New York Times*. November 8, 2023.

3. "Rule of Law in Hungary: Press Conference with Lead MEPs." European Parliament Press Release. May 30, 2023.

4. Shaun Walker and Flora Garamvolgyi, "Viktor Orbán Sparks Outrage with Attack on 'Race Mixing' in Europe." *The Guardian*. July 24, 2022.

has also cultivated alliances with states like Poland, the Czech Republic, and Slovakia, collectively known as the Visegrad Four, to resist EU efforts to discipline members that backslide on democratic principles.[5] Orbán's close ties with Russia and China further bolster his anti-democratic credentials while enhancing his leverage within the EU; Hungary remained the sole EU member maintaining close relations with Russia following its 2022 invasion of Ukraine.[6]

Faced with Orbán's disruptions, the EU has pursued a dual strategy of appeasement and sidelining. Appeasement has often been used to secure Hungary's cooperation on critical initiatives. During negotiations over the Multiannual Financial Framework and COVID-19 recovery fund in 2020, the EU agreed to dilute governance conditions aimed at ensuring that funds were not misused by member states.[7] The compromise included a two-step mechanism for addressing rule-of-law violations (Ladi and Wolff 2021), which critics argue diluted the impact of conditionality measures.[8] Proponents, however, defend the move as a necessary concession to preserve EU cohesion and avoid a deadlock.[9]

At the same time, the EU has not shied away from sidelining Hungary when appeasement has failed. For instance, when Hungary blocked a €50 billion aid package for Ukraine in 2023, the EU devised alternative financing mechanisms to bypass Budapest's veto, including the use of debt and carry-over plans.[10] Similarly, after Hungary left the UN Global Compact for Migration in 2018, the EU developed an "EU-minus-Hungary" negotiation strategy (Schuette and Dijkstra 2023), effectively isolating Orbán's government from key discussions.

Legal action has also been a recurring tool for sidelining Hungary. The EU has initiated numerous infringement procedures and brought cases before the

5. Lili Bayer and Jan Cienski, "The Not-So-Fantastic 4: Central Europe's Divided Visegrad Alliance." *Politico.* January 7, 2022.

6. Boldizsar Gyori, "US Says It Is 'Concerned' about Hungary's Relationship with Russia." *Reuters.* October 20, 2023.

7. "Parliaments Consent to the 2021–2027 MFF." *European Parliamentary Research Service.* December 15, 2020.

8. Joe Barnes, "Merkel Agrees Secret Deal With Orbán: True Cost of the 1.6 Trillion Euro EU Deal Revealed." *Express.* July 21, 2020.

9. "Parliament's Consent to the 2021–2027 MFF." *European Parliamentary Research Service.* December 15, 2020.

10. Paola Tamma and Henry Foy, "EU Readies 20bn Euro Plan B to Fund Ukraine." *Financial Times.* December 26, 2023.

European Court of Justice (ECJ) to challenge Orbán's anti-LGBTQ+ policies and other breaches of EU law.[11] In 2018, the EU invoked Article 7 proceedings against Hungary to address systemic violations of democratic principles, though the process remains fraught with political hurdles.

Beyond targeting Orbán directly via sidelining, the EU has sought to engage Hungarian citizens through public outreach. The Annual European Commission reports highlight Hungary's rule-of-law deficiencies,[12] while European Parliament resolutions call for the protection of democratic norms and civil liberties.[13] EU leaders, including the presidents of the European Commission and European Council, frequently address Hungary's actions in public statements and press briefings, aiming to foster transparency and accountability.[14] These efforts extend to the EU's broader electorate, as demonstrated by the New Pact on Migration and Asylum in 2023, which tightened migration policies to counter populist sentiment ahead of European Parliamentary elections.[15]

Finally, negotiations with Orbán often take place behind the scenes, out of view of Hungary's citizens. This ensures that Orbán does not face political blowback and gives him the political space to make compromises. In this way, the EU often sidelines Hungary's population from policy discussions.[16]

The EU's responses have thus far helped to retain Hungary's participation within the bloc and secure Orbán's support on key initiatives. However, these strategies come at a cost. Critics argue that appeasement undermines the EU's legitimacy by enabling Orbán to shape its agenda while simultaneously weaponizing EU policies for domestic political gain (Kelemen 2020). For instance, Orbán has framed the EU's conditionality measures

---

11. "Commission Refers Hungary to the Court of Justice of the EU Over Violation of LGBTIQ Rights." European Commission Press Release. July 15, 2022.

12. E.g., "2023 Country Report—Hungary." *European Commission*.

13. E.g., "Motion for a Resolution on the Situation in Hungary and Frozen EU Funds." *European Parliament*. January 16, 2024.

14. "Threats to Rule of Law and Fundamental Rights in Hungary." European Parliament Briefing. May 30, 2023; "Rule of Law in Hungary: Press Conference with Lead MEPs." European Parliament Press Release. May 30, 2023.

15. Anna Gawel, "10 Numbers That Defined Development in 2023." *Devex Newswire*. December 21, 2023.

16. Joe Barnes, "Merkel Agrees Secret Deal with Orbán: True Cost of the 1.6 Trillion Euro EU Deal Revealed." *Express*. July 21, 2020.

as "political blackmail,"[17] using them to rally support among Hungarian voters.[18]

While the EU's resilience in navigating Orbán's challenges is evident, the long-term implications of these strategies remain uncertain. The delicate balance between appeasing disruptive leaders and sidelining their influence underscores the broader challenges the EU faces in upholding its norms while maintaining unity in an era of rising populism.

8.2.   EU and May/Johnson

Before the UK's formal departure from the EU, British leaders like Nigel Farage, Boris Johnson, and Theresa May levied sharp critiques against the institution, rooted in familiar populist grievances. Their opposition echoed themes of anti-elitism and the defense of national sovereignty, framing the EU as an overbearing institution that stifled Britain's autonomy. Central to the "Leave" campaign was the promise of regaining control—reclaiming decision-making power over trade, immigration, and the broader regulatory agenda. Many skeptics of the EU resented the influence of the European Court of Justice over British law[19] and viewed EU-imposed regulations as needless constraints on domestic businesses (Gomez Arana et al. 2019). They also argued for Britain's ability to negotiate its own trade deals, free from EU oversight. The financial contributions Britain made to the EU budget became another focal point during the campaign, with populist rhetoric suggesting that those funds could be redirected to vital domestic needs, such as bolstering the National Health Service.[20] This messaging found fertile ground, particularly in deindustrialized regions and economically struggling areas outside London and in the Southeast, where resentment toward the EU resonated deeply.

To advance their agenda, British populists employed a barrage of hostile rhetoric and political maneuvers. Figures like Farage, along with his UK Independence Party and factions within the Conservative Party, framed the EU as

---

17. Lisa O'Carroll, "Secret EU Plan 'to Sabotage Hungarian Economy' Revealed as Anger Mounts at Orbán." *The Guardian.* January 29, 2024.

18. Krisztina Than and Andrew Gray, "EU Troublemaker Orbán Victorious at Home, Isolated in Brussels." *Reuters.* December 15, 2023.

19. "British PM May Sets Out Plans for Brexit." *Reuters.* January 17, 2017.

20. Jim Mann, "Britons and Europe: The Survey Results." *The Guardian.* March 20, 2016.

a bastion of elitism, detached from the needs and aspirations of ordinary citizens. They painted the campaign to leave as a battle against the establishment, leveraging public rallies, media appearances, and social media to amplify their message.[21] Their efforts culminated in the 2016 Brexit referendum, where a majority of voters opted to leave the EU, marking a seismic shift in Britain's relationship with Europe.

In response, the EU deployed several strategies aimed at mitigating the impact of Brexit while preserving its institutional integrity. Initially, it sought to appease the UK through concessions and reform discussions to retain its cooperation in key areas. Negotiations tackled issues like immigration, welfare benefits for EU citizens in the UK, and a reduction of regulatory burdens. One notable example was the 2018 "EU–UK Deal" (often referred to as "Cameron's Deal," alluding to Prime Minister David Cameron), which offered Britain provisions on its relationship with the euro, limited social benefits for EU migrants, and an "emergency brake" on in-work benefits.[22] These efforts reflected the EU's willingness to address British concerns while maintaining the broader framework of European integration.

Parallel to these negotiations, the EU launched a robust public relations campaign aimed at both internal and external audiences. Institutions like the European Commission and the European Council provided regular updates on Brexit negotiations, emphasizing the EU's commitment to preserving its single market and unity. High-profile leaders such as Jean-Claude Juncker, Donald Tusk, and Michel Barnier took center stage in press conferences and speeches, articulating the EU's positions.[23] This communication strategy extended to social media and dedicated online platforms designed to educate the public about Brexit's implications (Brändle, Galpin, and Trenz 2022). Such efforts sought to stem any contagion effect from Brexit by reinforcing confidence in the EU among its remaining member states and beyond.

However, not all negotiations unfolded in the public eye. Many aspects of the Brexit process were deliberately kept behind closed doors to allow for candid discussions and compromise on contentious issues. Confidential

---

21. Paul Lewis, "Rage, Rapture and Pure Populism: On the Road with Nigel Farage." *The Guardian*. May 19, 2019.

22. "EU Reform Deal: What Cameron Wanted and What He Got." *BBC News*. February 20, 2016.

23. See, e.g., "European Union Leaders on Brexit Deal Vote." *C-SPAN*. November 25, 2018.

negotiations enabled both UK and EU leaders to explore politically sensitive solutions without immediate public scrutiny, fostering an environment in which agreements could be reached on polarizing matters (Barnier 2021). Moreover, where the UK was able to extract concessions from the EU, secrecy prevented other countries from observing any potential benefits for them from an exit.

Despite these efforts, the UK officially left the EU in 2020, marking the first instance of a member state exiting the bloc. In the wake of Brexit, the EU adapted its strategies to sideline the UK while reinforcing its own cohesion. During leave negotiations, the EU maintained unity among its member states, isolating the UK diplomatically (Schuette 2023). After Britain's departure, the EU moved forward with a range of policies that reflected the new dynamics of the bloc. For instance, it adjusted its 2021–2027 Multiannual Financial Framework to redistribute budgetary commitments among member states and established a €5 billion Brexit Adjustment Reserve to support industries and regions most affected by the UK's exit.[24] These measures insulated vulnerable populations from Brexit's economic fallout and curtailed the risk of other countries following Britain's lead.

The EU also prioritized diversifying its global trade partnerships (Laffan and Telle 2023) to reduce its dependence on the UK. It advanced agreements with regional blocs like MERCOSUR (Zimmermann 2019) and bolstered cooperation on defense initiatives such as Permanent Structured Cooperation and the European Defense Fund (Sweeney and Winn 2020). These actions underscored the EU's commitment to maintaining its status as a global power and signaled its adaptability in navigating the post-Brexit landscape.

While the EU has largely maintained its cohesion and relevance after Brexit, this resilience is not costless. The EU's firm stance during negotiations may have solidified populist grievances within Britain, reinforcing narratives of EU inflexibility, though support for the EU seems to be on the upswing in the UK.[25] Additionally, populist leaders in other European countries have drawn on the rhetoric of the "Leave" campaign, criticizing the EU's handling of Brexit and leveraging it to bolster their own anti-EU platforms.

Nevertheless, the EU's capacity to weather Brexit and chart a stable path forward highlights its institutional adaptability and strategic pragmatism.

24. "The 2021–2027 EU budget: What's New?" *European Commission.*
25. Noah Keate, "Brits Would Vote to Rejoin EU in New Referendum, Poll Finds." *Politico.* August 13, 2024.

Despite losing one of its largest and most influential members, the bloc largely demonstrated a collective resolve to preserve the European project in the face of populist disruption.

8.3.   NATO and Erdoğan

NATO, a military alliance formed after World War II, stands as one of the most ambitious and expansive collective security pacts in history, comprising thirty-one member states. Anchored by Article V of its founding treaty, NATO operates on the principle of mutual defense: An attack against one member is considered an attack against all.

Turkish president Recep Tayyip Erdoğan has emerged as a vocal critic of NATO, frequently decrying what he sees as its elite-driven nature and the constraints it imposes on Turkish sovereignty (Destradi and Plagemann 2019). While Turkey remains a member, hosting key NATO military bases and contributing to joint operations in regions such as Afghanistan and Kosovo, Erdoğan's disdain for NATO's embrace of human rights and regional policies underscores this tension (Hazir 2022). Despite his criticisms, Erdoğan recognizes NATO's importance to Turkish national security. Turkey's military culture and standards are deeply intertwined with NATO, and its strategic geography places it at the forefront of operations against threats like the Islamic State and as a critical ally in NATO's support for Ukraine against Russian aggression (Kinacioğlu and Gürzel 2013).

Erdoğan has leveraged Turkey's importance within NATO to reshape the alliance to his advantage. For example, tensions flared between Erdoğan and NATO during Sweden and Finland's joint bid to join NATO after Russia's invasion of Ukraine in 2022.[26] Alarmed by the prospect of Russian expansion, these Nordic nations sought NATO membership to bolster their security. Turkey, however, held up their accession to the bloc, delaying Finland and Sweden's formal acceptance into the group until April 2023 and January 2024 respectively. In doing so, Erdoğan cited grievances over Sweden's past support

---

26. Susan Frazer and Robert Badendieck, "Turkey's Erdoğan Says Sweden Shouldn't Expect to Join NATO Any Time Soon." *Associated Press.* June 14, 2023.

for Kurdish groups and arms embargoes in the region as well as a series of anti-Muslim protests that Erdoğan condemned as inflammatory.[27]

To secure Erdoğan's approval, NATO and its member states employed a mix of appeasement and strategic negotiation. The alliance often softened its stance to retain Turkey's cooperation.[28] For instance, NATO appointed a Turkish assistant secretary-general in 2010 to address concerns about representation and frequently emphasized terrorism in its internal communications to align with Turkish priorities.[29] Regarding Sweden's membership, NATO facilitated a series of concessions: The United States advanced plans to sell Turkey forty F-16 fighter jets and modernization kits, Sweden pledged to reinvigorate Turkey's EU membership bid, and Sweden and Finland agreed to strengthen anti-terror laws and extradite individuals whom Turkey identified as terrorists. NATO itself adopted a more robust counterterrorism stance, appointing a special coordinator for these efforts.[30] Such moves went beyond paying lip service to Erdoğan's foreign policy priorities.

Negotiations over these items often took place in private, away from public scrutiny. At a pivotal 2023 NATO summit, NATO Secretary General Jens Stoltenberg held private meetings with Erdoğan and other leaders who were instrumental in resolving disputes, though the exact details remain confidential.[31]

At the same time, NATO employed sidelining tactics to pressure Erdoğan. The United States canceled plans for Erdoğan to visit Washington and imposed sanctions on Turkey, including the suspension of F-35 fighter jet sales following Turkey's purchase of Russian S-400 missile system.[32] These moves isolated Erdoğan diplomatically and signaled NATO's frustration with his obstructionist stance.[33]

27. Natasha Turak, "Right-Wing Quran Burning in Sweden Enrages Turkey and Throws a New Wrench in Nordic NATO Bid." *CNBC*. January 24, 2023.

28. Lili Bayer, "Turkey Is the Headache NATO Needs." *Politico*. April 3, 2023.

29. Lili Bayer, "Turkey Is the Headache NATO Needs." *Politico*. April 3, 2023.

30. "NATO Secretary General Stoltenberg Presses Turkey to Advance Sweden's Membership Application." PBS. October 12, 2023.

31. "Press Statement." *NATO*. July 10, 2023.

32. Henri Barkey, "Erdoğan's NATO Expansion Roadblock Will Only Harm Turkey." *Euractiv*. May 23, 2022.

33. Lili Bayer, "Turkey Is the Headache NATO Needs." *Politico*. April 3, 2023.

Publicly, NATO leaders, including Stoltenberg, used social media strategically to portray productive engagements with Erdoğan, emphasizing progress in the negotiations and framing Turkey's eventual cooperation as a mutual success. Tweets from Stoltenberg often showcased images of him with Erdoğan, accompanied by messages of shared achievements, which may have been an effort to bolster NATO's image among the Turkish public.[34]

Ultimately, Turkey approved NATO's expansion in 2024, marking a significant victory for the alliance. Despite ongoing disputes, Turkey remains a key player within NATO, contributing to counterterrorism efforts and regional stability. NATO continues to engage with Turkey, recognizing its strategic importance while managing the challenges posed by Erdoğan's populist rhetoric and policy demands (Giannotta 2020).

However, these prolonged disputes have allowed Erdoğan to bolster his populist image domestically. Concessions from NATO enabled him to claim victories in negotiations, reinforcing his narrative of standing up to elite powers and defending Turkish sovereignty. The canceled F-35 sale, in particular, became fodder for Erdoğan's rhetoric about NATO's perceived inequities, fueling anti-elite sentiment among his supporters.[35] While NATO's strategies have maintained Turkey's participation and secured key objectives, they may have also inadvertently amplified Erdoğan's populist agenda, highlighting the delicate balance the alliance must strike in dealing with populist leaders within its ranks.

8.4.   NATO and Trump

Similar to Erdoğan, US president Donald Trump's first term featured frequent clashes with NATO, particularly over funding. With the United States contributing roughly three-quarters of NATO's defense spending, Trump lambasted the alliance for placing a disproportionate financial burden on the United States. He repeatedly demanded that other member states increase their defense budgets to ease the strain on American resources. Trump's grievances extended beyond funding; he advocated for rapprochement with Russia (Schuette and Dijkstra 2023), in stark contrast to NATO's stance, and

34. Twitter. September 18, 2023; Twitter. July 10, 2023.

35. Barzou Daragahi, "Erdoğan's Foreign Policy Pivot Is All About Domestic Politics." *World Politics Review.* July 24, 2023.

called for a realignment of priorities, suggesting the alliance should focus solely on countering China.[36]

Trump's insistence on a more balanced distribution of financing across members became a focal point of his criticism. He declared that the United States would only guarantee the defense of members meeting the NATO guideline of allocating at least 2 percent of their GDP to defense, a policy first established in 2014.[37] His rhetoric escalated further when he suggested that the United States might withhold support from Baltic nations unless they fulfilled these obligations.[38] Trump's refusal to unequivocally endorse NATO's foundational Article V, which enshrines the principle of collective defense, alarmed allies.[39] At one point, Trump came perilously close to withdrawing the United States from NATO entirely, consistent with his pattern of exiting multilateral organizations during his presidency.

In response to Trump's criticisms and threats, NATO employed a range of strategies to manage the situation and preserve the alliance. One approach was to appease Trump by urging members to increase defense spending and framing these efforts as a direct result of his demands. Secretary General Jens Stoltenberg actively encouraged member states to boost their contributions and publicly credited Trump for these increases, positioning him as a driving force behind the alliance's financial changes.[40] Stoltenberg personally met with Trump in 2018, highlighting an additional $100 billion in defense commitments reportedly secured through Trump's pressure, a figure that was trumpeted by Trump as a major achievement.[41]

NATO also sought to appeal to Trump's base by leveraging public relations campaigns. Stoltenberg appeared on *Fox News*, a network favored by Trump and his supporters, to emphasize Trump's role in deterring Russia by

36. Robbie Gramer, "Trump Wants NATO's Eyes on China." *Foreign Policy.* January 2, 2024.

37. Julie Davis, "Trump Warns NATO Allies to Spend More on Defense, or Else." *New York Times.* July 2, 2018.

38. David E. Sanger and Maggie Haberman, "Donald Trump Sets Conditions for Defending NATO Allies Against Attack." *New York Times.* July 20, 2016.

39. Sophie Tatum, "Trump Seems to Question US Commitment to Defending All NATO Allies." CNN. July 18, 2018.

40. "AP Fact Check: Trump Falsely Claims Credit on NATO Spending." *PBS News Hour.* July 30, 2018.

41. "Fact-Checking Trump's 2019 State of the Union." *CBS News.* February 6, 2019.

spurring greater financial contributions from member states.[42] This strategy aimed to bolster Trump's domestic image as a leader securing tangible wins for the United States while reinforcing NATO's relevance to his core supporters. Efforts to "Trump-proof" the alliance included ensuring that public messaging resonated with populist narratives, particularly during high-profile summits.[43]

Behind the scenes, NATO relied on quiet diplomacy to navigate Trump's unpredictability. Stoltenberg engaged in private negotiations with Trump, allowing him to voice public criticisms while maintaining cooperation in practice (Dijkstra et al. 2022). These back-channel discussions fostered a working relationship between the NATO chief and Trump, enabling Stoltenberg to manage Trump's demands without alienating him (Dijkstra et al. 2022). By accommodating Trump's need to appear as a tough negotiator, NATO retained US participation and avoided outright confrontation.[44]

In areas where appeasement was unfeasible, NATO resorted to sidelining Trump's influence, particularly on matters related to Russia. While Trump advocated for closer ties with Moscow, most NATO members vehemently opposed this stance. Rather than directly challenging Trump, NATO leaders worked around him by engaging US institutions and individuals more aligned with NATO's traditional posture, such as the State Department, the Pentagon, and Congress (Schuette 2023). Figures like Defense Secretary James Mattis served as crucial intermediaries in maintaining continuity within the alliance. Additionally, NATO strategically kept Russia off the agenda during key meetings, preemptively securing agreements on declarations to limit Trump's ability to disrupt proceedings (Schuette 2023).

These strategies proved effective in many respects. Trump's public critiques of NATO persisted, but the United States remained engaged in the alliance throughout his first term. Defense spending among NATO members increased incrementally, and Trump publicly claimed victory, boasting during his 2019 State of the Union address that his leadership had secured billions in commitments from allies.[45] Despite Trump's initial reluctance, the United

42. Gregg Re, "NATO Head: Trump's Tough Talk Has Added $100B to Alliance, Helped Deter Russia." *Fox News.* January 27, 2019.

43. Tom Bateman, "US Allies Try to 'Trump-Proof' NATO—But Is That Even Possible?" *BBC News.* July 12, 2024.

44. David Jackson, "Donald Trump, NATO Leader Meet Amid Tensions Over Military Spending by US Allies." *USA Today.* April 2, 2019.

45. "Fact-Checking the State of the Union Address." *Washington Post.* February 5, 2019.

States continued to support NATO-led operations and maneuvers targeting Russian aggression.

However, appeasement and tactical maneuvering did not completely mollify Trump. On the campaign trail for the 2024 election, he revisited familiar criticisms of NATO, calling the alliance underfunded and questioning its value to the United States.[46] His rhetoric reignited concerns about a potential US withdrawal, underscoring the fragility of the alliance's relationship with populist leaders.[47] While NATO successfully managed Trump's first presidency without losing the United States as a member, his persistent skepticism highlights the challenges of navigating populist pressures within multilateral organizations.

8.5. UN Peacekeeping and Trump

UN peacekeeping operations, primarily managed by international political and security elites, have long relied on substantial financial backing from the United States. As the largest contributor to the UN peacekeeping budget, the United States was responsible for 27 percent of its funding in 2023, though a congressional cap formally limited contributions to 25 percent.[48] Beyond mandatory contributions, the United States also provides voluntary funding for specific programs, as well as critical training and logistical support. This dominance over financial support and expertise drew sharp criticism from Donald Trump, whose disdain for IOs made the UN a frequent target during his first presidency.

Trump especially rejected the authority of the UN's bureaucratic elites, favoring unilateral American leadership in conflicts such as Israel–Palestine and Kosovo–Serbia (Landau and Lehrs 2022). His administration dismissed prior UN resolutions as ineffective and largely disregarded the organization's role in these disputes. Trump's critiques extended to peacekeeping itself, as he threatened to defund its operations and demanded that the United States contribute significantly less to the UN's coffers.

---

46. Ben Blanchet, "Trump Unleashes His Doubts on NATO: 'We Don't Get So Much out of It.'" *Huffpost*. January 28, 2024.

47. "Fmr. Trump NSA: 'I'm Convinced' Trump 'Withdraw from NATO, Which Would Be a Catastrophic Mistake.'" *MSNBC*. January 31, 2024.

48. This cap had previously been waived. "Funding the United Nations: How Much Does the US Pay?" Council on Foreign Relations. August 22, 2023.

UN secretary general António Guterres sought to mitigate these tensions through a combination of appeasement, reform, and strategic diplomacy. Recognizing Trump's aversion to bureaucracy, Guterres reframed the UN's mission, emphasizing a "leaner, more efficient" institution that aligned with Trump's priorities.[49] He initiated structural reforms, such as opening the recruitment system to outsiders, consolidating departments into the streamlined Department of Peace Operations, and granting regional offices greater autonomy.[50] Under US pressure, the UN General Assembly cut $600 million from the peacekeeping budget in 2017—a concession that signaled responsiveness to Trump's fiscal demands.[51]

While Guterres publicly acknowledged Trump's criticisms, he also worked to sideline the administration's influence in key areas. He cultivated strong alliances with European and Latin American member states,[52] which allowed him to bypass internal pressures and focus on broader global priorities.[53] Guterres also leaned on collaborations with other IOs, civil society groups, and private corporations to fill gaps created by US skepticism. His efforts to incorporate technology into peacekeeping further reduced the organization's reliance on member states like the United States, which had become increasingly disengaged under Trump's leadership.[54]

Guterres concomitantly engaged Trump in private meetings, leveraging personal diplomacy to maintain the US commitment to the UN. These conversations allowed Trump to publicly posture as a critic while privately cooperating with the organization.[55] Guterres also appealed to the American public, countering Trump's inflammatory rhetoric on social media. For instance, when Trump derided the UN as "a club for people to get together, talk, and have a good time," Guterres responded on Snapchat by emphasizing

49. Janine Di Giovanni, "The U.N.'s Most Important Peacekeeping Mission: Trump. *Politico.* January 21, 2018.

50. Ibid.

51. Margaret Besheer, "UN Peacekeeping Budget Cut by $600 million." *Voice of America.* June 30, 2017.

52. Vesselin Popovski, "Can the United Nations Adapt to Donald Trump?" *The Conversation.* February 16, 2017.

53. Ibid.

54. Dulcie Leimbach, "Guterres's Grand Plan to Remake the UN's Peace and Security 'Pillar.'" *PassBlue.* October 20, 2017.

55. "Readout of President Donald J. Trump's Meeting with United Nations Secretary General António Guterres." *Trump White House Archives.* October 20, 2017.

the institution's untapped potential and his commitment to realizing it. He even extended goodwill to Trump by wishing him a swift recovery when he contracted COVID-19, signaling an effort to maintain a personal connection despite their differences.[56]

These strategies proved effective in tempering Trump's hostility. In May 2018, Trump tweeted praise for Guterres, lauding his efforts to "Make the United Nations Great Again" and highlighting cost savings achieved through reduced US involvement. Ultimately, Trump's funding cuts were more modest than his initial threats, with the US share of the peacekeeping budget decreasing from 28.5 percent to 25 percent, amounting to a reduction of $200 million in spending.[57] This was a nominal price for the UN to pay to maintain Trump's broad cooperation.

However, the long-term effects of Trump's policies remain uncertain. Many of the reforms implemented under his administration were reversed when President Biden restored US support for multilateral initiatives. Yet populist grievances regarding the UN persist, as evidenced by recent congressional debates over peacekeeping funds.[58] While Guterres's strategies effectively navigated Trump's first presidency, they underscore the precarious balance required to maintain US engagement in multilateral organizations amid growing populist pressures.

8.6.   WHO and Trump

The WHO possesses characteristics that, in many ways, make it a prime target for populist opposition. Staffed by international experts such as scientists and public health professionals, it operates in the realm of scientific data and health policy, areas often viewed skeptically by populists (as we showed in chapter 3). Its work inherently involves constraining state sovereignty, as member states are required to provide sensitive information on disease outbreaks, public health data, and vaccine research. The WHO's recommendations, ranging from quarantines to travel bans, can impose significant logistical, economic, and political challenges on nations. These measures, while essential for global health, are often resisted, particularly by populist leaders who view such

56. Twitter. December 26, 2016.

57. Michelle Nichols, "US Aims to Trim Its U.N. Peacekeeping Bill After Trump's Calls to Slash." *Reuters*. June 9, 2017.

58. Alex Rouhandeh, "House and Senate Republicans' Latest Infighting Is Over Peacekeeping Funds." *Newsweek*. July 14, 2023.

constraints as infringements on national autonomy (Carnegie and Carson 2023).

Donald Trump was an especially vocal critic of the WHO during his first term as US president, accusing it of bias toward China and pointing to what he labeled as "faulty recommendations" during the COVID-19 pandemic.[59] In April 2020, his administration thus announced a temporary suspension of US funding to the organization. By July of that year, the administration formally notified the United Nations of its intent to withdraw from the WHO entirely. Trump's criticism, amplified through social media, significantly undermined the organization, which depended heavily on US contributions for funding and on its engagement for legitimacy. For instance, the CDC and WHO have a long history of working together to address global health crises, such as Ebola outbreaks in sub-Saharan Africa. Echoing populist rhetoric, Trump administration officials framed their opposition in terms of safeguarding US sovereignty, rejecting the constraints the WHO was perceived to impose.[60]

The WHO responded to these challenges using strategies that aligned with its broader approach to populist opposition. To mitigate the damage from the US withdrawal, the WHO focused on carrying out its core functions—data collection, research, and pandemic response—by leveraging collaborations with other member states and IOs (Kuznetsova 2020). It coordinated efforts with partners such as UN agencies (e.g., UNICEF) and other global health organizations, ensuring a steady flow of expertise and resources. The Access to COVID-19 Tools (ACT) Accelerator exemplified these efforts, aiming to guarantee equitable access to diagnostics, treatments, and vaccines, particularly for developing countries (Moon et al. 2022).

Funding posed a significant challenge, but the WHO adapted by seeking support from other member states. The EU stepped up with additional financial contributions, and the WHO launched an unprecedented open-investment round to broaden its donor base and secure more predictable and flexible funding streams (Schuette and Dijkstra 2023). This initiative marked a turning point, reducing the organization's reliance on volatile member states like the United States and strengthening its financial resilience.[61]

Despite these efforts to sideline US disengagement, the WHO also sought to appease Trump. In response to his demands for an investigation into the

59. Twitter. April 7, 2020.
60. Helen Murphy, "Humanitarian Aid's Dismal Year." *Devex.* December 15, 2023.
61. "Pro Weekender Brief," *Devex.* Jan 28, 2024.

origins of COVID-19, the WHO convened the Global Study of the Origins of SARS-CoV-2 in 2020. The EU, too, advocated reforms designed to address US concerns, including calls for increased transparency, an independent on-site epidemiological assessment mechanism, and revisions to the system for declaring "Public Health Emergencies of International Concern" (Schuette and Dijkstra 2023). These measures were intended to assuage US skepticism and encourage re-engagement.

WHO director general Tedros Adhanom Ghebreyesus also took to social media to combat Trump's criticisms and rally international support. In a strategic shift, Tedros began retweeting endorsements from influential figures like Melinda Gates and former US president Jimmy Carter, as well as supportive statements from other member countries and peer IOs.[62] He emphasized messages of unity and resilience, aiming to strengthen public perception of the WHO as an essential actor in global health.[63] Behind the scenes, White House staff maintained occasional contact with WHO officials, although the specifics of these discussions remain unclear. These private meetings suggest an effort by the WHO to work around Trump's public antagonism and sideline domestic constituents while keeping lines of communication open.

Ultimately, while the WHO's strategies did not succeed in reversing Trump's decision to withdraw, they secured vital support from other international actors. The organization managed to weather the crisis by diversifying its funding sources, leveraging global partnerships, and maintaining its operational focus. Despite the strain, the WHO continued to work toward its mission, demonstrating resilience in the face of one of its most significant challenges.[64] However, Trump's actions left lasting stains on the institution, including reduced credibility and financial flexibility, illustrating the precarious position IOs face when confronted with populist opposition from key member states.

8.7. WTO and Trump

The WTO, originally established as the General Agreement on Tariffs and Trade after World War II, has long been a cornerstone of international trade governance. Founded by the United States and its Western allies, the

---

62. Twitter, September 15, 2020

63. Twitter, September 15, 2020.

64. Helen Murphy, "Humanitarian Aid's Dismal Year." *Devex*. December 15, 2023.

organization has historically enjoyed robust American support. Under the GATT/WTO framework, global trade has expanded dramatically, and tariff levels have plummeted, fueling economic growth and integration worldwide (Goldstein, Rivers, and Tomz 2007). Yet, the institution's trajectory shifted significantly with the arrival of Donald Trump in the White House in 2017. His administration mounted a sustained campaign against the WTO, marking a stark departure from decades of US advocacy for multilateral trade rules (Jones 2021).

The WTO embodies many of the features that populist leaders like Trump find objectionable. It is an elite-driven institution, staffed by a relatively small cadre of expert bureaucrats, international civil servants, and panels of adjudicators. Its mandate imposes far-reaching constraints on national sovereignty, requiring member states to abide by rules governing everything from intellectual-property rights and investment measures to anti-dumping policies and tariff schedules. Over time, successive rounds of negotiations have expanded both the scope and stringency of WTO regulations, amplifying its role as a global trade arbiter (Davis 2012). And unlike many organs of international law, the WTO is binding and can authorize costly retaliation against countries violating trade rules.

Trump's hostility toward the WTO was fueled in part by a series of adverse rulings issued by its dispute-settlement body against the United States. The administration accused the body of exceeding its mandate by interpreting trade law rather than adhering strictly to its text. These grievances dovetailed with broader populist concerns about sovereignty, as the Trump administration sought greater autonomy to craft US trade policy, particularly as it ramped up its trade war with China. Trump's preference for bilateral trade deals, which would maximize US leverage over individual partners, clashed with core WTO principles of reciprocity and nondiscrimination, which prohibit the very practices he sought to pursue (Bown 2022).

In pursuit of his agenda, Trump took steps to undermine the WTO's effectiveness. His administration withheld vital resources, most notably by blocking appointments to the Appellate Body, a move that crippled the WTO's dispute-settlement mechanism.[65] By December 2019, the Appellate Body was rendered inoperative, leaving disputes unresolved because losing parties could effectively stall rulings by appealing "into the void." This tactic

---

65. Stephanie Nebehay, "US Seals Demise of WTO Appeals Bench—Trade Officials." *Reuters.* December 9, 2019.

undercut the WTO's ability to enforce its rules, enabling member states to flout trade obligations without consequence.[66]

Trump's administration also violated WTO agreements by imposing unilateral tariffs on steel, aluminum, and other goods, targeting both adversaries like China and traditional allies. These actions bypassed the WTO's established dispute-resolution mechanisms, with the administration frequently invoking the nebulous "national security" exemption to justify its measures.[67] Coupled with sharp public criticism, including threats to withdraw from the organization,[68] Trump's rhetoric further eroded confidence in the WTO's impartiality and efficacy (Carnegie and Carson 2019).

The WTO, for its part, responded with a series of strategic countermeasures to mitigate the impact of US hostility. Recognizing the need to sideline Trump's obstructionism,[69] the WTO maintained its core functions, continuing to hear trade disputes, facilitate negotiations, and monitor compliance among the rest of its membership. When the Appellate Body became defunct, the organization worked with other states, notably the European Union, to establish a Multi-Party Interim Appeal Arrangement (MPIA). This innovative workaround allowed willing members to resolve disputes through independent arbitration, bypassing US opposition and preserving the integrity of the dispute-settlement system for participating countries.[70] Recent scholarship suggests that the MPIA has been an effective stopgap, making it a prime example of how institutions can successfully sideline populists (Pelc 2024).

The WTO also sought to strengthen partnerships with other trade organizations, such as the OECD and UNCTAD,[71] and embraced initiatives like plurilateral agreements that allowed subsets of members to negotiate rules

---

66. Jennifer Hillman, "A Reset of the World Trade Organization's Appellate Body." *Council on Foreign Relations.* January 14, 2020.

67. Ana Swanson, "W.T.O. Says American Tariffs on China Broke Global Trade Rules." *New York Times.* September 15, 2020.

68. Christine Wang, "Trump Threatens to Withdraw from World Trade Organization." *CNBC.* August 30, 2018.

69. "Isolate Trump at WTO, Says Former Top Trade Judge Bacchus." *Reuters.* October 3, 2018.

70. "Members Hold Informal Talks on WTO Reform." *World Trade Organization.* November 10, 2022.

71. E.g., "UNCTAD, ITC, and WTO Roll Out Tool to Help Businesses Trade Better." *UNCTAD News.* June 26, 2020.

on specific issues (Hoekman and Sabel 2021). These measures demonstrated the organization's adaptability and its commitment to advancing its mission despite external resistance.

Simultaneously, the WTO attempted to appease the Trump administration by addressing some of its grievances. It pursued discussions on reforming the dispute-settlement mechanism and improving transparency. Efforts by Japan and the EU included exploring ways to limit the binding nature of certain rulings and addressing US concerns about Chinese trade practices, such as state-owned enterprises and forced technology transfers (Hopewell 2021). The WTO also engaged the United States behind closed doors[72] as former director general Roberto Azevêdo maintained frequent contact with US trade representatives to seek common ground.[73] However, these efforts yielded limited success, as the administration repeatedly rejected proposed reforms without offering concrete alternatives.

Recognizing the importance of public perception, the WTO also reached out to American citizens, emphasizing the benefits of multilateralism and free trade.[74] Through social media campaigns and public statements, it highlighted how global trade rules promote economic stability and prosperity, aiming to counter the narrative that the WTO exclusively served elites or multinational corporations.[75]

Although the WTO survived Trump's first presidency, the damage dealt to its operations was significant. The Appellate Body remains incapacitated, and progress on multilateral trade negotiations has stalled. Yet the organization has demonstrated resilience. The MPIA has introduced innovative reforms (Pelc 2024), and the panel system continues to adjudicate disputes effectively, often adhering to the precedents set by the now-defunct Appellate Body (Howse and Langille 2023). Moreover, the WTO has retained its global membership, and its core functions remain intact.

The shadow of Trump's policies lingers, as his populist rhetoric continues to resonate with key segments of the US electorate.[76] His influence extended

72. Andrea Shalal, "No Meeting with Trump, but WTO Chief Sees US 'Sense of Urgency' on Trade Reforms." *Reuters.* February 4, 2020.

73. "Members Commit to Engagement on Dispute Settlement Reform." World Trade Organization. April 27, 2022.

74. Twitter. June 7, 2017.

75. Twitter. November 19, 2020.

76. Bryce Baschuk, "How Trump Could Deal Another Blow to Already Hobbled WTO." Bloomberg. September 4, 2023.

to the subsequent administration, with Biden largely maintaining Trump-era trade policies. With Trump back in office and escalating trade conflicts with a bevy of countries, the WTO faces an uphill battle, not only in addressing the structural issues that Trump has exposed but also in rebuilding trust and legitimacy among its members and constituents. Nonetheless, the organization's ability to adapt and endure offers hope for its continued role as a cornerstone of global trade governance.

8.8.   UNFPA and Trump

The United Nations Population Fund (UNFPA) operates in more than 150 countries, championing sexual and reproductive health and gender equality. Funded by voluntary member-state contributions, it has historically relied on substantial financial outlays from the United States, which is typically one of its largest donors.[77] The organization's staff comprises highly qualified professionals, including public health experts and economists, many of whom hold advanced degrees and elite credentials.

During Donald Trump's first presidency, the UNFPA became a prime target of his administration's ideological crusade to curtail US involvement in IOs and to reduce funding for initiatives linked to reproductive health. Trump's administration viewed the UNFPA as expendable, extending domestic Republican policies of cutting funds for abortion-related services to global health organizations. In 2017, the administration slashed $32.5 million in US contributions to the agency, citing its alleged support for coercive abortion practices in China, a claim the UNFPA vehemently denied.[78] Trump also demanded that the agency remove references to reproductive health from its communications regarding the COVID-19 response, fearing it might promote abortion as an essential service.[79]

Faced with this hostility, the UNFPA adopted several strategies to mitigate the damage. Anticipating potential funding cuts even before they were enacted, the organization proactively sought to diversify its donor base. It reached out to NGOs, charitable foundations, and both private-and public-sector partners, aiming to reduce its reliance on any single state's contributions (Hirschmann

77. UNFPA. "Resources and Funding." 2022.

78. Nurith Aizenman, "Citing Abortions in China, Trump Cuts Funds for U.N. Family Planning Agency." *NPR*. April 4, 2017.

79. Kylie Atwood, "US Asks for Abortion References to be Removed from UN Pandemic Response Plan." *CNN*. May 19, 2020.

2021). This diversification effort proved prescient, enabling the UNFPA to weather US funding cuts. By 2022, the agency announced plans to expand its donor base from 78 state contributors to 110, further safeguarding its financial independence.[80]

To appease the Trump administration, the UNFPA also sought to reframe its messaging, minimizing direct references to abortion and instead emphasizing broader goals like "sexual and reproductive health." This rhetorical shift was designed not only to placate Trump but also to appeal to conservative domestic audiences in member states (Hirschmann 2021). The organization expanded its communications and public relations efforts, hiring specialists to highlight the humanitarian nature of its work. These efforts increased public awareness and support within the United States, leading to individual and corporate donations that helped sustain the agency during this challenging period (Hirschmann 2021).

Behind the scenes, the UNFPA engaged in discreet lobbying efforts with the Trump administration, presenting itself as a humanitarian organization focused on critical issues like maternal health, gender equality, and emergency aid. By recasting its operations in this light, the agency aimed to soften its image and maintain some level of cooperation with US officials (Hirschmann 2021).

Ultimately, the UNFPA survived Trump's first term by securing alternative funding streams and navigating political headwinds until President Joe Biden restored US support. However, the agency continues to face challenges from far-right populist movements in the United States and abroad. Persistent opposition complicates long-term planning and threatens the stability of its programs. In Congress, for instance, some lawmakers have introduced bills to block federal funding for the UNFPA, underscoring the precariousness of its future.[81] Despite these obstacles, the UNFPA has demonstrated resilience, adapting to political adversity while striving to fulfill its global mandate.

8.9.   Paris Agreement and Trump

The Paris Agreement, adopted in 2015 at the 21st Conference of the Parties to the UN Framework Convention on Climate Change, stands as a landmark

---

80. *UNFPA.* "Resources and Funding." 2022.

81. Sandhya Raman, "Funding Uncertainty Weighs on UN Maternal Health Agency." *Roll Call.* January 11, 2023.

treaty aimed at curbing global emissions and slowing climate change. Signed by 196 countries, including all major emitters except Iran, the agreement requires each participant to set their own nationally determined contributions (NDCs), which outline their emissions targets and strategies for achieving them. While enforcement relies largely on transparency and public accountability, NDCs are publicly available, allowing NGOs, states, and citizens to apply pressure on leaders who fail to meet their commitments (Bodle, Donat, and Duwe 2016; Tingley and Tomz 2022; Casler, Clark, and Zucker 2024). Scientific expertise plays a crucial role in shaping these targets, as accurate data on emissions, mitigation strategies, and progress are vital for achieving the agreement's ambitious goals.

Under President Obama, the United States pledged to reduce emissions by 26 to 28 percent below 2005 levels by 2025, with a focus on expanding renewable energy and improving energy efficiency. However, Donald Trump, upon assuming office in 2017, announced his intention to withdraw the United States from the Paris Agreement, framing the decision as a reassertion of US sovereignty (Pavone 2018). Trump dismissed climate science as a "hoax" and often mocked the concept of global warming, using cold weather events to undermine the scientific consensus on climate change.[82] He criticized the Paris Agreement as unfair to the United States, claiming it disproportionately advantaged other nations while imposing unnecessary costs on American businesses. Trump's rhetoric, such as calling the agreement a "total con job"[83] and alleging that it was designed by China to harm US competitiveness,[84] resonated with his populist base and bolstered his anti-globalist narrative.

The US withdrawal dealt a significant blow to the Paris Agreement, as the country is both a major emitter and a global leader whose participation is critical to the pact's legitimacy. Recognizing this, world leaders and diplomats worked tirelessly to persuade Trump to remain in the agreement. At the 2017 G7 meeting, leaders from France, Japan, Canada, Italy, and the UK lobbied Trump intensively,[85] while French president Emmanuel Macron went so far

---

82. Helier Cheung, "What Does Trump Actually Believe on Climate Change?" *BBC*. January 23, 2020.

83. Twitter. December, 2013.

84. Twitter. November 6, 2012.

85. Kevin Liptak, "World Leaders Lobby Trump on Climate Change at G7." *CNN*. May 26, 2017.

as to host Trump in Paris in 2018, attempting to win him over with flattery.[86] These diplomatic efforts, conducted largely behind closed doors to sideline Trump's populist base, ultimately failed, as Trump had made withdrawal a highly visible campaign promise that he could not abandon without losing credibility among his supporters.

With Trump unyielding, the remaining signatories decided to move forward without the United States, sidelining his administration and focusing on preserving the agreement. UNFCCC officials and world leaders strengthened coalitions with nonstate actors, such as local governments and private organizations, to fill the void left by US nonparticipation (Dijkstra et al. 2022). European countries took on leadership roles in global climate efforts.[87] The EU ramped up its Paris commitments with initiatives like the European Green Deal, which set a target of net-zero emissions by 2050. Additionally, the EU began incorporating compliance with the Paris Agreement as a condition in its trade agreements and lobbied other major emitters, including China, to uphold their commitments (Schuette and Dijkstra 2023). China, for its part, has emerged as a global leader on climate change mitigation and renewable energy.[88]

Efforts to bypass the Trump administration extended to engaging subnational actors and civil society within the United States. The UNFCCC launched initiatives like the Lima-Paris Action Agenda and the Momentum of Change Initiative, encouraging local governments, businesses, and NGOs to take the lead on climate action.[89] These efforts inspired the "We're Still In" movement, wherein states, cities, and corporations (including 3,900 CEOs) across the United States pledged to uphold the goals of the Paris Agreement despite the federal withdrawal.[90] This grassroots mobilization underscored a broader commitment to climate action within the United States, even as the federal government resisted.

---

86. Paul Pradier, "French President Macron Flatters Trump, But Fails to Convince Him: Experts." *ABC News*. November 8, 2018.

87. "Leaders Ramp Up Climate Fight, with 'Momentum' from Trump." *CNN*. December 12, 2017.

88. Julia Simon, "How Will China Impact the Future of Climate Change? You Might Be Surprised." *NPR*. November 22, 2024.

89. Emma Bryce, "Food at COP21: Three New Initiatives Spotlight Food Insecurity, Soils, Waste." *Guardian*. December 4, 2015.

90. Madeleine Sheehan Perkins, "A Group Representing $6.2 Trillion of the US Economy Says They're 'Still in' the Paris Climate Agreement." *Business Insider*. January 5, 2017.

In the short term, these strategies succeeded in keeping the Paris Agreement alive. The agreement continued to function, with global momentum sustained through the leadership of the EU and other key actors. When President Biden assumed office in 2021, the United States re-entered the agreement, restoring its role as a central player in global climate governance.

However, longer-term challenges remain. *The Economist* has warned of a growing transnational populist backlash against climate policies, fueled by the perception that green initiatives are imposed undemocratically by elites, infringing on national sovereignty.[91] While the international community's efforts to circumvent Trump preserved the Paris Agreement during his first term, the failure to directly confront these populist concerns left the door open for future resistance, threatening the sustainability of global climate efforts.

8.10.   Paris Agreement and Bolsonaro

Jair Bolsonaro, like Donald Trump, emerged as a vocal populist opponent of the Paris Agreement, expressing outright disdain for its emissions-reduction targets and the accountability mechanisms it imposed. Brazil's commitment under the Agreement included an ambitious goal to reduce carbon emissions by 43 percent by 2030 from 2005 levels, with a particular emphasis on curbing deforestation in the Amazon. Such an aggressive target reflected Brazil's long-standing position as a global leader on climate change. As the world's largest carbon sink, the Amazon plays a critical role in mitigating climate change and offsetting the negative effects of global warming, such as extreme weather patterns.[92]

However, Bolsonaro viewed these commitments through the lens of populist ideology, rejecting the Agreement as a symbol of elite interference and an affront to Brazil's sovereignty.[93] He argued that conservation efforts posed a threat to Brazil's economic development and control over its resources, fueling his broader narrative of resistance to external constraints. Bolsonaro's administration actively dismantled environmental protections, cutting funding for

91. "The Global Backlash Against Climate Policies Has Begun." *The Economist*. October 11, 2023.

92. See Brazil's climate pledge on the UNFCCC site.

93. Yasmeen Serhan, "The Real Reason Behind Bolsonaro's Climate Promises." *The Atlantic*. November 12, 2021.

ecological programs and removing scientists who reported on the alarming rate of Amazonian deforestation. Denying the very existence of climate change, Bolsonaro frequently attacked environmentalists, labeling them the "self-proclaimed climate elite" and amplifying his administration's alignment with agribusiness interests, which stood to benefit from deforestation (Mendes Motta and Hauber 2023).

Bolsonaro's hostility extended to the Paris Agreement itself, which he initially threatened to abandon. While he later agreed to remain in the pact, partially as a result of widespread public support for it within Brazil, his cooperation came with significant caveats. He demanded assurances that Brazil would retain sovereignty over its natural resources, including the Amazon rainforest, and called for financial compensation in exchange for curbing emissions. Bolsonaro's rhetoric was unequivocal: Brazil would not cede control of its land to "native tribes or international jurisdiction," and any preservation efforts would have to be economically beneficial for Brazil.[94]

In response, members of the Paris Agreement employed a range of strategies to manage Bolsonaro's defiance. The EU sought to appease him by leveraging a long-negotiated trade deal with MERCOSUR, tying the agreement to Brazil's continued participation in the Paris framework.[95] The proposed deal, which offered significant economic benefits for Brazil, created pressure for Bolsonaro to remain in the climate pact, as abandoning it could alienate other MERCOSUR members and disrupt Brazil's economic aspirations. Similarly, the Biden administration signaled that Brazil's disregard for climate action would hinder any efforts to deepen bilateral relations, adding further diplomatic pressure.[96]

These tactics politicized Brazil's Paris membership and mobilized domestic and international stakeholders to counter Bolsonaro's narrative. In Brazil, where climate change is broadly recognized as a serious issue, civil society groups, environmental advocates, and international partners capitalized on public opinion to challenge Bolsonaro's stance. Data from the World Values Survey revealed that 90 percent of Brazilians view climate change as

94. Rodrigo Viga Gaier, "Brazil's Bolsonaro Scraps Pledge to Quit Paris Climate Deal." *Reuters*. October 25, 2018.

95. "Trade Deal Binds Brazil to Paris Agreement, Says Top EU Official." *Climate Home News*. July 16, 2019.

96. Travis Waldron, "Brazil Is Key to Biden's Global Climate Ambitions. The Only Problem? Bolsonaro." *Huffpost*. April 21, 2021.

a significant concern, and 60 percent prioritize environmental protection over economic growth.[97] Leveraging this public sentiment, activists and international actors kept climate issues at the forefront of political discourse, rallying support for Brazil's continued engagement with the Paris Agreement.[98]

In the short term, these combined efforts succeeded in keeping Brazil within the Agreement. Bolsonaro ultimately backtracked on his threats to withdraw, preserving Brazil's formal commitments to global climate goals. However, the underlying populist opposition to environmental policies remains entrenched among segments of the Brazilian electorate, particularly those aligned with agribusiness and skeptical of indigenous rights. This persistent anti-environmentalist sentiment poses a long-term challenge to meaningful climate action in Brazil, risking continued deforestation and weakening international efforts to address the climate crisis (Rached 2022). If left unaddressed, this populist resistance may further undermine progress, perpetuating conflict over the Amazon and complicating Brazil's role in global environmental governance.

8.11.   IMF and Tsipras

In 2010, Greece secured a bailout from the EU, IMF, and ECB—collectively known as the "troika"—in exchange for implementing a stringent austerity program (Henning 2017). This program included deeply unpopular measures such as tax hikes, pension cuts, and labor market reforms, fueling widespread discontent across the country. By January 2015, this discontent culminated in the electoral victory of Syriza, a left-wing populist party led by Alexis Tsipras, which had campaigned on a staunchly anti-austerity and anti-IMF platform. Syriza's rise to power escalated tensions with the troika, as its supporters lambasted the IMF and EU as elitist institutions enforcing policies that disproportionately harmed ordinary Greeks.

Syriza's rhetoric painted the IMF as the architect of Greece's suffering. The party accused the "elites" at the IMF and EU of imposing austerity measures that exacerbated economic hardship while benefiting banks rather than the Greek people. Syriza supporters often referred to the "euro elite" as exploiting

---

97. Data come from the 2014 wave of the WVS.

98. Michael Jacobs, "High Pressure for Low Emissions: How Civil Society Created the Paris Climate Agreement." *IPPR*. March 14, 2016.

Greece for their gain,[99] amplifying claims that troika-imposed austerity had brought widespread poverty and spiraling debt. Such anti-elite sentiment, combined with Syriza's threats to exit the eurozone, created a fraught relationship between Greece and the troika (Henning 2017).

Faced with the prospect of Syriza's galvanizing of public opinion against its programs, the IMF adopted a strategy to counteract the rising tide of populism. Central to this effort was re-framing its image and policies to resonate with Greek citizens.[100] Recognizing the potential for public opposition to derail necessary reforms, the IMF employed populist-style messaging to recast itself as a champion of ordinary Greeks. In particular, it sought to highlight how reforming Greece's tax administration—one of the core conditions of its program—could reduce inequality, with the burden of payment falling on wealthy elites rather than on everyday citizens. As one senior IMF official explained, the Fund attempted to position itself as "a friend of the ordinary Greeks," emphasizing the benefits of targeting tax evasion by wealthy individuals and politically connected families.[101]

The IMF also sought to shift public perceptions through an aggressive communication campaign on social media.[102] Key figures like Christine Lagarde used platforms like Twitter to advocate for fairer tax systems and governance reforms. Lagarde tweeted messages such as "We need a tax system where multinational companies and wealthy individuals contribute a fair share to the public purse" and "Solid fiscal frameworks together with good governance and transparency give citizens confidence that fiscal policy serves the good of all, not just the wealthy or well-connected." These efforts were designed to align the IMF's image with the broader interests of working-class Greeks and to counter Syriza's narrative of the Fund as an elitist and oppressive institution.[103]

In addition to its public outreach, the IMF sought to placate Greece's populist government by pushing for more lenient debt-restructuring terms. This stance put the Fund at odds with European institutions, which maintained

99. Seumas Milne, "The Crucifixion of Greece Is Killing the European Project." *The Guardian.* July 16, 2005.

100. Poul Thomsen, "The IMF and the Greek Crisis: Myths and Realities." Transcript of speech delivered at the London School of Economics on September 30, 2019.

101. Senior IMF official. Interview by authors. October 2022.

102. Senior IMF official. Interview by authors. October 2022.

103. Christopher Colford, "Amid the Rescue and Recovery in Greece." *World Bank Blogs.* 2015.

a hard-line approach to conditionality.[104] The IMF advocated for reducing the number of loan conditions imposed on Greece, with the total number of conditions dropping significantly, from forty-six in 2014 to just eight in 2015, coinciding with Syriza's ascent to power (Kentikelenis, Stubbs, and King 2016). However, the reduction in conditions may also reflect the winding down of the IMF's program in Greece, complicating efforts to attribute the shift solely to Syriza's influence.

Despite these efforts, the IMF faced an uphill battle in restoring its image among Greek citizens. While it managed to sustain Greece's engagement with the bailout program during much of Syriza's tenure, public sentiment toward the Fund remained overwhelmingly negative. The narrative of the IMF as an institution serving elites rather than ordinary people endured, with populist factions continuing to scapegoat it for Greece's economic struggles (Handlin, Kaya, and Günaydin 2023). This enduring tension underscores the challenges IOs face when navigating the intersection of populist resistance and the need for economic reform.

8.12. ICC and Various

The ICC, headquartered in The Hague, Netherlands, prosecutes individuals accused of crimes against humanity, genocide, war crimes, and crimes of aggression. Established in 1998 and operational since 2002, the ICC wields considerable authority, particularly over states that have ratified the Rome Statute, its founding document. Staffed by elite legal experts, judges, and investigators, the ICC is a highly constraining institution that enforces accountability for war crimes within its members' territories.

The ICC has faced significant pushback from African nations, which have been disproportionately represented in its prosecutions. This dynamic has sparked accusations of bias and infringements on state sovereignty, particularly from populist leaders in the region. Presidents Pierre Nkurunziza of Burundi, Yahya Jammeh of The Gambia, Jacob Zuma of South Africa, and Kenya's former president Raila Odinga have all voiced fierce opposition to the Court, claiming it unfairly targets African leaders (Voeten 2020).

Kenya's Parliament set the stage for this backlash in 2013 when it passed a motion to withdraw from the ICC, though the country ultimately did not

104. Angelos Chryssogelos and Matthew Oxenford, "Greek Bailout: IMF and Europeans Diverge on Lessons Learnt." *Chatham House.* August 16, 2018.

follow through. The situation escalated in 2016 when Burundi, The Gambia, and South Africa initiated withdrawal efforts, with Burundi's Parliament overwhelmingly voting to leave. President Nkurunziza promptly signed the motion into law, making Burundi the first and only African nation to officially exit the Rome Statute. In early 2017, the African Union even adopted a nonbinding resolution advocating for a collective withdrawal from the ICC, further amplifying these challenges.[105]

The rhetoric surrounding these withdrawal efforts heavily emphasized claims of injustice and bias. South African leaders pointed out that only Africans had been charged in the six ICC cases at the time, fueling perceptions of systemic prejudice (Voeten 2020). Gambian information minister Sheriff Bojang went further, branding the ICC the "International Caucasian Court" and accusing it of targeting people of color, especially Africans.[106] Specific flashpoints, such as the arrest warrant issued for Sudanese president Omar al-Bashir and the ICC's criticism of South Africa for allowing al-Bashir to attend an African Union Summit in 2015, further inflamed tensions (Souris 2020).

Despite this wave of hostility, the ICC managed to retain most of its African membership, with only Burundi completing its withdrawal. In The Gambia, presidential candidate Adama Barrow campaigned on reversing Jammeh's withdrawal decision,[107] and upon his election in 2017, he reinstated the country's ICC membership.[108] Similarly, South Africa's courts blocked its withdrawal, deeming the motion unconstitutional.[109] These reversals underscored the resilience of the ICC in the face of populist challenges.

To address this backlash, the ICC employed a variety of strategies to maintain its legitimacy and membership. It worked closely with civil society organizations and nonpopulist governments to rally support. Seminars, advocacy campaigns, and partnerships with regional organizations emphasized

---

105. Abdoulie John, "Gambia Will Reverse Its ICC Withdrawal, EU Official Says." *Associated Press.* February 9, 2017.

106. Siobhan O'Grady, "Gambia: The ICC Should Be Called the International Caucasian Court." *Foreign Policy.* October 26, 2016.

107. Alieu Manneh, "Opposition Leader Promises Return of Gambia to ICC." *AA.* November 28, 2016.

108. Abdoulie John, "Gambia Will Reverse its ICC Withdrawal, EU Official Says." *Associated Press.* February 9, 2017.

109. Norimitsu Onishi, "South Africa Reverses Withdrawal from International Criminal Court." *New York Times.* March 8, 2017.

the ICC's role in ensuring justice.[110] Countries like Senegal, Botswana, Sierra Leone, and Nigeria publicly defended the Court, providing a counternarrative to the populist critiques in the region.[111] Regional coalitions, including the African Group for Justice and Accountability, also mobilized to encourage countries like South Africa to reconsider withdrawal.[112] Connections with these international partners served to isolate skeptical leaders.

The ICC also sought to appease critics by broadening its focus beyond Africa, thereby addressing accusations of regional bias. In 2016, it opened investigations into crimes committed in Afghanistan and Georgia and later initiated inquiries into Venezuela's government and the Russian invasion of Ukraine.[113] These actions demonstrated the Court's willingness to pursue justice on a global scale, not just within African states. The ICC also facilitated open debates about its operations, providing forums for member states and the public to voice concerns and propose reforms.[114]

Despite these efforts, populist opposition to the ICC remains a persistent and evolving challenge. While the Court successfully retained most of its African membership, skepticism about its fairness and efficacy continues to resonate among populist leaders and their supporters (Helfer and Showalter 2017). This ongoing hostility underscores the broader tension between IOs and populist movements, which frequently invoke sovereignty concerns and anti-elitism to challenge global governance. The ICC's long-term success will depend on its ability to navigate these ideological divides while maintaining its commitment to justice.

8.13.   Implications and Discussion

Our case studies illustrate a consistent pattern: No matter the nature of the state led by populists or the type of IO they challenge, IOs have responded in ways that align with the strategies we theorize—appeasing and sidelining

110. Sarah Lansky, "Africans Speak Out Against ICC Withdrawal." *Human Rights Watch.* November 2, 2016.

111. Ibid.

112. "South Africa: Continent Wide Outcry at ICC Withdrawal." *Human Rights Watch.* October 22, 2016.

113. "Georgia." ICC. ICC-01/15. David Bosco, "Exclusive: International Criminal Court Poised to Open Investigation into War Crimes in Afghanistan." *Foreign Policy.* October 31, 2016.

114. Franck Kuwonu, "ICC: Beyond the Threats of Withdrawal." *UN Africa Renewal.* May–July 2017.

leaders and their constituents. Across a wide range of examples, we see IOs and their members offering tangible concessions to populist leaders, such as fighter jets, trade incentives, and policy adjustments, while simultaneously reinforcing alliances with other states and organizations to mitigate risks if appeasement efforts fell short. Concurrently, IOs have worked to engage and mollify populist constituents, leveraging social media platforms like Twitter to share their narratives and offering assurances of potential gains if populists lost power. IOs also conducted behind-the-scenes negotiations with populist leaders to cultivate cooperation free from public scrutiny. These multifaceted responses have often, though not always, bolstered IOs' resilience, allowing them to weather populist challenges and adapt to evolving threats.

The concluding chapter of this book synthesizes these findings, presenting a comprehensive overview of how IOs have navigated the populist challenge and outlining strategies to bolster their resilience in the future. We propose a forward-looking framework that equips IOs with the tools to anticipate and counter populist opposition while preserving their legitimacy, fairness, and efficacy. This discussion not only highlights the importance of a proactive, multipronged approach but also addresses the broader normative implications of these strategies, raising critical questions about the role of IOs in an era of intensifying populism. By reflecting on these dynamics, we aim to chart a path for IOs to remain vital and effective in the face of ongoing global challenges.

9

Conclusion

POPULISTS OFTEN target IOs, accusing them of eroding national sovereignty and being dominated by global elites. This antagonism has sparked alarm among scholars and policymakers, raising doubts about the endurance of the primary pillars of global governance and the liberal international order they uphold. Such concerns are heightened by the fact that populist leaders enjoy significant support in countries that were instrumental in creating the post–World War II global framework. Many fear that the continued rise of populism could accelerate the unraveling of the liberal international order.

Global Governance Under Fire challenges the assumption that populism poses an existential threat to liberal internationalism and multilateral cooperation. We argued that IOs are not powerless in the face of populist opposition. On the contrary, they possess a range of tools and strategies with which to counteract such threats. Through our analysis, we revealed how IOs have effectively employed these tools to reinforce themselves and navigate mounting resistance. Moreover, we demonstrated that their efforts have, to a large extent, enabled the liberal international order to endure despite this turbulence.

However, critical questions linger about the future resilience of IOs as populist challenges continue to evolve and intensify. How can IOs, policymakers, and practitioners best position themselves to counter populism in the years ahead? What are the normative implications of the actions IOs take to safeguard their missions? How do these strategies affect perceptions of their legitimacy, fairness, and resilience?

In this concluding chapter, we address these pressing questions. We begin by offering practical recommendations for policymakers seeking to shield IOs from populist pressures. We then explore the broader implications of our findings, considering how IOs can balance the need for self-defense with their commitments to democratic values and multilateral cooperation. Through this lens, we aim to provide a road map for sustaining and strengthening global governance in an era of rising populist sentiment.

9.1.   How to Insulate IOs Against Populist Pressure

Our study has highlighted how IOs can defend themselves against populist resistance, but the question remains: How can they proactively fortify themselves against future challenges? Populist parties have assumed power across various regions, and their critiques of global governance show no signs of abating. By anticipating hostility, IOs can not only mitigate damage in a reactionary fashion but also position themselves as resilient pillars of multilateral cooperation. This chapter offers strategies for policymakers and practitioners seeking to reinforce IOs, examining the risks, benefits, and untapped potential of these approaches. We argue that drawing from the full spectrum of strategies we outline—preemptive appeasement and sidelining of leaders and constituents—can provide a powerful toolkit for bolstering IOs against populist threats. These strategies are outlined in table 9.1.

9.1.1.   *Preemptive Sidelining*

We have shown that IOs often sideline populist leaders, seeking out information and other resources from peer IOs and nonpopulist states to increase their resilience. Here, we consider whether and how IOs might sideline populists preemptively rather than in response to resource shortfalls. We suggest that IOs can pursue sidelining strategies that diversify the suppliers of critical resources, raise the costs of disengagement, and increase institutional readiness to withstand their attacks.

DIVERSIFICATION AND REDUNDANCY

IOs can fortify their operations against populist withdrawals by embedding redundancy and flexibility into their systems, ensuring resilience in the face of disruption. One of the most effective ways to achieve this is by diversifying their funding sources as well as their providers of expertise and information. For instance, IFIs increasingly rely on co-financing arrangements with private sector actors, peer IOs, and bilateral aid agencies (Clark 2021). In this vein, UNICEF has successfully garnered support from companies like Unilever and

TABLE 9.1. Strategies for insulating IOs against populist pressure

Tactic	Subtactic	Examples
Preemptive sidelining	Diversification and redundancy	Diversify funding sources (e.g., UNICEF partnerships with Unilever, IKEA Foundation); leverage private-sector data and technology (e.g., WTO using private company data); build operational flexibility (e.g., UN peacekeeping funds).
	Raising barriers to exit	Paris Agreement's one-year exit waiting period; EU's clause allowing sanctions for treaty violations; US congressional requirement for NATO withdrawal.
	Reducing barriers to re-entry	Paris Agreement's seamless US re-entry under Biden; WHO and UNESCO's simplified re-admission policies; IMF and World Bank observer roles for nonmembers.
Preemptive appeasement	Institutional concessions	Redistributing voting power in IOs to include rising powers (e.g., China, India); appointing critics to leadership roles (e.g., Trump appointing David Malpass to World Bank).
	Retrenchment	WTO's judicial economy on sensitive issues; operational IOs focusing on friendly political environments (e.g., World Bank conditional lending); regional partnerships to address local concerns.
Preemptive sidelining of constituents	Secrecy mechanisms	UN Security Council closed-door sessions; IMF and WTO redacted meeting minutes; technological investments for secure data handling.
Preemptive appeasement of constituents	Benefiting local populations	IMF hospital donation in a program country; World Bank's Women Entrepreneurs Finance Initiative (We-Fi) microloans to female entrepreneurs.
	Media campaigns	Social media campaigns countering populist narratives; visible IO branding near funded infrastructure projects (e.g., showcasing public health or disaster-relief contributions).

the IKEA Foundation,[1] while the WHO has collaborated with pharmaceutical firms to expand vaccine access. Similarly, the UNDP has worked alongside tech giants like Microsoft and SAP,[2] and the World Bank has drawn on resources from the Gates Foundation.[3] These diversified funding streams provide a financial cushion, allowing IOs to build reserves that can be tapped during periods of state-level disengagement. The UN, for example, has set aside more than $1 billion to ensure that peacekeepers can be deployed rapidly, even when traditional funding sources falter.[4]

Strategic flexibility in operations can also enable IOs to navigate shifts in political climates. Consider Haiti's Transitional Presidential Council, which requested that its international security mission transition to a UN peacekeeping operation. This adjustment would enable the UN to draw upon its broader peacekeeping budget, mitigating the risk of funding cuts from a potentially hostile US administration under Trump.[5] By proactively leveraging such mechanisms, the UN could secure long-term commitments to critical missions before political headwinds intensify.

Collaboration among IOs and other stakeholders also strengthens resilience. As explored in chapter 4, IOs often share information to counteract the impact of populist withdrawals. For example, the WTO regularly taps into data provided by private companies to maintain its operations (Carnegie and Carson 2020). Similarly, advances in technology have further amplified IOs' ability to operate autonomously—tools such as satellite imagery and drones have enabled the UN to gather information on troop movements and warring parties directly (as opposed to relying on member states to transmit such information; Dorn 2009). NGOs, whose capabilities have similarly expanded through technological advances, also serve as valuable partners in supplying critical data (Bush and Hadden 2019). These innovations enable IOs to function as interconnected networks, capable of seamlessly accruing resources and information from within their own ecosystems or from partner

---

1. "Private Sector Partnerships: Paving the Way for a Sustainable Future." *United Nations System Staff College*. August 22, 2023.

2. "UNDP and Microsoft to Create Joint Initiative to Empower Youth in Asia with AI Fluency and Skills for the Future." *UNDP*. May 31, 2023.

3. "World Bank and the Foundation Team Up to Improve Financial Data Collection." *Bill & Melinda Gates Foundation*. November 2010.

4. Peacekeeping Budgets A: New Missions." *United Nations*. December 23, 2000.

5. "Weighing the Case for a New Peacekeeping Mission to Haiti." *International Crisis Group*. November 1, 2024.

organizations. In this way, threats to individual IOs are mitigated by the broader collaborative framework in which they operate.

Subnational entities like cities and states are another critical component of IOs' strategic partnerships. In large, politically diverse countries like the United States, local governments often remain committed to international cooperation, even when federal administrations withdraw. During Trump's first presidency, the UNFCCC successfully engaged with pro-environmental states like California and cities such as Los Angeles and New York to sustain progress on climate goals under the Paris Agreement. These partnerships enabled the UN to maintain dialogue and resource sharing with American officials, bypassing federal opposition.

Flexible operational structures and voluntary membership arrangements further bolster IO resilience. As the preceding chapter discussed, the MPIA, established by a coalition of WTO members, provides a compelling example. When Trump's refusal to confirm judges rendered the WTO's Appellate Body nonfunctional, the MPIA stepped in as a stopgap mechanism for resolving trade disputes, and appears to have played a helpful role (Pelc 2024). Similarly, the Paris Agreement's design allows for voluntary commitments, enabling countries to pursue ambitious climate policies even in the absence of populist-led states like the United States. This framework proved crucial when the United States exited the agreement in 2017, as the Paris Agreement continued to function, with other nations stepping up to fill the leadership void.

By embracing redundancy, fostering diverse partnerships, and embedding operational flexibility, IOs can preemptively safeguard their missions against populist resistance. These strategies not only ensure continuity but also position IOs as adaptive, forward-thinking institutions capable of thriving in a rapidly evolving global landscape.

RAISING BARRIERS TO EXIT

IOs and nonpopulist governments can also curtail the disruptive impacts of populist leaders by raising the barriers to exit, creating frameworks that discourage states from disengaging and making noncompliance a costly endeavor. Such measures not only deter withdrawal but also ensure that states contemplating exit face clear material consequences that isolate and penalize them for undermining collective commitments. Legislative bodies within member states play a pivotal role to this end by enacting domestic laws that complicate or delay the process of withdrawal. For instance, under the Biden administration, the United States sought to introduce a requirement for congressional approval before any future withdrawal from NATO.[6] This measure aimed to prevent unilateral exits by populist administrations.

Another effective way to reinforce states' commitments to IOs is to draw out the withdrawal process. The Paris Agreement offers a prime example, requiring a one-year waiting period after a country signals its intention to exit. This deliberate delay provides a crucial window for civil society, advocacy groups, and other stakeholders to mobilize and campaign for continued membership, exerting pressure on governments to reverse course. Additionally, this buffer period allows time for political shifts, potentially ushering in leadership more favorable to the IO before the withdrawal process is finalized.

Beyond procedural delays, IOs can also raise the stakes for exit by introducing tangible penalties for treaty violations or withdrawals. Sanctions tied to treaty compliance serve as a powerful deterrent. For example, in its 1990 preferential trade agreement with the EU, Chile agreed to a clause permitting the EU to impose sanctions in the event of human-rights violations or democratic backsliding (Hafner-Burton 2011). This type of automatic punitive mechanism could be adapted to modern IOs, providing clear and enforceable consequences for countries that choose to sever their commitments. By embedding such clauses into agreements, IOs not only heighten the cost of disengagement but also signal their seriousness about upholding collective values and rules.

These measures, individually and collectively, help fortify IOs against populist-driven attempts to undermine multilateral cooperation. By increasing the procedural and material costs of exit, IOs can foster greater stability and commitment among member states, safeguarding the integrity and longevity of the international system.

REDUCING BARRIERS TO RE-ENTRY

IOs can further strengthen their resilience by reducing barriers to re-entry and re-engagement, making it easier for states to rejoin after a populist-led withdrawal. When countries formally exit an IO, rejoining often requires meeting stringent accession criteria, even if a more cooperative political environment emerges. By streamlining re-entry processes, IOs can diminish concerns about

6. Tim Kaine, "Congress Approves Bill Barring Presidents from Unilaterally Exiting NATO." December 16, 2023. https://www.kaine.senate.gov/in-the-news/congress-approves-bill-barring-presidents-from-unilaterally-exiting-nato.

prolonged or permanent disengagement, ultimately reducing the risks and costs associated with sidelining hostile states.

Some IOs have already embraced flexible re-entry mechanisms, ensuring that states can return with minimal disruption. For instance, the Paris Agreement features a re-entry process that enabled the United States to rejoin swiftly under the Biden administration. This design reflects a conscious effort to foster continued global participation and minimize bureaucratic hurdles, encouraging states to re-engage without unnecessary delays. Similarly, the Biden administration quickly re-engaged with the WHO and UNESCO, benefiting from their straightforward re-admission policies that bypassed cumbersome accession requirements. These approaches demonstrate how IOs can create pathways for re-entry that are as seamless as possible, facilitating rapid alignment with multilateral goals once political climates shift.

In addition to easing re-entry, IOs can extend opportunities for non-member states to participate in dialogue and decision making. Institutions like the World Bank and the IMF allow nonmembers to join as observers, granting access to technical assistance and other multilateral benefits without requiring full membership. Such inclusive policies keep the channels of communication open even after states exit an institution, allowing such disengaged states to maintain a presence and contribute to global governance. This approach not only preserves relationships but also provides a bridge for smoother re-engagement once political transitions pave the way for renewed cooperation.

By prioritizing flexibility and inclusivity, IOs can ensure that they remain accessible and adaptable, ready to welcome back states after periods of populist disruption. These strategies help maintain the continuity of international cooperation and underscore the enduring value of multilateralism, even in the face of political volatility.

9.1.2. Preemptive Appeasement

A second policy tool at IOs' disposal is preemptive appeasement. By proactively offering tangible benefits, IOs can make continued participation advantageous enough that even populist leaders and their skeptical constituencies find disengagement an unattractive option. This strategy hinges on creating incentives—such as critical services, resources, and economic opportunities—that clearly outweigh the perceived costs of international cooperation.

When IOs establish a framework in which the rewards of membership are substantial and unmistakable, they elevate the stakes of withdrawal. These benefits can range from financial aid and trade advantages to access to vital expertise and support networks, ensuring that the value of staying engaged is evident not just to leaders but to the broader public.

INSTITUTIONAL CONCESSIONS

IOs often find themselves in the crosshairs of populist leaders who perceive them as bastions of global elitism that constrain national sovereignty. These tensions are rooted in historical imbalances, as many long-standing IOs were designed in the aftermath of World War II, heavily influenced by Western powers like the United States, the UK, and France. Over time, emerging powers such as Brazil, India, and China have grown increasingly frustrated with their limited representation in institutions like the World Bank, IMF, and UN (Pratt 2021). Meanwhile, smaller states often criticize these IOs as tools of neocolonialism that impose liberal norms at the expense of sovereignty (Voeten 2020). These grievances are fertile ground for populist leaders, who amplify such discontent by framing IOs as elitist and detached from the interests of ordinary citizens.

One avenue to address these underlying tensions is for IOs to redistribute voting power and leadership roles more equitably among member states. This would involve reducing the disproportionate influence of the United States and its wealthy allies and increasing representation for middle- and low-income countries, including rising powers like China (Kaya 2015). Greater voice and influence within IOs would allow these countries to align institutional policies with their foreign policy goals, reducing the temptation to exit or disengage.

IOs could also address perceptions of elitism by adjusting their hiring practices and increasing transparency. Many IOs are staffed by individuals from Western countries, often with advanced degrees from prestigious institutions (Weaver 2008; Nelson 2017). These technocrats make decisions through opaque processes, presenting outcomes as inevitable while leaving little room for public input or dissent. This dynamic fuels resentment, as individuals who disagree with these policies have no opportunity to hold international bureaucrats accountable at the ballot box (Zürn 2022).

To counter this, IOs could diversify their leadership and staff to include more representatives from non-Western and developing countries. Diverse bureaucracies tend to be perceived as more legitimate, particularly among audiences in the Global South (McDowell et al. 2024). For example, recent calls for greater inclusivity in IO leadership, including at the World Bank and IMF, have aimed to address these concerns. Furthermore, IOs could engage directly with local communities and governments in program design, procurement, and implementation, demonstrating sensitivity to local needs and perspectives. This approach aligns with the localization movement in foreign aid, which emphasizes empowering local actors in decision-making processes.

Transparency and accountability are equally critical. By reducing the opacity of their decision-making processes, IOs can foster trust among member states, making countries feel more included and valued. Reforms aimed at improving efficiency, accountability, and responsiveness to members' concerns have already been initiated by institutions like the World Bank and the IMF. The EU, in response to populist critiques, has also made efforts to modify its immigration policies, demonstrating an ability to adapt to member states' evolving needs.

Another strategy IOs can employ is to tightly integrate the benefits they offer, making the cost of withdrawal prohibitively high. For example, the EU's single market, customs union, and eurozone have created deep economic interdependence among member states. Even during the eurocrisis, when Greece considered leaving the EU, the economic and logistical challenges of de-integration made remaining in the union the more viable option. Similarly, the protracted and costly Brexit negotiations served as a cautionary tale for other populist leaders contemplating a rollback of European integration.

Ultimately, IOs must balance structural reforms with proactive engagement in order to address the challenges posed by populism. By tackling long-standing grievances, enhancing inclusivity and transparency, and demonstrating their tangible benefits, IOs can strengthen their resilience and ensure their continued relevance.

RETRENCHMENT

IOs can strategically scale back their operations as a preemptive measure to minimize vulnerabilities in the face of populist challenges. By narrowing their focus to core issues, steering clear of polarizing areas, and respecting state sovereignty, IOs can demonstrate responsiveness to the common grievances of populist leaders and their constituents. This kind of retrenchment not only addresses populist demands but also positions IOs as pragmatic and adaptable institutions.

This strategy is already evident in the behavior of various IOs. The WTO, for instance, has practiced judicial economy by exercising discretion in selecting which disputes to adjudicate, particularly those involving politically sensitive issues (Busch and Pelc 2010). Such cautious decision making helps avoid fueling populist ire. Similarly, international and regional courts, which often face populist backlash, can mitigate tensions by refraining from rulings likely to provoke significant discontent (Voeten 2020). Meanwhile, operational IOs like the World Bank and the Asian Development Bank can direct their conditional lending to politically friendly environments or introduce adjustments gradually, working collaboratively with governments in more adversarial contexts.

A particularly effective approach is for global IOs to partner with regional institutions, which are often perceived as more attuned to local needs and less intrusive by populist regimes. These partnerships allow IOs to benefit from such local knowledge, while also deflecting some of the criticisms that populists often levy against larger, more centralized global institutions.

In retrenching their activities, IOs can also grant greater domestic control in areas that are especially contentious for populist governments. This aligns with the concept of "embedded liberalism," which suggests that multilateralism should support governments in managing their economies and preserving domestic stability (Ruggie 1982). For example, recent scholarship advocates for IOs to accommodate industrial policies that allow states to strategically shape their economies in pursuit of public goals (Juhász, Lane, and Rodrik 2023).

Importantly, retrenchment does not have to be permanent or formalized through structural reforms. Informal, reversible measures enable IOs to ramp up activities once populist pressures subside. Foreign aid is a clear example of this flexibility: Aid flows can be targeted, scaled back, or adjusted to meet evolving political climates without overhauling institutional frameworks. Similarly, IOs might periodically reassess their operations to address issues of mission creep—instances where bureaucratic ambition and insufficient oversight have led organizations to expand beyond their original mandates (Barnett and Finnemore 1999). By clearly defining the boundaries of their activities, IOs can reassure member states of their commitment to preserving sovereignty and limiting overreach.

Ultimately, such strategic retrenchment allows IOs to weather populist storms while maintaining their relevance and capacity to act. By tailoring their focus to immediate priorities and remaining adaptable, IOs can strike a balance between responsiveness to populist concerns and their broader mission of fostering international cooperation.

9.1.3. Preemptive Sidelining of Constituents

IOs can proactively establish mechanisms that allow states to engage in global governance discreetly, effectively sidelining public scrutiny while fostering productive collaboration. As explored in chapter 6, populist leaders often use these private channels to engage constructively with IOs and member states, even as they publicly criticize these institutions. To ensure that skeptical leaders have avenues for meaningful yet covert participation, IOs can develop and enhance their secrecy infrastructure well in advance of a tangible threat.

Confidential participation is already an established practice within many IOs. For instance, the UN Security Council frequently holds closed-door sessions when deliberating on sensitive issues, with meeting minutes either classified or summarized in ways that obscure individual members' positions. Similarly, at the IMF, member states can openly discuss economic matters during board meetings, with their remarks sealed from public release for a period of five to seven years. The WTO adopts a comparable approach, heavily redacting documents from dispute-resolution processes to protect sensitive or proprietary information provided by member states and firms. These measures create a secure environment for candid dialogue, encouraging participation from even the most skeptical actors.

However, maintaining such confidentiality requires more than promises of discretion; it demands tangible investments in robust technologies, clear protocols, and sometimes specialized personnel. Secure communication channels, advanced encryption systems, and secure data storage solutions are essential. For instance, IOs may store sensitive information physically in highly restricted archives or rely on fortified online systems to safeguard data. Access to such information must be tightly controlled, with clearance granted only to select staff. Additionally, IOs may need to collaborate with specialized firms to acquire cutting-edge security tools or build their own internal capacities to manage sensitive information effectively.

While technological advancements have made many security tools more accessible and cost-effective, IOs must remain vigilant against risks such as leaks or cyberattacks. Ensuring the trust of member states means implementing rigorous security measures that minimize vulnerabilities and protect the integrity of confidential interactions. Failure to do so risks undermining confidence in these mechanisms, which could deter states from fully utilizing them.

By investing in the infrastructure and protocols necessary for private engagement, IOs can provide a secure forum for dialogue that accommodates the needs of populist leaders and skeptical governments. This approach not only preserves trust but also ensures that even contentious states can contribute meaningfully to the global governance process, shielding these interactions from potentially damaging public scrutiny while promoting collaboration behind the scenes.

9.1.4.   *Preemptive Appeasement of Constituents*

IOs can actively work to shape favorable public opinion, reducing the support that populists can rally against them during campaigns or while in office. Populist leaders often gain traction by opposing IOs, framing them as symbols of elitism and threats to national sovereignty. However, if the general public views these organizations positively, populist attacks on multilateralism lose their appeal and can even backfire, sparking domestic backlash against leaders who denounce international cooperation.

To build public support, IOs must prioritize consistent and effective communication with domestic audiences. This involves leveraging media outreach, forming partnerships with local businesses and civil society groups, and crafting effective social media campaigns. By promoting their successes and showcasing the tangible benefits they deliver, IOs can connect with everyday citizens and counter perceptions of being distant or elite. For example, visible branding near infrastructure projects funded by IOs or clear messaging about their contributions to public health, education, or disaster relief can help highlight their relevance and positive impact.

Simplifying how IOs communicate is equally important. Using accessible, plain language to explain their work and the advantages of international cooperation can make these organizations more relatable and dismantle the perception that they operate exclusively for elites. By focusing on transparency and storytelling that resonates with people's daily lives, IOs can demonstrate that their efforts are directly aligned with citizens' well-being and prosperity.

In short, by engaging with the public thoughtfully and consistently, IOs can foster goodwill, making it harder for populists to rally opposition and ensuring that multilateralism continues to be valued as a cornerstone of global progress.

BENEFITING LOCAL POPULATIONS

Development banks are increasingly shifting their focus toward fostering local ownership by designing projects and policy reforms that resonate with the priorities of governments and local communities. The UNDP, for instance, frequently partners with local governments to implement initiatives tailored to specific national needs. This approach ensures that development efforts are not only more relevant but also more sustainable by aligning with the aspirations of the communities they serve.

Similarly, the IMF has found ways to directly engage with local communities. Beyond its financial programs, the IMF has occasionally supported charitable endeavors in program countries, demonstrating a commitment to grassroots impact. In one notable instance, the IMF made a significant donation to a local hospital after an on-the-ground staffer identified a critical funding gap.[7] Acts like these not only address immediate needs but also help to humanize IOs, reinforcing the perception that they are invested in the well-being of ordinary citizens rather than catering exclusively to elites.

Aid organizations have also made strides in directly empowering vulnerable populations through targeted programs. For example, the World Bank's Women Entrepreneurs Finance Initiative (We-Fi) offers microloans to female entrepreneurs in regions with low female labor-force participation.[8] By providing small-scale financial support, initiatives like We-Fi help individuals, and particularly women, build businesses, improve livelihoods, and foster economic resilience in their communities.

These efforts underscore a broader trend among IOs: connecting more directly with the people they serve. By supporting local priorities, addressing critical needs, and empowering underserved populations, IOs demonstrate that their mission is not just about macrolevel development but also about uplifting individuals and communities at the grassroots level.

7. Interview with former IMF Resident Representative, November 7, 2024.

8. World Bank. "Women Entrepreneurs." https://www.worldbank.org/ja/programs/women -entrepreneurs.

MEDIA CAMPAIGNS

In chapter 7, we explored how how social media has transformed the way IOs engage with the public. These platforms offer IOs a direct line to domestic audiences, enabling them to counter populist narratives and adopt people-centric language that resonates with ordinary citizens. Historically, IOs have often been perceived as opaque, elitist, and disconnected from the public, largely because their communication has typically been channeled through domestic leaders and policy officials. As a result, their rhetoric has rarely reached the everyday people whose lives their policies aim to improve.

Social media provides a unique opportunity for IOs to break down these barriers and foster a sense of accessibility and transparency. By engaging directly with domestic audiences, IOs can demystify their actions and intentions, making them appear more relatable and accountable. This strategy can also serve to enhance their legitimacy, as transparency builds trust and undercuts populist attempts to scapegoat IOs or misrepresent their policies. Research shows that such outreach can increase public awareness and bolster trust in IOs, particularly in advanced democracies where skepticism toward multilateral institutions is often high (Dellmuth and Tallberg 2023).

By adopting these strategies proactively, IOs can better position themselves to handle the challenges posed by populist leaders in influential member states. We hope the specific policy options outlined in this section serve as valuable tools for policymakers within IOs and member-state governments, equipping them to strengthen institutional resilience.

WHICH COMBINATION OF TACTICS SHOULD IOS EMPLOY?

As we have argued, IOs confronting populist backlash must employ a diverse portfolio of strategies, which we have categorized across two dimensions: the target of the strategy (leaders versus constituents) and the approach (appeasement versus sidelining). We suggest that IOs that fail to balance these tactics, instead relying primarily on one or two types, are particularly vulnerable to legitimacy crises and policy paralysis. Normative concerns arise when certain combinations of tactics dominate, leading to outcomes ranging from populist co-optation to total state disengagement.

To illustrate these dynamics, table 9.2 provides our preliminary expectations of populist responses, depending on whether appeasement or sidelining strategies dominate for both populist leaders and their constituents. As the

TABLE 9.2. Typology of combinations of IO responses to populism

	Appease leader	Sideline leader
Appease constituents	Co-optation	Muddle along
Sideline constituents	Participation/co-optation	Disengagement/ hostility

table shows, when an IO simultaneously appeases both populist leaders and their constituencies, it risks co-optation, such that the IO realigns in support of the populist agenda. While the IO may continue to enjoy some participation and engagement, its independence and authority are likely to be eroded.

In such a scenario, the organization's behavior is increasingly driven by populist demands and rhetoric, internalizing populist critiques rather than constraining them. IOs may even reduce their commitments to multilateralism in favor of nationalist objectives. While this may prevent populist withdrawal, it undermines the IO's credibility among nonpopulist actors. Moreover, co-optation may be unstable; as the IO becomes more accommodating, populists may escalate their demands, further hollowing out the organization.

At the opposite extreme lies the strategy of dual sidelining, in which IOs deliberately distance themselves from both populist leaders and their domestic bases. While normatively appealing to many nonpopulists, especially those in favor of globalization, this strategy is likely to accelerate populist disengagement from the IO.

In this situation, populist leaders are deprived of influence, and constituents are denied recognition or material benefits. Consequently, neither the elites nor the populist public sees continued IO participation as worthwhile. This increases the likelihood of defection, noncompliance, or active sabotage from within. Taken to the extreme, it may result in formal withdrawal or the creation of parallel institutions that better reflect the populist agenda. Importantly, disengagement may not reduce the IO's vulnerability to populist attacks; in fact, exclusion may feed domestic narratives of victimization and illegitimacy.

A third combination of strategies allows IOs to appease populist leaders while sidelining their constituents. This strategy may involve granting policy concessions, elevating populist leaders into prestigious roles, or allowing rule-bending behavior in exchange for continued cooperation. At the same time, IOs may neglect public outreach, engagement with civil society, or social investment within populist-led states, working out of public view or actively supporting nonpopulist members of the public.

This asymmetric accommodation risks empowering leaders while ignoring the grievances and expectations of the public that brought them to power. While such an arrangement may reduce public pressure for withdrawal or confrontation, it creates a permissive environment for elite manipulation and democratic backsliding. If leaders are excessively appeased, the boundary between participation and co-optation becomes thin, which can delegitimize the IO in the eyes of both populist and nonpopulist audiences.

Finally, IOs may sideline populist leaders while continuing to engage and appease their constituents. This could take the form of direct communication with civil society, investment in subnational projects, or policies that address populist voters' material concerns. Though such efforts may be met with elite hostility, they can help sustain public support for the IO.

In this configuration, the IO may experience low-level populist obstruction but avoid full-scale defection or delegitimation. By cultivating popular legitimacy even without the buy-in of populist leaders, IOs can survive political turbulence and avoid the most damaging outcomes. However, this is a delicate balance: Efforts to bypass populist leaders may be viewed as interference. The success of this strategy depends on the IO's ability to demonstrate tangible benefits to the public while avoiding perceptions of overreach.

Taken together, these options highlight the trade-offs IOs face in responding to populist challenges. Appeasement and sidelining are not binary choices but dimensions along which IOs can vary their engagement across both elites and mass publics. Our framework suggests that the effectiveness and legitimacy of IO responses depend on their ability to calibrate these strategies in a balanced way. Overreliance on any single quadrant, especially dual appeasement or dual sidelining, is likely to generate backlash, co-optation, or withdrawal.

9.2.   Which IOs Can Reform? The Role of Institutional Frameworks

We have examined the strategies of appeasement and sidelining that IOs can use to bolster their resilience against populist pressures. However, an IO's capacity to employ these approaches often depends on its existing institutional framework, including governing rules, decision-making procedures, and operational norms. These institutional characteristics can either enable or constrain reform efforts, shaping how effectively IOs can navigate populist challenges. Here, we outline some key limitations inherent in these structures, focusing particularly on how decision-making rules influence an IO's ability to adapt.

One critical determinant of an IO's effectiveness in addressing populist resistance lies in its decision-making rules. These frameworks vary widely across organizations, each offering unique advantages and trade-offs. However, IOs with more agile and adaptable decision-making structures are generally better equipped to counteract hostile actors. Most IOs employ a combination of rules tailored to their mandates and organizational needs, ranging from unanimity requirements to majority voting or executive-driven decisions.

Unanimity-based decision making is a common feature in many IOs, particularly for sensitive issues such as foreign policy or major reforms. While unanimity ensures that every member has an equal voice, it also risks paralysis when consensus cannot be achieved. For example, the EU's requirement for unanimity on foreign policy decisions has frequently led to deadlock, with individual member states wielding veto power to block collective action. The same goes for the passage of sweeping trade legislation at the WTO. Such rigidity can make it exceedingly difficult to implement appeasement or sidelining strategies, especially when such measures require formal votes on contentious issues like restructuring voting shares or imposing conditionality. Conversely, certain actions, such as informal information-sharing agreements or administrative reforms, may bypass these constraints and be executed directly by bureaucrats or institutional leaders.

Other IOs employ supermajority or qualified majority voting systems, which balance inclusivity with the need for efficiency. For instance, the UN General Assembly requires a two-thirds majority for key decisions, while the IMF employs weighted voting that reflects member states' financial contributions. These systems can accelerate decision making compared with unanimity but may also amplify the influence of powerful states. This dynamic can complicate efforts to address populism if influential populist leaders use their weighted votes to stall or derail initiatives. On the flip side, countries with limited vote share may find themselves marginalized, which populist leaders can exploit to rally domestic opposition by claiming their voices are ignored.

Rotational voting systems and leadership structures provide another avenue for decision making. For example, the UN Security Council's rotation of nonpermanent members allows different states temporary influence in shaping policies. While this ensures a degree of equity and inclusivity, it can create inconsistencies in how IOs address populist challenges, as leadership priorities shift over time. Conversely, centralized decision making vested in a secretariat or director general, as seen in the WTO and some UN agencies, can enable swifter responses to crises. However, this concentration of power may also draw populist criticism, reinforcing claims that IOs are run by unaccountable elites.

Rigid decision-making frameworks, particularly those requiring unanimity, often leave IOs struggling to respond effectively to populist threats. The EU exemplifies this challenge—its governance structure is frequently criticized for its inflexibility and has been slow to address violations of rule-of-law norms because of its reliance on unanimous consent. For instance, Hungary's Viktor Orbán has repeatedly used procedural delays and veto power to evade EU sanctions under Article 7. These delays allow populist leaders to enact controversial policies while IOs remain entangled in bureaucratic processes, effectively neutralizing potential consequences.

By contrast, IOs with adaptable governance models, such as those led by centralized secretariats or flexible voting arrangements, are better positioned to withstand populist pressures. These organizations can make decisions more quickly, minimizing the window of opportunity for populists to undermine collective action. As IOs face an evolving landscape of challenges, re-examining their decision-making rules to enhance agility and responsiveness may be key to ensuring their continued resilience and relevance in a world increasingly shaped by populist politics.

9.3. Normative Implications

The strategies IOs use to defend themselves against populist threats often create significant ripple effects, shaping their operations and structures long after an immediate challenge has passed. These downstream consequences vary in magnitude depending on whether the chosen response involves minor adjustments or sweeping reforms. IOs can adapt more flexibly if their actions are reversible, such as launching people-focused social media campaigns or temporarily relaxing loan conditions for populist-led states. These adjustments can be undone without much difficulty once the political climate shifts.

In contrast, structural reforms that reconfigure power dynamics or alter institutional frameworks tend to have enduring impacts. These changes often become deeply entrenched as a result of institutional inertia and the tendency to maintain the status quo. For instance, creating secret channels for engagement or granting populist states substantial influence within an IO can fundamentally reshape the organization. Even when nonpopulist leaders return to power, they may have limited leverage or fear political backlash if they attempt to undo these changes. A case in point is the Biden administration's decision not to restore the WTO Appellate Body, which remained incapacitated following the Trump administration's efforts to block judicial appointments. This illustrates how major policy shifts can become difficult to reverse, even under more favorable political conditions (Howse and Langille 2023).

When confronting populist pressures, IOs must carefully consider the potential longevity of their policy responses. Short-term solutions may be preferable to measures that risk permanent institutional transformation. However, IOs may sometimes feel compelled to adopt less easily reversible measures. This could be due to a lack of viable alternatives or a calculated decision to prioritize long-term institutional resilience. For instance, building alliances with peer organizations may create "sticky" relationships that are difficult to disentangle but offer lasting benefits, such as bolstered resources or shared expertise. In some cases, IOs might conclude that the populist threat is not a transient phenomenon and implement permanent defenses designed to outlast populist administrations. These could include reforms that enhance procedural safeguards or diversify sources of support, ensuring the IO's stability even under prolonged challenges.

Ultimately, the choice between reversible adjustments and enduring reforms reflects a strategic trade off, one that balances immediate needs against long-term implications for the institution. By carefully considering the potential durability of their responses, IOs can position themselves to navigate populist pressures effectively while preserving their core missions and institutional integrity.

9.3.1. *Legitimacy*

IOs operate on the foundation of legitimacy—the belief that their authority is rightful and their processes and decisions are fair and effective. Such perceptions are critical for IOs to fulfill their mandates. Without legitimacy, states are less inclined to cooperate, skilled bureaucrats may hesitate to work for IOs, and donors may withhold essential funding (Hurd 1999; Tallberg, Backstrand, and Scholte 2018). Yet IOs' strategies to navigate populist challenges, particularly through appeasement and secrecy, can inadvertently erode legitimacy.

Appeasement, while sometimes necessary to keep populist-led states engaged, raises significant questions about fairness, which is tightly intertwined with legitimacy. Preferential treatment for populist states, such as doling out concessions or other benefits, can undermine trust among member states, especially those that view such actions as inequitable or ethically dubious. This perception can erode the integrity of IO decision-making processes and fuel resentment. Critics may interpret these concessions as bribes or instances of corruption, damaging the IO's standing. For instance, the WTO has faced backlash for privileging small, exclusive groups of powerful states in trade negotiations, while eschewing broader membership discussions (Davis 2003). Similarly, the IMF has been accused of favoritism, particularly toward US allies, prompting questions about the organization's impartiality and fairness (Stone 2011).

Such appeasement strategies risk undermining the premise of IO legitimacy: the idea that states participate because they recognize IOs as rightful arbiters in global politics (Hurd 1999; Buchanan and Keohane 2006). IOs are meant to deliver collective benefits and welfare-enhancing outcomes to their members (Pollack 1997). Visible appeasement strategies, however, may create the impression that IOs cater disproportionately to the loudest or most demanding members, weakening trust among observers—whether member states, domestic publics, or elite stakeholders like NGOs.

Secrecy presents another challenge to legitimacy, particularly by casting doubt on the fairness and transparency of IO processes. When IOs obscure the decision-making mechanisms behind their actions, they undermine the public's ability to assess their processes and decisions. Transparency and inclusivity are cornerstones of democratic governance, and their absence in IO operations can lead to skepticism and diminished trust. If stakeholders suspect that IO decisions are being made behind closed doors, without accountability, it becomes harder to maintain confidence in these institutions.

Conversely, strategic efforts to bolster transparency and expand outreach to domestic audiences can enhance IO legitimacy. By engaging directly with citizens, explaining decisions in clear and accessible terms, and demonstrating the tangible benefits of their work, IOs can counter populist narratives that frame them as elitist or out-of-touch. Similarly, efforts to curb member states' disengagement or withdrawal while maintaining fairness can reinforce the perception that IOs are functional, unified, and essential components of global governance.

The impact of appeasement and sidelining strategies on IO legitimacy depends on the balance struck between these approaches. While appeasement may secure short-term cooperation, it risks long-term damage if perceived as unfair. Secrecy may protect sensitive negotiations but can erode trust if it compromises transparency. Meanwhile, proactive engagement and clear communication can rebuild public confidence and solidify support for multilateralism. Policy officials must weigh these trade-offs carefully, considering not only the immediate challenges posed by populism but also the broader implications for the legitimacy and resilience of IOs moving forward.

9.3.2. *Adaptability*

IOs are often criticized for succumbing to status quo bias, which limits their ability to adapt to changing circumstances. Yet our findings reveal that IOs do evolve in the face of populist threats. In fact, populist pushback can act as a catalyst for reform.

Absent external shocks or major crises, IOs are notoriously resistant to change, with reforms typically incremental and slow-moving (Page 2006; Carnegie and Clark 2023). The IMF, for example, has faced criticism for its reluctance to redistribute voting shares to reflect the growing influence of rising powers like China and India (Kaya 2015). This inertia stems from a combination of bureaucratic hurdles, entrenched institutional cultures, and member states' competing interests. Additionally, IOs' risk-averse nature often discourages them from departing from established procedures, as they fear the unintended consequences of significant deviations.

Many reforms are inherently a zero-sum game for resource-constrained IOs. Granting more influence, resources, or benefits to one member often comes at the expense of another, creating resistance from those who stand to lose. This dynamic makes proactive appeasement difficult, as reforms require extensive negotiation, resources, and political will. Moreover, many IOs operate through consensus-based decision-making, either formally (e.g., the WTO) or informally (e.g., the IMF and World Bank), further complicating the process of implementing change.

However, history shows that systemic shocks, such as global security or financial crises, can break through this inertia and prompt transformative reforms (Wallander 2000; Ikenberry 2011b). The aftermath of World War II, for instance, spurred the creation of the multilateral institutions that underpin today's liberal order, while the financial crises of the late 2000s pushed organizations like the IMF to rethink their roles in the global economy. In these moments, a shared sense of urgency and external pressure from member states, civil society, and private actors often drive IOs to implement rapid and meaningful changes. Crises not only galvanize political will but also create the conditions for resource mobilization and mandate expansion.

Populist takeovers, especially in hegemonic powers like the United States or across a critical mass of member states, can rise to the level of such a crisis. The threat that populists pose to IOs through funding cuts, public delegitimization, or outright withdrawal can cripple institutional operations and destabilize global governance. The scale and nature of IOs' responses tend to correspond to the perceived severity of the populist challenge. When threats are localized or deemed minor, IOs often employ incremental strategies like appeasement or sidelining, making small but cumulative adjustments to their operations and culture over time (Carnegie and Clark 2023). Such small and targeted changes are unlikely to have long-term repercussions for perceptions of legitimacy and fairness. However, when populist influence becomes widespread or entrenched, IOs may pursue more sweeping reforms, such as altering institutional rules or redistributing power within the organization.

That said, the effectiveness of these strategies diminishes as populism grows in prevalence. When populist-led states constitute a significant portion of an IO's membership, sidelining becomes impractical—replacing the contributions of multiple key members simultaneously is a difficult task. Similarly, appeasement becomes untenable when too many concessions are required, particularly if they involve zero-sum trade-offs like redistributing voting shares or financial benefits. For instance, the EU has struggled to appease euroskeptic parties through budgetary adjustments as their influence within the bloc has grown (Sadeh, Raskin, and Rubinson 2022).

Moreover, appeasement and sidelining strategies face limitations when used frequently or visibly. Repeated secrecy measures can undermine public trust, while efforts to engage broader audiences may encounter diminishing returns as these audiences grow more diverse and diffuse.

In sum, while populism poses clear challenges for IOs, it can also serve as a wake-up call for IOs to address inefficiencies and inequities. The extent and success of these reforms depends on the severity and scope of the populist threat, as well as the willingness of member states and IO leadership to rise to the occasion.

9.3.3.   Autonomy

When IOs face populist threats, they often seek to bolster their autonomy by enhancing their expertise, expanding their operational capabilities, and forging stronger ties with peer institutions. While such moves can enable IOs to navigate around hostile actors and safeguard their missions, they also carry significant implications for global governance.

On the positive side, greater autonomy can make IOs more efficient and adaptable. Autonomy empowers IOs to employ in-house experts who can develop innovative solutions to complex, transnational problems. Freed from the need for constant member approval, autonomous organizations can experiment with cutting-edge strategies, streamline operations, and adopt flexible funding models. For instance, the AIIB was specifically designed with fewer procedural checks compared with the World Bank, enabling it to disburse loans more rapidly. This streamlined approach highlights how a lean bureaucracy and concentrated executive authority can enhance agility, particularly in responding to crises or emerging political and economic disruptions like populism.

However, IOs that function with minimal member-state oversight are also susceptible to mission creep, where they venture into areas beyond their original mandates. This can lead to the diversion of resources from core priorities to peripheral issues, overextending their capabilities and creating inefficiencies. Institutional overlap, in turn, may encourage "forum shopping," where states and other actors choose among competing IOs to find one that aligns with their interests (Busch 2007), further diluting the effectiveness of global governance structures.

Accountability poses another significant challenge. As IOs gain autonomy, they may become less responsive to their member states, fueling perceptions of a democratic deficit. Decisions made without robust member input can deepen concerns over sovereignty, particularly among populist leaders and their constituents, who often see autonomous IOs as encroachments on national self-determination. This perceived detachment can exacerbate populist opposition and diminish trust in IOs, particularly if member states feel sidelined from key decisions affecting their interests.

Finally, unchecked autonomy can lead to accusations of inefficiency or corruption, further undermining an IO's legitimacy. Without clear mechanisms for accountability, autonomous IOs risk alienating the very states and stakeholders they aim to serve. Weighing the benefits of autonomy with the need for member engagement and transparency is thus critical for ensuring that IOs remain effective, credible, and resilient in the face of populist pressures. In navigating these trade-offs, IOs must tread carefully to preserve their independence while maintaining the trust and cooperation of their member states and the broader public.

9.3.4.   Transparency

We have identified secrecy as a potent mechanism enabling IOs to engage constructively with populists while allowing populists to avoid domestic backlash. Secrecy measures thus serve as a strategic tool to mitigate populist resistance, offering significant advantages. Indeed, many IOs already operate covertly in certain areas, capitalizing on the benefits secrecy can provide. Yet its overuse or mismanagement can lead to negative repercussions.

In terms of benefits, secrecy enhances international cooperation in critical ways. It allows IOs to secure sensitive information, as demonstrated by the UN Security Council, where classified discussions about conflict zones protect lives and preserve fragile peace processes. It also fosters open and candid dialogue by providing a confidential space for member states to voice concerns, negotiate disputes, and explore compromises that might be politically untenable in public settings. For example, the WTO's private negotiation mechanisms encourage forthright communication, helping to resolve disputes without the pressures of public scrutiny (Kucik and Pelc 2016). Additionally, secrecy shields IOs from premature media sensationalism and public backlash, which can derail delicate negotiations or generate misunderstandings. In peace talks or complex global initiatives, early leaks can provoke adverse reactions to incomplete or out-of-context information, jeopardizing the entire process.

However, an excessive reliance on secrecy can undermine an IO's legitimacy and effectiveness. Transparency is fundamental to ensuring accountability, enabling the public, member states, and stakeholders to evaluate an organization's performance, adherence to norms, and use of resources. When IOs operate behind closed doors, they risk eroding public trust and fostering skepticism about their motives. This perceived opacity can amplify the very grievances populists often exploit, portraying IOs as distant, elitist, and disconnected from the people they serve.

Moreover, a lack of transparency can result in poorer decision making. Public awareness and input often contribute to more informed and robust policies, particularly when IOs address issues with broad societal implications, such as climate change, health crises, or global inequality. NGOs and civil society actors are invaluable partners in these areas, providing local insights and amplifying IO initiatives. For instance, if the WHO were excessively secretive in an effort to collect data on disease transmissions during a health emergency without disrupting states' economic activity, public understanding could suffer, and compliance with health measures might falter.

Secrecy can also create perceptions of hypocrisy, especially when IOs demand transparency from their member states while keeping their own operations opaque. Institutions like the IMF and World Bank often make transparency a condition of their financial assistance, aiming to combat corruption and foster domestic accountability. When IOs fail to hold themselves to the same standard, they risk accusations of double standards and elitism.

In striking a balance, IOs must carefully manage secrecy, ensuring that it facilitates cooperation and protects sensitive negotiations without undermining their transparency, legitimacy, or accountability. A judicious approach can help IOs navigate the challenges of engaging with populist actors while maintaining public trust and organizational integrity.

9.4.   Concluding Thoughts

In an era when populist forces challenge the very foundations of international cooperation, IOs find themselves at a pivotal juncture. These institutions, long considered the bedrock of global governance, face mounting pressure to adapt or risk obsolescence. Populist leaders and movements, with their aggressive pro-sovereignty rhetoric and disdain for global elites, threaten to unravel decades of progress in fostering multilateralism and addressing transnational challenges. Yet, as this book has revealed, IOs are far from passive observers. They are resilient, adaptive, and capable of meeting these threats head-on.

By embracing strategies to counter populist pressures—appeasing and sidelining populist leaders and their constituents—IOs have demonstrated remarkable ingenuity and flexibility. Their ability to navigate these turbulent waters has kept the primary organs of global governance functioning, safeguarding international cooperation at a time when it is vital to address mounting challenges, including climate change and global health crises. From quiet diplomacy and issuing strategic concessions to forging alliances and leveraging technology, IOs have shown that they possess both the tools and the will to confront populist challenges.

However, this resilience comes with risks and trade-offs. As IOs reform to counter populism, they must carefully balance their actions to preserve legitimacy and maintain public trust. Appeasement, while often effective in the short term, can erode perceptions of fairness and fuel further criticism. Secrecy, though a valuable tool in sensitive negotiations, can alienate publics and exacerbate the democratic deficit that populists often decry. The challenge for IOs is to evolve in ways that strengthen their capacity to address global issues while avoiding the pitfalls that could undermine their credibility.

The stakes in this confrontation between populism and multilateralism could not be higher. The choices IOs make today will not only shape their own survival but also determine the future of collective action on humanity's most urgent challenges. If IOs rise to the occasion, they have the potential to reaffirm the value of multilateral cooperation, demonstrating its indispensability in an interconnected world. Failure to do so, however, risks a fracturing of global governance, with profound implications for international peace, stability, and prosperity.

As this book has shown, IOs are not powerless in the face of populist resistance. They are powerful agents capable of innovation, reform, and leadership. The path forward will not be without obstacles, but IOs have proven that they can adapt to shifting political landscapes. Their survival, and the continued ability of the world to tackle collective challenges, depends on their capacity to act decisively, creatively, and transparently. In the enduring struggle between populism and multilateralism, IOs have the opportunity to emerge stronger, more inclusive, and better equipped to lead the world into an uncertain future.

Appendix: List of Interviews

THIS TABLE summarizes the interviews from which we quote evidence in this book. We also talked with a number of other officials who were unwilling to be quoted, even anonymously, but their insights inform deep background. We are extremely grateful to our interviewees for sharing their experiences and expertise.

Interview subject	Date
IMF official	January 2018
Official from regional development bank	January 2021
Senior official at an environmental IO	January 2021
Official at a leading health IO	January 2021
Former senior IMF official	January 2021
Former senior IMF official	February 2021
Former senior IMF official	February 2021
Senior official at an environment and energy IO	February 2021
IMF official	August 2021
Senior IMF official	October 2022
WTO official	October 2022
IMF official	October 2022
Former IMF Resident Representative	November 2024

ABBREVIATIONS

ADB	Asian Development Bank
AfDB	African Development Bank
AIIB	Asian Infrastructure Investment Bank
BDEAC	Development Bank of the Central African States
BDEGL	Development Bank of the Great Lakes States
CDC	Centers for Disease Control and Prevention
EADB	East African Development Bank
ECJ	European Court of Justice
EDB	Eurasian Development Bank
EU	European Union
GATT	General Agreement on Tariffs and Trade
GDP	Gross Domestic Product
GRIPE	Global Research in International Political Economy
IADB	Inter-American Development Bank
IAEA	International Atomic Energy Agency
IBRD	International Bank for Reconstruction and Development
ICC	International Criminal Court
IDA	International Development Association
IFI	international financial institution
IMF	International Monetary Fund
IO	international organization
IPES	International Political Economy Society
ITC	International Trade Commission
MEPS	Members of the European Parliament
MFF	multiannual financial framework
MPIA	Multi-Party Interim Appeal Arbitration Agreement
NATO	North Atlantic Treaty Organization
NDB	New Development Bank

NDCs	Nationally Determined Contributions
NGO	nongovernmental organization
NRC	National Research Council
OECD	Organisation for Economic Co-operation and Development
UN	United Nations
UNCTAD	United Nations Conference on Trade and Development
UNDP	United Nations Development Programme
UN-FCCC	United Nations Framework Convention on Climate Change
UNFPA	United Nations Population Fund
UNICEF	United Nations Children's Fund
WDI	World Development Indicators
WHO	World Health Organization
WTO	World Trade Organization

REFERENCES

Abbott, Kenneth W., and Duncan Snidal. 1998. "Why States Act Through Formal International Organizations." *The Journal of Conflict Resolution* 42(1):3–32.

Abbott, Kenneth W., Philipp Genschel, Duncan Snidal, and Bernhard Zangl, eds. 2015. *International Organizations as Orchestrators*. Cambridge: Cambridge University Press.

Ackroyd, Stephen, and Paul Thompson. 2003. *Organizational Misbehaviour*. London: SAGE.

Adler-Nissen, Rebecca. 2021. "Struggles for Recognition: The Liberal International Order and the Merger of Its Discontents." *International Organization* 75(S2):611–34.

Akkerman, Tjitske, and Matthijs Rooduijn. 2015. "Pariahs or Partners? Inclusion and Exclusion of Radical Right Parties and the Effects on Their Policy Positions." *Political Studies* 63(5):1140–57.

Alonso-Muñoz, Laura, and Andreu Casero-Ripollés. 2020. "Populism Against Europe in Social Media: The Eurosceptic Discourse on Twitter in Spain, Italy, France, and United Kingdom During the Campaign of the 2019 European Parliament Election." *Frontiers in Communication* 5:54.

Alter, Karen J., and Sophie Meunier. 2009. "The Politics of International Regime Complexity." *Perspectives on Politics* 7(1):13–24.

Ambrose, Maureen L., Mark A. Seabright, and Marshall Schminke. 2002. "Sabotage in the Workplace: The Role of Organizational Injustice." *Organizational Behavior and Human Decision Processes* 89(1):947–65. Amsterdam: Elsevier.

Andersen, Thomas Barnebeck, Henrik Hansen, and Thomas Markussen. 2006. "US Politics and World Bank IDA-Lending." *The Journal of Development Studies* 42(5):772–94.

Arias, Sabrina B. 2022. "Who Sets the Agenda? Diplomatic Capital and Small State Influence in the United Nations." Working paper presented at APSA 2022.

Arias, Sabrina B., Richard Clark, and Ayse Kaya. 2024. "Power by Proxy: Participation and Influence in Global Governance." *Review of International Organizations* (Forthcoming).

Autesserre, Severine. 2014. *Peaceland: Conflict Resolution and the Everyday Politics of International Intervention*. New York: Cambridge University Press.

Baccini, Leonardo, and Stephen Weymouth. 2021. "Gone for Good: Deindustrialization, White Voter Backlash, and U.S. Presidential Voting." *American Political Science Review* 115(2):550–67.

Bailey, Michael A. 2003. "The Politics of the Difficult: Congress, Public Opinion, and Early Cold War Aid and Trade Policies." *Legislative Studies Quarterly* 28(2):147–77.

Bailey, Michael A., Anton Strezhnev, and Erik Voeten. 2017. "Estimating Dynamic State Preferences from United Nations Voting Data." *Journal of Conflict Resolution* 61(2):430–456.

Bakker, Bert N., Gijs Schumacher, and Matthijs Rooduijn. 2021. "The Populist Appeal: Personality and Antiestablishment Communication." *The Journal of Politics* 83(2):589–601.

Ballard-Rosa, Cameron, Mashail Malik, Stephanie Rickard, and Kenneth Scheve. 2021. "The Economic Origins of Authoritarian Values: Evidence from Local Trade Shocks in the United Kingdom." *Comparative Political Studies* 54(13):2321–53.

Barisione, M., and A. Michailidou. 2017a. "Do We Need to Rethink EU Politics in the Social Media Era? An Introduction to the Volume" [in:] Social Media and European Politics.

Barisione, Mauro, and Asimina Michailidou. 2017b. *Social Media and European Politics: Rethinking Power and Legitimacy in the Digital Era*. New York: Springer.

Barnett, Jon, and W. Neil Adger. 2007. "Climate Change, Human Security and Violent Conflict." *Political Geography* 26(6):639–55. http://www.sciencedirect.com/science/article/pii/S096262980700039X

Barnett, Michael N., and Martha Finnemore. 1999. "The Politics, Power, and Pathologies of International Organizations." *International Organization* 53(4):699–732.

Barnier, Michel. 2021. *My Secret Brexit Diary: A Glorious Illusion*. Hoboken, N.J.: John Wiley & Sons.

Barrett, Scott. 2003. *Environment and Statecraft: The Strategy of Environmental Treaty-Making*. New York: Oxford University Press.

Bearce, David H., and Brandy Joliff Scott. 2018. "Popular Opposition to International Organizations: How Extensive and What Does This Represent?" Political Economy of International Organization Annual Meeting. https://www.peio.me/wp-content/uploads/2018/01/PEIO11_paper_31.pdf

Bellodi, Luca, Massimo Morelli, and Matia Vannoni. 2024. "A Costly Commitment: Populism, Economic Performance, and the Quality of Bureaucracy." *American Journal of Political Science* 68(1):193–209.

Bennett, Andrew, and Colin Elman. 2006. "Complex Causal Relations and Case Study Methods: The Example of Path Dependence." *Political Analysis* 14:250–67.

Besley, Timothy, and Robin Burgess. 2002. "The Political Economy of Government Responsiveness: Theory and Evidence from India." *Quarterly Journal of Economics* 117(4): 1415–1451.

Bjola, Corneliu, and Ruben Zaiotti. 2020. *Digital Diplomacy and International Organisations: Autonomy, Legitimacy and Contestation*. New York: Routledge.

Blair, Robert A., Robert Marty, and Philip Roessler. 2022. "Foreign Aid and Soft Power: Great Power Competition in Africa in the Early Twenty-First Century." *British Journal of Political Science* 52(3):1355–1376.

Blyth, Mark. 2002. *Great Transformations: Economic Ideas and Institutional Change in the Twentieth Century*. New York: Cambridge University Press.

Bodle, Ralph, Lena Donat, and Matthias Duwe. 2016. "The Paris Agreement: Analysis, Assessment and Outlook." *Carbon and Climate Law Review* 10(1): 5–22.

Bonucci, Nicola, Gabrielle Marceau, André-Philippe Ouellet, and Rebecca Walker. 2022. "IGOs' Initiatives as a Response to Crises and Unforeseen Needs." *International Organizations Law Review*, 19(2), 423–82.

Bordia, Prashant, Elizabeth Jones, Cindy Gallois, Victor J. Callan, and Nicholas DiFonzo. 2006. "Management Are Aliens! Rumors and Stress During Organizational Change." *Group & Organization Management* 31(5):601–621.

Borzel, Tanja A., and Michael Zürn. 2021. "Contestations of the Liberal International Order: From Liberal Multilateralism to Postnational Liberalism." *International Organization* 75(SI-2):282–305.

Bosco, David. 2012. "Espionage in International Organizations: Brussels Edition." *Foreign Policy.* https://foreignpolicy.com/2012/09/19/espionage-in-international-organizations-brussels -edition/

Bown, Chad P. 2022. "Trump Ended WTO Dispute Settlement. Trade Remedies Are Needed to Fix it." *World Trade Review* 21(3):312–329. New York: Cambridge University Press. https://www.cambridge.org/core/journals/world-trade-review/article/trump-ended-wto -dispute-settlement-trade-remedies-are-needed-to-fix-it/902DFA6AA116AE7B3E0301F47 0FC87C2

Brändle, Verena K., Charlotte Galpin, and Hans-Jörg Trenz. 2022. "Brexit as 'Politics of Division': Social Media Campaigning after the Referendum." *Social Movement Studies* 21(1-2):234–253.

Brewer, Mark D. 2016. "Populism in American Politics." *The Forum* 14(3): 249–64.

Brewer, Paul R. 2001. "Value Words and Lizard Brains: Do Citizens Deliberate about Appeals to Their Core Values?" *Political Psychology* 22(1):45–64. https://doi.org/10.1111/0162-895X .00225.

Brown, Douglas J., and Robert G. Lord. 2003. *Leadership Processes and Follower Self-identity.* New York: Psychology Press.

Broz, J. Lawrence. 2008. "Congressional Voting on Funding the International Financial Institutions." *The Review of International Organizations* 3(4):351–74.

Broz, J. Lawrence, Jeffry Frieden, and Stephen Weymouth. 2021. "Populism in Place: The Economic Geography of the Globalization Backlash." *International Organization* 75(S2): 464–94.

Brutger, Ryan. 2021. "The Power of Compromise: Proposal Power, Partisanship, and Public Support in International Bargaining." *World Politics* 73(1):128–66.

Brutger, Ryan, and Josh Kertzer. 2018. "A Dispositional Theory of Reputation Costs." *International Organization* 72(3):693–724.

Brutger, Ryan, Joshua D. Kertzer, Jonathan Renshon, Dustin Tingley, and Chagai M. Weiss. 2022. "Abstraction and Detail in Experimental Design." *American Journal of Political Science* 67(4): 979–995.

Brutger, Ryan, and Richard Clark. 2022. "At What Cost? Power, Payments, and Public Support of International Organizations." *The Review of International Organizations* 18(3): 431–65.

Buchanan, Allen, and Robert O. Keohane. 2006. "The Legitimacy of Global Governance Institutions." *Ethics and International Affairs* 20(4):405–37.

Bulir, Ales, and Soojin Moon. 2004. "Is Fiscal Adjustment More Durable When the IMF Is Involved?" *Comparative Economic Studies* 46(3):373–99.

Busby, Ethan C., Joshua R. Gubler, and Kirk A. Hawkins. 2019. "Framing and Blame Attribution in Populist Rhetoric." *Journal of Politics* 81(2):616–30.

Busch, Marc L. 2007. "Overlapping Institutions, Forum Shopping, and Dispute Settlement in International Trade." *International Organization* 61(4):735–61.

Busch, Marc L., and Krzysztof J. Pelc. 2010. "The Politics of Judicial Economy at the World Trade Organization." *International Organization* 64(2):257–79.

Bush, Sarah Sunn, and Jennifer Hadden. 2019. "Density and Decline in the Founding of International NGOs in the United States." *International Studies Quarterly* 63(4):1133–46.

Campbell, John L. 2021. *Institutional Change and Globalization*. Princeton, NJ: Princeton University Press.

Caraway, Teri L., Stephanie J. Rickard, and Mark S. Anner. 2012. "International Negotiations and Domestic Politics: The Case of IMF Labor Market Conditionality." *International Organization* 66(1):27–61.

Carnegie, Allison, and Austin Carson. 2019. "Reckless Rhetoric? Compliance Pessimism and International Order in the Age of Trump." *The Journal of Politics* 81(2):739–46.

Carnegie, Allison, and Austin Carson. 2020. *Secrets in Global Governance: Disclosure Dilemmas and the Challenge of International Cooperation*. New York: Cambridge University Press.

Carnegie, Allison, and Austin Carson. 2023. "Scared to Share: Why Fighting Pandemics Requires Secrecy, Not Transparency." *Global Perspectives* 4(1):1–12.

Carnegie, Allison, and Richard Clark. 2023. "Reforming Global Governance: Power, Alliance, and Institutional Performance." *World Politics* 75(3):523–565.

Carnegie, Allison, Richard Clark, and Ayse Kaya. 2024. "Private Participation: How Populists Engage with International Organizations." *The Journal of Politics* 86(3):877–91.

Carnegie, Allison, Richard Clark, and Lisa Fan. 2024. "Multilateral Messaging: International Organizations, Social Media, and Public Opinion." Working paper.

Carnegie, Allison, Richard Clark, and Noah Zucker. 2024. "Global Governance Under Populism: The Challenge of Information Suppression." *World Politics* 76(4):639–66.

Casler, Don, and Dylan Groves. 2023. "Perspective Taking Through Partisan Eyes." *Journal of Politics* 85(4):1471–86.

Casler, Don, Richard Clark, and Noah Zucker. 2024. "Do Pledges Bind? The Mass Politics of International Climate Targets." Working paper.

Chan, Ho Fai, Bruno Frey, Ahmed Skali, and Benno Torgler. 2019. "Political Entrenchment and GDP Misreporting." CESifo Working paper. https://www.ifo.de/en/cesifo/publications /2019/working-paper/political-entrenchment-and-gdp-misreporting

Chwieroth, Jeffrey M. 2015. "Professional Ties That Bind: How Normative Orientations Shape IMF Conditionality." *Review of International Political Economy* 22(4):757–87.

Cialdini, Robert B., and Noah J. Goldstein. 2004. "Social Influence: Compliance and Conformity." *Annual Review of Psychology* 55(1):591–621. https://doi.org/10.1146/annurev.psych.55 .090902.142015

Clark, Richard. 2021. "Pool or Duel? Cooperation and Competition Among International Organizations." *International Organization* 75(4):1133–53.

Clark, Richard. 2022. "Bargain Down or Shop Around? Outside Options and IMF Conditionality." *Journal of Politics* 84(3):1791–1805.

Clark, Richard. 2024. "The Populist Challenge." In *The Oxford Handbook of the International Monetary Fund*, ed. Mark Hibben and Bessma Momani. Oxford: Oxford University Press.

Clark, Richard. 2025. *Cooperative Complexity: The Next Level of Global Economic Governance.* New York: Cambridge University Press.

Clark, Richard, and Anna M. Meyerrose. 2025. "Austerity and Aggression: IMF Programs and the Initiation of Interstate Disputes." *World Politics* (Forthcoming).

Clark, Richard, and Lindsay R. Dolan. 2021. "Pleasing the Principal: U.S. Influence in World Bank Policymaking." *American Journal of Political Science* 65(1):36–51.

Clark, Richard, Lindsay R. Dolan, and Alexandra O. Zeitz. 2025. "Accountable to Whom? Public Opinion of Aid Conditionality in Recipient Countries." International Studies Quarterly. Forthcoming. https://www.peio.me/wp-content/uploads/PEIO15/PEIO15_paper _56.pdf.

Clark, Richard, and Noah Zucker. 2024. "Climate Cascades: IOs and the Prioritization of Climate Action." *American Journal of Political Science* 68(4):1299–1314.

Clark, Richard, and Tyler Pratt. 2024. "The Art of Imitation: IO Legitimacy and Strategic Treaty Design." Working paper. https://static1.squarespace.com/static/65d64df20aab017d8f9f0 3e6/t/673cf56649c8f727d4d9c9c3/1732048230609/Treaty_Language.pdf

Clemens, Elisabeth S., and James M. Cook. 1999. "Politics and Institutionalism: Explaining Durability and Change." *Annual Review of Sociology* 25(1):441–66.

Clemens, Michael A., and Michael Kremer. 2016. "The New Role for the World Bank." *Journal of Economic Perspectives* 30(1):53–76.

Coe, Andrew J., and Jane Vaynman. 2020. "Why Arms Control Is So Rare." *American Political Science Review* 114(2):342–355.

Colgan, Jeff, Jessica F. Green, and Thomas Hale. 2021. "Asset Revaluation and the Existential Politics of Climate Change." *International Organization* 75(2):586–610.

Copelovitch, Mark, and Jon C.W. Pevehouse. 2019. "International Organizations in a New Era of Populist Nationalism." *Review of International Organizations* 14(2):169–86.

Copelovitch, Mark S. 2010. "Master or Servant? Common Agency and the Political Economy of IMF Lending." *International Studies Quarterly* 54(1):49–77.

Copelovitch, Mark S., and Tonya L. Putnam. 2014. "Design in Context: Existing International Agreements and New Cooperation." *International Organization* 68:471–93.

Copelovitch, Mark, and Stephanie Rickard. 2021. "Partisan Technocrats: How Leaders Matter in International Organizations." *Global Studies Quarterly* 1(3).

Cory, Jared, Michael Lerner, and Iain Osgood. 2021. "Supply Chain Linkages and the Extended Carbon Coalition." *American Journal of Political Science* 65(1):69–87.

Cruz, Cesi, and Christina J. Schneider. 2017. "Foreign Aid and Undeserved Credit Claiming." *American Journal of Political Science* 61(2):396–408.

Csehi, Robert, and Edit Zgut. 2021. "'We Won't Let Brussels Dictate Us': Eurosceptic Populism in Hungary and Poland." *European Politics and Society* 22(1):53–68.

Dahl, Robert A. 1999. "Can International Organizations Be Democratic?" In *Democracy's Edges,* ed. Ian Shapiro and Casiano Hacker-Cordon. New York: Cambridge University Press.

Dai, Xinyuan. 2002. "Information Systems in Treaty Regimes." *World Politics* 54(4):405–36.

Davis, Christina L. 2003. *Food Fights over Free Trade: How International Institutions Promote Agricultural Trade Liberalization.* Princeton, NJ: Princeton University Press.

Davis, Christina L. 2004. "International Institutions and Issue Linkage: Building Support for Agricultural Liberalization." *American Political Science Review* 98(1):153–69.

Davis, Christina L. 2009. "Overlapping Institutions in Trade Policy." *Perspectives on Politics* 7(1):25–31.

Davis, Christina L. 2012. *Why Adjudicate? Enforcing Trade Rules in the WTO.* Princeton, NJ: Princeton University Press.

Davis, Christina L. 2023. *Discriminatory Clubs: The Geopolitics of International Organizations.* Princeton, NJ: Princeton University Press.

Davis, Christina L., and Tyler Pratt. 2020. "The Forces of Attraction: How Security Interests Shape Membership in Economic Institutions." *Review of International Organizations* 16: 903–29.

Dellmuth, Lisa M. 2018. "Individual Sources of Legitimacy Beliefs: Theory and Data." In *Legitimacy in Global Governance: Sources, Processes, and Consequences*, ed. Jonas Tallberg, Karin Bäckstrand, and Jan Part Scholte. Oxford: Oxford University Press.

Dellmuth, Lisa, Jan Aart Scholte, Jonas Tallberg, and Soetkin Verhaegen. 2021. "The Elite-Citizen Gap in International Organization Legitimacy." *American Political Science Review.* Forthcoming.

Dellmuth, Lisa, and Jonas Tallberg. 2023. *Legitimacy Politics: Elite Communication and Public Opinion in Global Governance.* Cambridge: Cambridge University Press.

Destradi, Sandra, and Johannes Plagemann. 2019. "Populism and International Relations: (Un)predictability, Personalisation, and the Reinforcement of Existing Trends in World Politics." *Review of International Studies* 45(5):711–30.

Dietrich, Simone, and Matthew S. Winters. 2015. "Foreign Aid and Government Legitimacy." *Journal of Experimental Political Science* 2(2):164–71.

Dietrich, Simone, Minhaj Mahmud, and Matthew S. Winters. 2018. "Foreign Aid, Foreign Policy, and Domestic Government Legitimacy: Experimental Evidence from Bangladesh." *Journal of Politics* 80(1):133–48.

Dietrich, Simone, Susan Hyde, and Matthew Winters. 2019. "Overseas Credit Claiming and Support for Foreign Aid." *Journal of Experimental Political Science* 6:159–79.

Dijkstra, Hylke, Laura von Allwörden, Leonard A Schuette, and Giuseppe Zaccaria. 2022. "Donald Trump and the Survival Strategies of International Organisations: When Can Institutional Actors Counter Existential Challenges?" *Cambridge Review of International Affairs*, 1–24.

Dingwerth, Klaus, Henning Schmidtke, and Tobias Weise. 2020. "The Rise of Democratic Legitimation: Why International Organizations Speak the Language of Democracy." *European Journal of International Relations* 26(3):714–41.

Dolan, Lindsay R., and Helen V. Milner. 2023. "Low-Skilled Liberalizers: Support for Globalization in Africa." *International Organization* 77(4):848–70.

Dorn, Walter. 2009. "Intelligence-Led Peacekeeping: The United Nations Stabilization Mission in Haiti (MINUSTAH), 2006–07." *Intelligence and National Security* 24(6):805–35.

Downs, George W., David M. Rocke, and Peter N. Barsoom. 1996. "Is the Good News about Compliance Good News about Cooperation?" *International Organization* 50(3):379–406.

Dreher, Axel. 2009. "IMF Conditionality: Theory and Evidence." *Public Choice* 141:233–67.

Dreher, Axel, Andreas Fuchs, Bradley Parks, Austin Strange, and Michael J. Tierney. 2022. *Banking on Beijing: The Aims and Impacts of China's Overseas Development Program.* Cambridge: Cambridge University Press.

Dreher, Axel, Jan-Egbert Sturm, and James Raymond Vreeland. 2009. "Development Aid and International Politics: Does Membership on the UN Security Council Influence World Bank Decisions?" *Journal of Development Economics* 88(1):1–18.

Dreher, Axel, Jan-Egbert Sturm, and James Raymond Vreeland. 2015. "Politics and IMF Conditionality." *Journal of Conflict Resolution* 59(1):120–48.

Dreher, Axel, and Nathan M. Jensen. 2007. "Independent Actor or Agent? An Empirical Analysis of the Impact of U.S. Interests on International Monetary Fund Conditions." *The Journal of Law & Economics* 50(1):105–24.

Dreher, Axel, Valentin Lang, B. Peter. Rosendorff, and James Raymond Vreeland. 2018. "Buying Votes and International Organizations: The Dirty Work-Hypothesis." CEPR discussion paper no. DP13290. https://papers.ssrn.com/sol3/papers.cfm?abstract_id=3278665.

Drezner, Daniel W. 2017. "The Angry Populist as Foreign Policy Leader: Real Change or Just Hot air?" *Fletcher F. World Aff.* 41:23.

Ebrahim, Alnoor. 2002. "Information Struggles: The Role of Information in the Reproduction of NGO–Funder Relationships." *Nonprofit and Voluntary Sector Quarterly* 31(1):84–114. https://doi.org/10.1177/0899764002311004

Ecker-Ehrhardt, Matthias. 2018a. "International Organizations 'Going Public'? An Event History Analysis of Public Communication Reforms 1950–2015." *International Studies Quarterly* 62(4):723–36.

Ecker-Ehrhardt, Matthias. 2018b. "Self-Legitimation in the Face of Politicization: Why International Organizations Centralized Public Communication." *Review of International Organizations* 13:519–46.

Eichengreen, Barry. 2018. *The Populist Temptation: Economic Grievance and Political Reaction in the Modern Era*. New York: Oxford University Press.

Eilstrup-Sangiovanni, Mette. 2021. "Ordering Global Governance Complexes: The Evolution of the Governance Complex for International Civil Aviation." *Review of International Organizations* 17:293–322.

Ernst, Nicole, Sven Engesser, Florin Buchel, Sina Blassnig, and Frank Esser. 2017. "Extreme Parties and Populism: An Analysis of Facebook and Twitter Across Six Countries." *Information, Communication & Society* 20(9):1347–64.

Etter, Michael, Davide Ravasi, and Elanor Colleoni. 2019. "Social Media and the Formation of Organizational Reputation." *Academy of Management Review* 44(1):28–52. Valhalla, NY: Academy of Management. https://journals.aom.org/doi/10.5465/amr.2014.0280

Ezzamel, Mahmoud, Hugh Willmott, and Frank Worthington. 2001. "Power, Control and Resistance in 'The Factory That Time Forgot.'" *Journal of Management Studies* 38(8): 1053–79.

Farrell, Henry, and Abraham L. Newman. 2021. "The Janus Face of the Liberal International Information Order: When Global Institutions Are Self-Undermining." *International Organization* 75(SI-2):333–58.

Fearon, James D. 1994. "Domestic Political Audiences and the Escalation of International Disputes." *American Political Science Review* 88(3):577–92.

Findley, Michael G., Daniel L. Nielson, and J.C. Sharman. 2014. "Causes of Noncompliance with International Law: A Field Experiment on Anonymous Incorporation." *American Journal of Political Science* 59:146–61. https://doi.org/10.1111/ajps.12141.

Fleming, Peter, and André Spicer. 2007. *Contesting the Corporation: Struggle, Power and Resistance in Organizations*. Cambridge: Cambridge University Press. https://www.cambridge .org/core/books/contesting-the-corporation/E65BE93C8096E7E1EE47D79E39A65456

Fombrun, Charles, and Mark Shanley. 1990. "What's in a Name? Reputation Building and Corporate Strategy." *The Academy of Management Journal* 33(2):233–58. Valhalla, NY: Academy of Management. https://www.jstor.org/stable/256324

Freeman, John, Glenn R. Carroll, and Michael T. Hannan. 1983. "The Liability of Newness: Age Dependence in Organizational Death Rates." *American Sociological Review* 48(5):692–710.

Frieden, Jeffry. 2021. "International Cooperation in the Age of Populism." In *Economic Globalization and Governance*, ed. Luis Brites Pereira, Maria Eugenia Mata, and Miguel Rocha De Sousa. Cham: Springer International Publishing, 303–14.

Funke, Manuel, Moritz Schularick, and Christoph Trebesch. 2023. "Populist Leaders and the Economy." *American Economic Review* 113(12):3249–88.

Gartzke, Erik. 2007. "The Capitalist Peace." *American Journal of Political Science* 51(1):166–191.

Ge, Zoe Xincheng. 2022. "Empowered by Information: Disease Outbreak Reporting at the World Health Organization." Working paper. https://bit.ly/3LsfdGR

Giacalone, Robert A., and Jerald Greenberg. 1997. *Antisocial Behavior in Organizations*. Thousand Oaks, CA: Sage Publications.

Giacalone, Robert A., and Stephen B. Knouse. 1990. "Justifying Wrongful Employee Behavior: The Role of Personality in Organizational Sabotage." *Journal of Business Ethics* 9(1):55–61. New York: Springer. https://www.jstor.org/stable/25072004

Giannotta, Valeria. 2020. Turkey and NATO: A Fluctuating Relationship. In *NATO and Transatlantic Relations in the 21st Century*. Oxfordshire: Routledge, 207–23.

Gil de Zúñiga, Homero, Karolina Koc Michalska, and Andrea Römmele. 2020. "Populism in the Era of Twitter: How Social Media Contextualized New Insights into an Old Phenomenon." *New Media & Society* 22(4):585–94.

Goes, Iasmin, and Terrence Chapman. 2024. "Can 'Soft' Advice from International Organizations Catalyze Natural Resource Sector Reform?" *International Studies Quarterly* 68(2).

Goldstein, Judith L., Douglas Rivers, and Michael Tomz. 2007. "Institutions in International Relations: Understanding the Effects of the GATT and the WTO on World Trade." *International Organization* 61(01):37–67.

Goldstein, Judith, and Robert Gulotty. 2021. "America and the Trade Regime: What Went Wrong?" *International Organization* 75(SI2):524–57.

Gomez Arana, Arantza, Jay Rowe, Alex de Ruyter, Rebecca Semmens-Wheeler, and Kimberley Hill. 2019. "Brexit: 'Revolt' Against the 'Elites' or Trojan Horse for More Deregulation?" *The Economic and Labour Relations Review* 30(4):498–512. Thousand Oaks, CA: Sage Publications. https://doi.org/10.1177/1035304619881271

Gray, Julia. 2018. "Life, Death, or Zombie? The Vitality of International Organizations." *International Studies Quarterly* 62(1):1–13.

Green, Donald P., Bradley Palmquist, and Eric Schickler. 2002. *Partisan Hearts and Minds: Political Parties and the Social Identities of Voters*. New Haven, Conn.: Yale University Press.

Green, Jessica. 2022. "Hierarchy in Regime Complexes: Understanding Authority in Antarctic Governance." *International Studies Quarterly* 66(1).

Grieco, Joseph M. 1988. "Anarchy and the Limits of Cooperation: A Realist Critique of the Newest Liberal Institutionalism." *International Organization* 42(3):485–507.

Grossman, Gene M., and Elhanan Helpman. 1994. "Protection for Sale." *The American Economic Review* 84(4):833–50.

Guisinger, Alexandra. 2009. "Determining Trade Policy: Do Voters Hold Politicians Accountable?" *International Organization* 63(3):533–57.

Guisinger, Alexandra, and Elizabeth Saunders. 2017. "Mapping the Boundaries of Elite Cues: How Elites Shape Mass Opinion across International Issues." *International Studies Quarterly* 61(3):425–41.

Hadden, Jennifer, and Sarah Sunn Bush. 2020. "What's Different about the Environment? Environmental INGOs in Comparative Perspective." *Environmental Politics* 30(1–2):202–23.

Hafner-Burton, Emilie M. 2008. "Sticks and Stones: Naming and Shaming the Human Rights Enforcement Problem." *International Organization* 62:689–716.

Hafner-Burton, Emilie M. 2011. *Forced to Be Good: Why Trade Agreements Boost Human Rights.* Ithaca, NY: Cornell University Press.

Hafner-Burton, Emilie M. 2012. "International Regimes for Human Rights." *Annual Review of Political Science* 15:265–86.

Hafner-Burton, Emilie M., Zachary C. Steinert-Threlkeld, and David G. Victor. 2016. "Predictability Versus Flexibility: Secrecy in International Investment Arbitration." *World Politics* 68(3):413–53.

Handlin, Sam, Ayse Kaya, and Hakan Günaydin. 2023. "Sovereignty Intrusion: Populism and Attitudes Toward the International Monetary Fund." *International Studies Quarterly* 67(4).

Hazir, Ümit Nazmi. 2022. "Anti-Westernism in Turkey's Neo-Ottomanist Foreign Policy under Erdoğan." *Russia in Global Affairs* 20(2):164–183.

Heinzel, Mirko, and Andrea Liese. 2021. "Managing Performance and Winning Trust: How World Bank Staff Shape Recipient Performance." *The Review of International Organizations.* Forthcoming.

Helfer, Laurence R. 2004. "Regime Shifting: The TRIPS Agreement and New Dynamics of International Intellectual Property Lawmaking." *Yale J.Int'l L.* 29:1.

Helfer, Laurence R., and Annie E. Showalter. 2017. "Opposing International Justice: Kenya's Integrated Backlash Strategy Against the ICC." *International Criminal Law Review* 17(1): 1–46.

Henning, C. Randall. 2017. *Tangled Governance: International Regime Complexity, the Troika, and the Euro Crisis.* First edition ed. Oxford, United Kingdom: Oxford University Press.

Henning, C. Randall. 2011. "Coordinating Regional and Multilateral Financial Institutions." Working Paper 11-9. https://www.piie.com/publications/working-papers/coordinating -regional-and-multilateral-financial-institutions

Henning, C. Randall, and Tyler Pratt. 2020. "Hierarchy and Differentiation in International Regime Complexes: A Theoretical Framework for Comparative Research." *Review of International Political Economy* 30(6):22178–2205. https://doi.org/10.1080/09692290.2023 .2259424

Hirose, Kentaro, Gabriella R. Montinola, Matthew S. Winters, and Masaru Kohno. 2024. "A Matter of Trust: Public Support for Country Ownership over Aid." *The Review of International Organizations*, 1–29.

Hirschman, Albert O. 2004. *Exit, Voice, and Loyalty: Responses to Decline in Firms, Organizations, and States.* Cambridge, MA: Harvard University Press.

Hirschmann, Gisela. 2021. "International Organizations' Responses to Member State Contestation: From Inertia to Resilience." *International Affairs* 97(6):1963–1981.

Hoekman, Bernard, and Charles Sabel. 2021. "Plurilateral Cooperation as an Alternative to Trade Agreements: Innovating One Domain at a Time." *Global Policy* 12(S3):49–60. https://onlinelibrary.wiley.com/doi/abs/10.1111/1758-5899.12923

Hollyer, James R., B. Peter Rosendorff, and James R. Vreeland. 2014. "Measuring Transparency." *Political Analysis* 22(4):413–434.

Hollyer, James R., B. Peter Rosendorff, and James Raymond Vreeland. 2018. *Information, Democracy, and Autocracy: Economic Transparency and Political (In)Stability.* Ithaca, NY: Cornell University Press.

Honig, Dan. 2018. *Navigation by Judgment: Why and When Top-Down Management of Foreign Aid Doesn't Work.* New York: Oxford University Press.

Hopewell, Kristen. 2021. "Trump & Trade: The Crisis in the Multilateral Trading System." *New Political Economy* 26(2):271–82.

Howse, Robert, and Joanna Langille. 2023. "Continuity and Change in the World Trade Organization: Pluralism Past, Present, and Future." *American Journal of International Law* 117(1):1–47. https://www.cambridge.org/core/journals/american-journal-of-international-law/article/continuity-and-change-in-the-world-trade-organization-pluralism-past-present-and-future/C4D2467D46520D4E7C5D1B715D052627

Hurd, Ian. 1999. "Legitimacy and Authority in International Politics." *International Organization* 53(2):379–408.

Hyde, Susan D. 2011. *The Pseudo-Democrat's Dilemma: Why Election Monitoring Became an International Norm.* Ithaca, NY: Cornell University Press.

Ikenberry, G. John. 2001. *After Victory: Institutions, Strategic Restraint, and the Rebuilding of Order after Major Wars.* Princeton, NJ: Princeton University Press.

Ikenberry, G. John. 2011a. *Liberal Leviathan.* Princeton, NJ: Princeton University Press.

Ikenberry, G. John. 2011b. Crisis of the World Order. In *Liberal Leviathan: The Origins, Crisis, and Transformation of the American World Order.* Princeton, NJ: Princeton University Press.

Ikenberry, G. John. 2018. "The End of Liberal International Order?" *International Affairs* 94(1):7–23.

Imai, Kosuke, In Song Kim and Erik H. Wang. 2023. "Matching Methods for Causal Inference with Time-Series Cross-Sectional Data." *American Journal of Political Science* 67:587–605. https://doi.org/10.1111/ajps.12685

Imerman, Dane. 2018. "Contested Legitimacy and Institutional Change: Unpacking the Dynamics of Institutional Legitimacy." *International Studies Review* 20:74–100.

Jaggers, Keith, and Ted Robert Gurr. 1995. "Tracking Democracy's Third Wave with the Polity III Data." *Journal of Peace Research* 32(4):469–82.

Johnson, Tana. 2014. *Organizational Progeny: Why Governments Are Losing Control over the Proliferating Structures of Global Governance.* Oxford: Oxford University Press.

Johnston, Alastair Ian. 2008. *Social States: China in International Institutions, 1980–2000.* Princeton Studies in International History and Politics Princeton, NJ: Princeton University Press.

Jones, Kent. 2021. "Populism, Trade, and Trump's Path to Victory." In *Populism and Trade: The Challenge to the Global Trading System*. New York: Oxford University Press. https://doi .org/10.1093/oso/9780190086350.003.0004

Jones, Matthew T., and Paul Hilbers. 2004. "Stress Testing Financial Systems: What to Do When the Governor Calls."

Juhász, Réka, Nathan J. Lane, and Dani Rodrik. 2023. "The New Economics of Industrial Policy." Technical report, National Bureau of Economic Research.

Jupille, Joseph Henri, Walter Mattli, and Duncan Snidal. 2013. *Institutional Choice and Global Commerce*. New York: Cambridge University Press.

Kahneman, Daniel, and Amos Tversky. 1979. "Prospect Theory: An Analysis of Decision under Risk." *Econometrica* 47(2): 263–291.

Kaja, Ashwin, and Eric Werker. 2010. "Corporate Governance at the World Bank and the Dilemma of Global Governance." *The World Bank Economic Review* 24(2):171–98.

Kaya, Ayse. 2015. *Power and Global Economic Institutions*. New York: Cambridge University Press.

Kelemen, R. Daniel. 2017. "Europe's Other Democratic Deficit: National Authoritarianism in Europe's Democratic Union." *Government & Opposition* 52(S2):211–38.

Kelemen, R. Daniel. 2020. "The European Union's Authoritarian Equilibrium." *Journal of European Public Policy* 27(3):481–99. https://doi.org/10.1080/13501763.2020.1712455

Kelley, Judith. 2009. "The More the Merrier? The Effects of Having Multiple International Election Monitoring Organizations." *Perspectives on Politics* 7(1):59–64.

Kelley, Judith Green. 2012. *Monitoring Democracy: When International Election Observation Works, and Why It Often Fails*. Princeton, N.J.: Princeton University Press.

Kentikelenis, Alexander E., Thomas H. Stubbs, and Lawrence P. King. 2016. "IMF Conditionality and Development Policy Space, 1985–2014." *Review of International Political Economy* 23(4):543–82.

Keohane, Robert O. 1984. *After Hegemony: Cooperation and Discord in the World Political Economy*. Princeton, NJ: Princeton University Press.

Keohane, Robert O., and David G. Victor. 2011. "The Regime Complex for Climate Change." *Perspectives on Politics* 9(1):7–23.

Kilby, Christopher. 2011. "Informal Influence in the Asian Development Bank." *The Review of International Organizations* 6(3–4):223.

Kilby, Christopher. 2013. "An Empirical Assessment of Informal Influence in the World Bank." *Economic Development and Cultural Change* 61(2):431–464.

Kim, In Song. 2017. "Political Cleavages Within Industry: Firm-level Lobbying for Trade Liberalization." *American Political Science Review* 111(1):1–20.

Kinacioğlu, Müge, and Aylin G. Gürzel. 2013. "Turkey's Contribution to NATO's Role in Post–Cold War Security Governance: The Use of Force and Security Identity Formation." *Global Governance* 19(4):589–610. Boulder, CO: Lynne Rienner Publishers. https://www.jstor .org/stable/24526395

Kiratli, Osman Sabri. 2021. "Politicization of Aiding Others: The Impact of Migration on European Public Opinion of Development Aid." *JCMS: Journal of Common Market Studies* 59(1):53–71.

Knack, Stephen. 2001. "Aid Dependence and the Quality of Democratic Governance: Cross-Country Empirical Tests." *Southern Economic Journal* 68(2):310–329.

Kono, Daniel Y. 2006. "Optimal Obfuscation: Democracy and Trade Policy Transparency." *American Political Science Review* 100(3):369–384.

Kramer, Roderick M. 1999. "Trust and Distrust in Organizations: Emerging Perspectives, Enduring Questions." *Annual Review of Psychology* 50(1):569–598. https://doi.org/10.1146/annurev.psych.50.1.569

Krasner, Stephen D. 1976. "State Power and the Structure of International Trade." *World Politics* 28(3):317–347.

Krasner, Stephen D. 1978. *Defending the National Interest: Raw Materials Investments and U.S. Foreign Policy.* Princeton, NJ: Princeton University Press.

Krcmaric, Daniel, Stephen C. Nelson, and Andrew Roberts. 2020. "Studying Leaders and Elites: The Personal Biography Approach." *Annual Review of Political Science* 23:133–151.

Kucik, Jeffrey, and Krzysztof J. Pelc. 2016. "Measuring the Cost of Privacy: A Look at the Distributional Effects of Private Bargaining." *British Journal of Political Science* 46(4): 861–89.

Kuznetsova, Lidia. 2020. "COVID-19: The World Community Expects the World Health Organization to Play a Stronger Leadership and Coordination Role in Pandemics Control." *Frontiers in Public Health* 8. https://www.frontiersin.org/articles/10.3389/fpubh.2020.00470

Kyle, Jordan, and Brett Meyer. 2020. "High Tide? Populism in Power, 1990–2020." Technical report, Tony Blair Institute for Global Change. https://www.institute.global/insights/geopolitics-and-security/high-tide-populism-power-1990-2020

Ladi, Stella, and Sarah Wolff. 2021. "The EU Institutional Architecture in the Covid-19 Response: Coordinative Europeanization in Times of Permanent Emergency." *Journal of Common Market Studies* 59(Suppl 1):32–43. https://www.ncbi.nlm.nih.gov/pmc/articles/PMC8657326/

Laffan, Brigid, and Stefan Telle. 2023. *The EU's Response to Brexit: United and Effective.* London: Palgrave Macmillan.

Lake, David A., Lisa L. Martin, and Thomas Risse. 2021. "Challenges to the Liberal Order: A Reflection on International Organization." *International Organization* 75(S2):225–57.

Lall, Ranjit. 2016. "How Multiple Imputation Makes a Difference." *Political Analysis* 24(4): 414–43.

Landau, Dana M., and Lior Lehrs. 2022. "Populist Peacemaking: Trump's Peace Initiatives in the Middle East and the Balkans." *International Affairs* 98(6):2001–19.

Lawrence, Thomas B., and Sandra L. Robinson. 2007. "Ain't Misbehavin': Workplace Deviance as Organizational Resistance." *Journal of Management* 33(3):378–94. Thousand Oaks, CA: Sage Publications. https://doi.org/10.1177/0149206307300816

Lenz, Tobias, Alexandr Burilkov, and Lora Anne Viola. 2019. "Legitimacy and the Cognitive Sources of International Institutional Change: The Case of Regional Parliamentarization." *International Studies Quarterly* 63(4):1094–1107.

Lenz, Tobias, and Fredrik Söderbaum. 2023. "The Origins of Legitimation Strategies in International Organizations: Agents, Audiences and Environments." *International Affairs* 99(3):899–920.

Li, Handi. 2017. "Political Effect of Economic Data Manipulation: Evidence from Chinese Protests." PhD thesis, Duke University.

Li, Larry, Malick Sy, and Adela McMurray. 2015. "Insights into the IMF Bailout Debate: A Review and Research Agenda." *Journal of Policy Modeling* 37:891–914.

Likert, Rensis. 1967. *The Human Organization: Its Management and Values.* New York: McGraw-Hill.

Lim, Daniel Yew Mao, and James Raymond Vreeland. 2013. "Regional Organizations and International Politics: Japanese Influence over the Asian Development Bank and the UN Security Council." *World Politics* 65(1):34–72.

Lipscy, Philip Y. 2015. "Explaining Institutional Change: Policy Areas, Outside Options, and the Bretton Woods Institutions." *American Journal of Political Science* 59(2):341–56.

Lipscy, Phillip Y. 2017. *Renegotiating the World Order: Institutional Change in International Relations.* New York: Cambridge University Press.

Loughran, Tim, and Bill McDonald. 2011. "When Is a Liability Not a Liability? Textual Analysis, Dictionaries, and 10-Ks." *The Journal of Finance* 66(1):35–65.

Mahoney, James, and Kathleen Thelen. 2010. "A Theory of Gradual Institutional Change." In *Explaining Institutional Change: Ambiguity, Agency, and Power.* New York: Cambridge University Press, pp. 1–37.

Malhotra, Neil, Yotam Margalit, and Cecilia Hyunjung Mo. 2013. "Economic Explanations for Opposition to Immigration: Distinguishing Between Prevalence and Conditional Impact." *American Journal of Political Science* 57(2):391–410. https://onlinelibrary.wiley.com/doi/abs/10.1111/ajps.12012.

Malik, Rabia, and Randall W. Stone. 2018. "Corporate Influence in World Bank Lending." *The Journal of Politics* 80(1):103–18.

McDowell, Daniel, David A Steinberg, Selim Erdem Aytaç, and Dimitar Gueorguiev. 2024. "Developing-Country Representation and Public Attitudes Toward International Organizations: The Case of IMF Governance Reform." *International Studies Quarterly* 68(3).

McGarity, Thomas O., and Wendy E. Wagner. 2010. *Bending Science: How Special Interests Corrupt Public Health Research.* Cambridge, MA: Harvard University Press.

Mearsheimer, J. J. 1995. "The False Promise of International Institutions." *International Security* 19(3):5–49.

Mearsheimer, John J. 2001. *The Tragedy of Great Power Politics.* New York: Norton.

Mearsheimer, John J. 2019. "Bound to Fail: The Rise and Fall of the Liberal International Order." *International Security* 43(4):7–50.

Mechanic, David. 1962. "Sources of Power of Lower Participants in Complex Organizations." *Administrative Science Quarterly* 7(3): 349–64.

Mendes Motta, Filipe, and Gabriella Hauber. 2023. "Anti-environmentalism and Proto-authoritarian Populism in Brazil: Bolsonaro and the Defence of Global Agri-business." *Environmental Politics* 32(4):642–62.

Meyerrose, Anna M. 2020. "The Unintended Consequences of Democracy Promotion: International Organizations and Democratic Backsliding." *Comparative Political Studies* 53(10–11):1547–81.

Michailidou, Asimina. 2008. "Democracy and New Media in the European Union: Communication or Participation Deficit?" *Journal of Contemporary European Research* 4(4):346–68.

Milner, Helen V., Daniel L. Nielson, and Michael G. Findley. 2016. "Citizen Preferences and Public Goods: Comparing Preferences for Foreign Aid and Government Programs in Uganda." *Review of International Organizations* 11(2):219–45.

Milner, Helen V., and Dustin H. Tingley. 2012. "The Choice for Multilateralism: Foreign Aid and American Foreign Policy." *Review of International Organizations* 8(3):313–41.

Moon, Suerie, Jana Armstrong, and Brian Hutler et al. 2022. "Governing the Access to COVID-19 Tools Accelerator: Towards Greater Participation, Transparency, and Accountability." *Lancet* 399(10323):487–94. https://www.ncbi.nlm.nih.gov/pmc/articles/PMC8797025/

Moravcsik, Andrew. 2004. "Is There a 'Democratic Deficit' in World Politics? A Framework for Analysis." *Government and Opposition* 39(2):336–63.

Morgenthau, Hans. 1948. *Politics among Nations: The Struggle for Power and Peace.* New York: Knopf.

Morse, Julia C., and Robert O. Keohane. 2014. "Contested Multilateralism." *Review of International Organizations* 9(4):385–412.

Mudde, Cas, and Cristóbal Rovira Kaltwasser. 2017. *Populism: A Very Short Introduction.* New York: Oxford University Press.

Mudde, Cas, and Cristóbal Rovira Kaltwasser. 2018. "Studying Populism in Comparative Perspective: Reflections on the Contemporary and Future Research Agenda." *Comparative Political Studies* 51(13):1667–93.

Muller, Jan-Werner. 2016. *What Is Populism?* Philadelphia: University of Pennsylvania Press.

Nelson, Stephen C. 2017. *The Currency of Confidence: How Economic Beliefs Shape the IMF's Relationship with Its Borrowers.* Ithaca, NY: Cornell University Press.

Neuman, Joel H., and Robert A. Baron. 2005. "Aggression in the Workplace: A Social–Psychological Perspective." In *Counterproductive work behavior: Investigations of actors and targets.* Washington: American Psychological Association, 13–40.

Nielson, Daniel L., and Michael J. Tierney. 2003. "Delegation to International Organizations: Agency Theory and World Bank Environmental Reform." *International Organization* 57(2):241–76.

Novosad, Paul, and Eric Werker. 2019. "Who Runs the International System? Nationality and Leadership in the United Nations Secretariat." *Review of International Organizations* 14(1):1–33.

O'Leary, Rosemary. 2010. "Guerrilla Employees: Should Managers Nurture, Tolerate, or Terminate Them?" *Public Administration Review* 70(1):8–19. https://onlinelibrary.wiley.com/doi/abs/10.1111/j.1540-6210.2009.02104.x

Oliver, Eric, and Thomas Wood. 2014. "Conspiracy Theories and the Paranoid Style(s) of Mass Opinion." *American Journal of Political Science* 58(4):952–66.

Oliver, Eric, and Wendy Rahn. 2016. "Rise of the Trumpenvolk: Populism in the 2016 Election." *Annals of the American Academy of Political and Social Science* 667(1):189–206.

Oliveros, Virginia, Rebecca Weitz-Shapiro, and Matthew S. Winters. 2023. "Credit Claiming by Labeling." *Comparative Political Studies* 56(13):2099–2127.

Oreskes, Naomi, and Erik M. Conway. 2011. *Merchants of Doubt: How a Handful of Scientists Obscured the Truth on Issues from Tobacco Smoke to Global Warming.* New York: Bloomsbury.

Özdemir, Sina Furkan, and Christian Rauh. 2022. "A Bird's Eye View: Supranational EU Actors on Twitter." *Politics and Governance* 10(1): 133–145.

Page, Scott E. 2006. "Path Dependence." *Quarterly Journal of Political Science* 1:87–115.

Parízek, Michal. 2017. "Control, Soft Information, and the Politics of International Organizations Staffing." *The Review of International Organizations* 12(4):559–83.

Pavone, Ilja Richard. 2018. "The Paris Agreement and the Trump Administration: Road to Nowhere?" *Journal of International Studies* 11(1):34–49.

Pearson, Christine M., Lynne M. Andersson, and Judith W. Wegner. 2001. "When Workers Flout Convention: A Study of Workplace Incivility." *Human Relations* 54(11): 1387–1419.

Pelc, Krzysztof. 2024. "Institutional Innovation in Response to Backlash: How Members Are Circumventing the WTO Impasse." *Review of International Organizations* (Online first). https://dx.doi.org/10.2139/ssrn.4718668.

Pevehouse, Jon C., Timothy Nordstrom, and Kevin Warnke. 2004. "The Correlates of War 2 International Governmental Organizations Data Version 2.0." *Conflict Management and Peace Science* 21(2):101–19.

Pfeffer, J., and G. R. Salancik. 1978. *The External Control of Organizations: A Resource Dependence Perspective.* New York: Harper & Row.

Pollack, Mark A. 1997. "Delegation, Agency, and Agenda Setting in the European Community." *International Organization* 51(1):99–134.

Potter, Rachel Augustine. 2021. "Buying Evidence? Government Research as a Presidential Prerogative." Working paper. https://www.augustinepotter.com/research.html

Pratt, Tyler. 2018. "Deference and Hierarchy in International Regime Complexes." *International Organization* 72(3):561–590.

Pratt, Tyler. 2021. "Angling for Influence: Institutional Proliferation in Development Banking." *International Studies Quarterly* 65(1):95–108.

Putnam, Robert D. 1988. "Diplomacy and Domestic Politics: The Logic of Two-Level Games." *International Organization* 42(3):427–460.

Rached, Danielle Hanna. 2022. "Right-Wing Populists and the Global Climate Agenda." In *Verfassungsblog: On Matters Constitutional.* https://verfassungsblog.de/right-wing-populists-and-the-global-climate-agenda/.

Reinsberg, Bernhard, Thomas Stubbs, and Alexander Kentikelenis. 2022. "Compliance, Defiance, and the Dependency Trap: IMF Program Interruptions and their Impact on Capital Markets." *Regulation and Governance* 16(4): 1022–41.

Rho, Sungmin, and Michael Tomz. 2017. "Why Don't Trade Preferences Reflect Economic Self-Interest?" *International Organization* 71(S1):S85–S108.

Rico, Guillem, Marc Guinjoan, and Eva Anduiza. 2017. "The Emotional Underpinnings of Populism: How Anger and Fear Affect Populist Attitudes." *Swiss Political Science Review* 23(4):444–461.

Rigney, Daniel. 1991. "Three Kinds of Anti-intellectualism: Rethinking Hofstadter." *Sociological Inquiry* 61(4):434–451.

Roberts, Margaret E., Dustin Tingley, Brandon M. Stewart, and Edoardo M. Airoldi. 2013. "The Structural Topic Model and Applied Social Science." *Advances in Neural Information Processing Systems Workshop on Topic Models: Computation, Application, and Evaluation.* https://bstewart.scholar.princeton.edu/sites/g/files/toruqf4016/files/bstewart/files/stm nips2013.pdf.

Robinson, Sandra L., and Rebecca J. Bennett. 1995. "A Typology of Deviant Workplace Behaviors: A Multidimensional Scaling Study." *Academy of Management Journal* 38(2): 555–572.

Rodrik, Dani. 2017. "Populism and the economics of globalization." Technical report, National Bureau of Economic Research.

Rovira Kaltwasser, Cristóbal, and Paul Taggart. 2016. "Dealing with Populists in Government: A Framework for Analysis." *Democratization* 23(2):201–20.

Ruggie, John Gerard. 1982. "International Regimes, Transactions, and Change: Embedded Liberalism in the Postwar Economic Order." *International Organization* 36(2):379–415.

Russett, Bruce M., and John R. Oneal. 2001. *Triangulating Peace: Democracy, Interdependence, and International Organizations.* New York: Norton.

Sadeh, Tal, Yoav Raskin, and Eyal Rubinson. 2022. "Big Politics, Small Money: Euroscepticism's Diminishing Return in EU Budget Allocations." *European Union Politics* 23(3):437–61.

Sasso, Greg, and Massimo Morelli. 2021. "Bureaucrats under Populism." *Journal of Public Economics* 202.

Schlipphak, Bernd, Paul Meiners, and Osman Sabri Kiratli. 2022. "Crisis Affectedness, Elite Cues and IO Legitimacy." *Review of International Organizations* 17(1):877–98.

Schneider, Christina J., and Jennifer L. Tobin. 2016. "Portfolio Similarity and International Development Aid." *International Studies Quarterly* 60(4):647–64.

Schneider, Christina J., and Jennifer L. Tobin. 2020. "The Political Economy of Bilateral Bailouts." *International Organization* 74(1):1–29.

Schuessler, John M. 2010. "The Deception Dividend: FDR's Undeclared War." *International Security* 34(4):133–65.

Schuette, Leonard August. 2023. "IO Survival Politics: International Organisations amid the Crisis of Multilateralism." *Journal of European Public Policy* 31(11), 3812–38. https://doi.org/10.1080/13501763.2023.2276757.

Schuette, Leonard, and Hylke Dijkstra. 2023. "The Show Must Go On: The EU's Quest to Sustain Multilateral Institutions since 2016." *JCMS: Journal of Common Market Studies* 1318–1336.

Schöll, Nikolas, Aina Gallego, and Gaël Le Mens. 2024. "How Politicians Learn from Citizens' Feedback: The Case of Gender on Twitter." *American Journal of Political Science* 68(2): 557–74.

Serenko, Alexander. 2019. "Knowledge Sabotage as an Extreme Form of Counterproductive Knowledge Behavior: Conceptualization, Typology, and Empirical Demonstration." *Journal of Knowledge Management* 23(7):1260–88. Leeds, UK: Emerald Publishing Limited. https://doi.org/10.1108/JKM-01-2018-0007

Snyder, Jack. 2019. "The Broken Bargain: How Nationalism Came Back." *Foreign Affairs* 98(2):54–60.

Söderbaum, Fredrik, Kilian Spandler, and Agnese Pacciardi. 2021. *Contestations of the Liberal International Order: A Populist Script of Regional Cooperation.* New York: Cambridge University Press.

Souris, Renée Nicole. 2020. "African Challenges to the International Criminal Court: An Example of Populism?" In *Democracy, Populism, and Truth,* edited by Mark Christopher Navin and Richard Nunan. New York: Springer.

Spandler, Kilian, and Fredrik Söderbaum. 2023. "Populist (De)legitimation of International Organizations." *International Affairs* 99(3):1023–41. https://doi.org/10.1093/ia/iiado48

Stasavage, David. 2004. "Open-Door or Closed-Door? Transparency in Domestic and International Bargaining." *International Organization* 58(4):667–703.

Stone, Randall W. 2008. "The Scope of IMF Conditionality." *International Organization* 62(4):589–620.

Stone, Randall W. 2011. *Controlling Institutions: International Organizations and the Global Economy.* New York: Cambridge University Press.

Streeck, Wolfgang, and Kathleen Thelen. 2005. *Beyond Continuity: Institutional Change in Advanced Political Economies.* New York: Oxford University Press.

Sweeney, Simon, and Neil Winn. 2020. "EU Security and Defence Cooperation in Times of Dissent: Analysing PESCO, the European Defence Fund and the European Intervention Initiative (EI2) in the Shadow of Brexit." *Defence Studies* 20(3):224–49.

Taggart, Paul. 2000. *Populism: Concepts in the Social Sciences.* Philadelphia: Open University Press.

Tallberg, J., K. Backstrand, and J. A. Scholte. 2018. *Legitimacy in Global Governance: Sources, Processes, and Consequences.* Oxford: Oxford University Press.

Tallberg, Jonas, and Michael Zürn. 2019. "The Legitimacy and Legitimation of International Organizations: Introduction and Framework." *Review of International Organizations* 14(2):581–606.

Taylor, Paul. 1991. "The United Nations System under Stress: Financial Pressures and Their Consequences." *Review of International Studies* 17:365–382.

Terman, Rochelle, and Erik Voeten. 2018. "The Relational Politics of Shame: Evidence From the Universal Periodic Review." *Review of International Organizations* 13(1):1–23.

Thorne, Leslie. 1992. "IAEA Nuclear Inspections in Iraq." *IAEA Bulletin* 1:16–24.

Tingley, Dustin, and Michael Tomz. 2022. "The Effects of Naming and Shaming on Public Support for Compliance with International Agreements: An Experimental Analysis of the Paris Agreement." *International Organization* 76(2):445–68.

Tomz, Michael. 2007. "Domestic Audience Costs in International Relations: An Experimental Approach." *International Organization* 61(4):821–40.

Trachtenberg, Marc. 2012. "Audience Costs: An Historical Analysis." *Security Studies* 21(1):3–42. http://dx.doi.org/10.1080/09636412.2012.650590

Tucker, James. 1993. "Everyday Forms of Employee Resistance." *Sociological Forum* 8(1):25–45. https://www.jstor.org/stable/684283

Twiplomacy. 2017. "International Organizations on Social Media." https://twiplomacy.com/blog/international-organisations-on-social-media-2017

Twitter. 2022. "How to Get the Blue Checkmark on Twitter." https://help.twitter.com/en/managing-your-account/about-twitter-verified-accounts

Urpelainen, Johannes, and Thijs Van de Graaf. 2015. "Your Place or Mine? Institutional Capture and the Creation of Overlapping International Institutions." *British Journal of Political Science* 45(4):799–827.

Varoufakis, Yanis. 2017. *Adults in the Room: My Battle with the European and American Deep Establishment.* New York: Farrar, Straus and Giroux.

Vaubel, Roland. 1991. "The Political Economy of the IMF: A Public Choice Analysis." In *The Political Economy of International Organizations*, ed. Roland Vaubel and Thomas Willett. Boulder, CO: Westview Press, pp. 204–44.

Verdier, Daniel. 1994. *Democracy and International Trade: Britain, France, and the United States, 1860–1990*. Princeton, NJ: Princeton University Press.

Voeten, Erik. 2005. "The Political Origins of the UN Security Council's Ability to Legitimate the Use of Force." *International Organization* 59(3):527–57.

Voeten, Erik. 2020. "Populism and Backlash Against International Courts." *Perspectives on Politics* 18(2):407–22.

Voeten, Erik. 2021. *Ideology and International Institutions*. Princeton, NJ: Princeton University Press.

von Borzyskowski, Inken, and Felicity Vabulas. 2019a. "Credible Commitments? Explaining IGO Suspensions to Sanction Political Backsliding." *International Studies Quarterly* 63(1):139–52.

von Borzyskowski, Inken, and Felicity Vabulas. 2019b. "Hello, Goodbye: When Do States Withdraw from International Organizations?" *Review of International Organizations* 14(2): 335–66.

von Borzyskowski, Inken, and Felicity Vabulas. 2024a. "Public Support for Withdrawal from International Organizations: Experimental Evidence from the US." *Review of International Organizations* 19(4):809–45.

von Borzyskowski, Inken, and Felicity Vabulas. 2024b. "When Do Member State Withdrawals Lead to the Death of International Organizations?" *European Journal of International Relations* 30(3):756–86.

Vreeland, James R. 1999. "The IMF: Lender of Last Resort or Scapegoat." Unpublished manuscript. https://www.files.ethz.ch/isn/30242/1999-03.pdf

Vreeland, James R. 2003. *The IMF and Economic Development*. Cambridge: Cambridge University Press.

Vreeland, James R. 2005. "The International and Domestic Politics of IMF Programs." Unpublished manuscript.

Vreeland, James R., James R. Hollyer, and B. Peter Rosendorff. 2011. "Democracy and Transparency." *The Journal of Politics* 73(4):1191–1205.

Vreeland, James Raymond, and Axel Dreher. 2014. *The Political Economy of the United Nations Security Council: Money and Influence*. New York: Cambridge University Press.

Wajner, Daniel F. 2022. "Global Populism." In *The Palgrave Handbook of Populism*, edited by Michael Oswald. New York: Springer.

Wallander, Celeste A. 2000. "Institutional Assets and Adaptability: NATO after the Cold War." *International Organization* 54(4):705–35.

Weaver, Catherine. 2008. *Hypocrisy Trap: The World Bank and the Poverty of Reform*. Princeton, NJ: Princeton University Press.

Weiss, Jessica Chen. 2013. "Authoritarian Signaling, Mass Audiences, and Nationalist Protest in China." *International Organization* 67:1–35.

Weiss, Jessica Chen, and Jeremy L. Wallace. 2021. "Domestic Politics, China's Rise, and the Future of the Liberal International Order." *International Organization* 75(S2):635–64.

White House Archives. 2020. "President Trump: We Have Rejected Globalism and Embraced Patriotism."

Worsnop, Catherine Z. 2019. "Concealing Disease: Trade and Travel Barriers and the Timeliness of Outbreak Reporting." *International Studies Perspectives* 20(4):344–72.

Zaller, John. 1992. *The Nature and Origins of Mass Opinion*. Cambridge: Cambridge University Press.

Zimmermann, Hubert. 2019. "Brexit and the External Trade Policy of the EU." *European Review of International Studies* 6(1):27–46.

Zürn, Michael. 2022. "How Non-majoritarian Institutions Make Silent Majorities Vocal: A Political Explanation of Authoritarian Populism." *Perspectives on Politics* 20(3):788–807.

Zvogbo, Kelebogile. 2019. "Human Rights versus National Interests: Shifting US Public Attitudes on the International Criminal Court." *International Studies Quarterly* 63(4):1065–78.

INDEX

Page references in *italics* indicate a figure; page references in **bold** indicate a table.

A NOTE ON THE TYPE

This book has been composed in Arno, an Old-style serif typeface in the classic Venetian tradition, designed by Robert Slimbach at Adobe.

GPSR Authorized Representative: Easy Access System Europe - Mustamäe tee
50, 10621 Tallinn, Estonia, gpsr.requests@easproject.com

www.ingramcontent.com/pod-product-compliance
Lightning Source LLC
Chambersburg PA
CBHW030349270326
41926CB00009B/1029